Chi's Sweet Home

チーズ スイートホーム

8

Konami Kanata

contents
homemade 129~146+🐾

129 a cat manifests   3

130 a cat anticipates   11

131 a cat cases   19

132 a cat is wowed   27

133 a cat has a blast   35

134 a cat is pursued   43

135 a cat is hemmed   51

136 a cat leaps   59

137 a cat returns   67

138 a cat relaxes   75

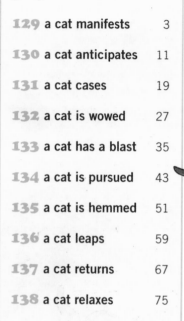
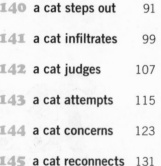

139 a cat monitors   83

140 a cat steps out   91

141 a cat infiltrates   99

142 a cat judges   107

143 a cat attempts   115

144 a cat concerns   123

145 a cat reconnects   131

146 a cat sheds tears   139

🐾   **Let's Make a Chi Face**
     147

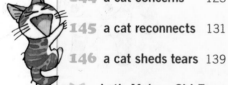

homemade 129: a cat manifests

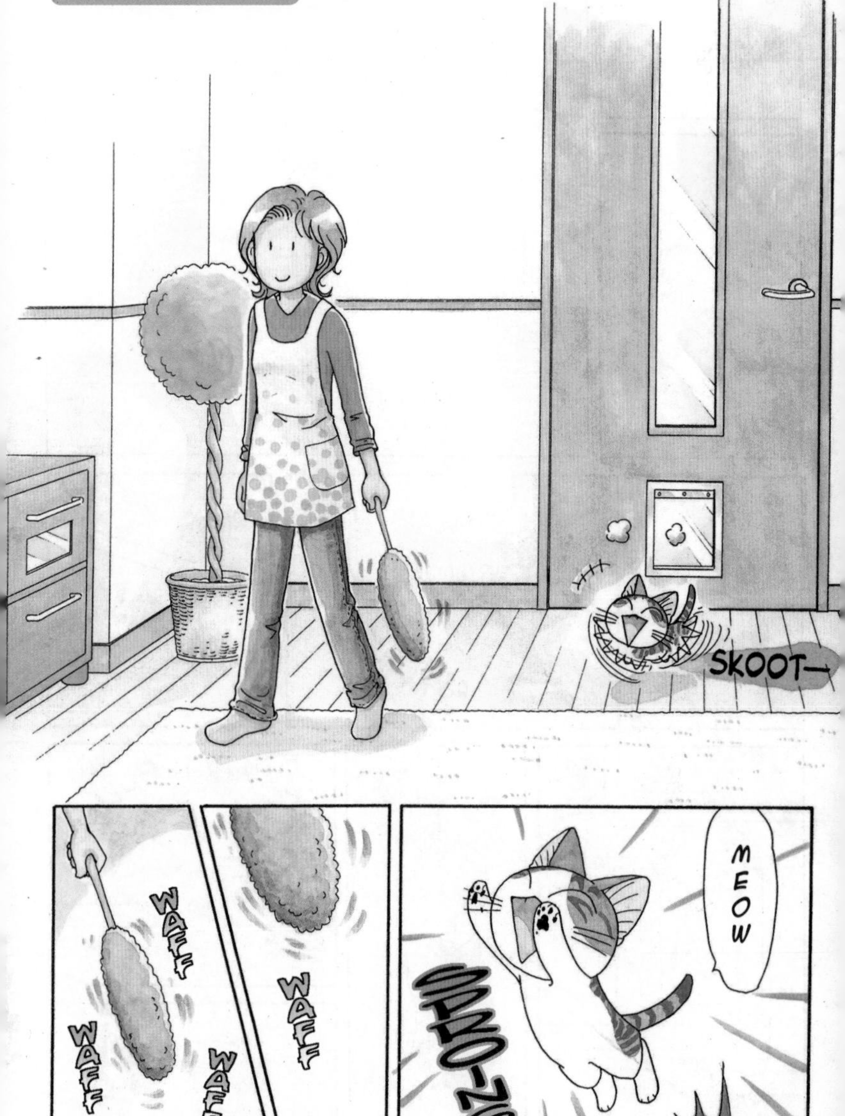
SKOOT—
WAFF
WAFF
WAFF
WAFF
SPRO-NG
MEOW

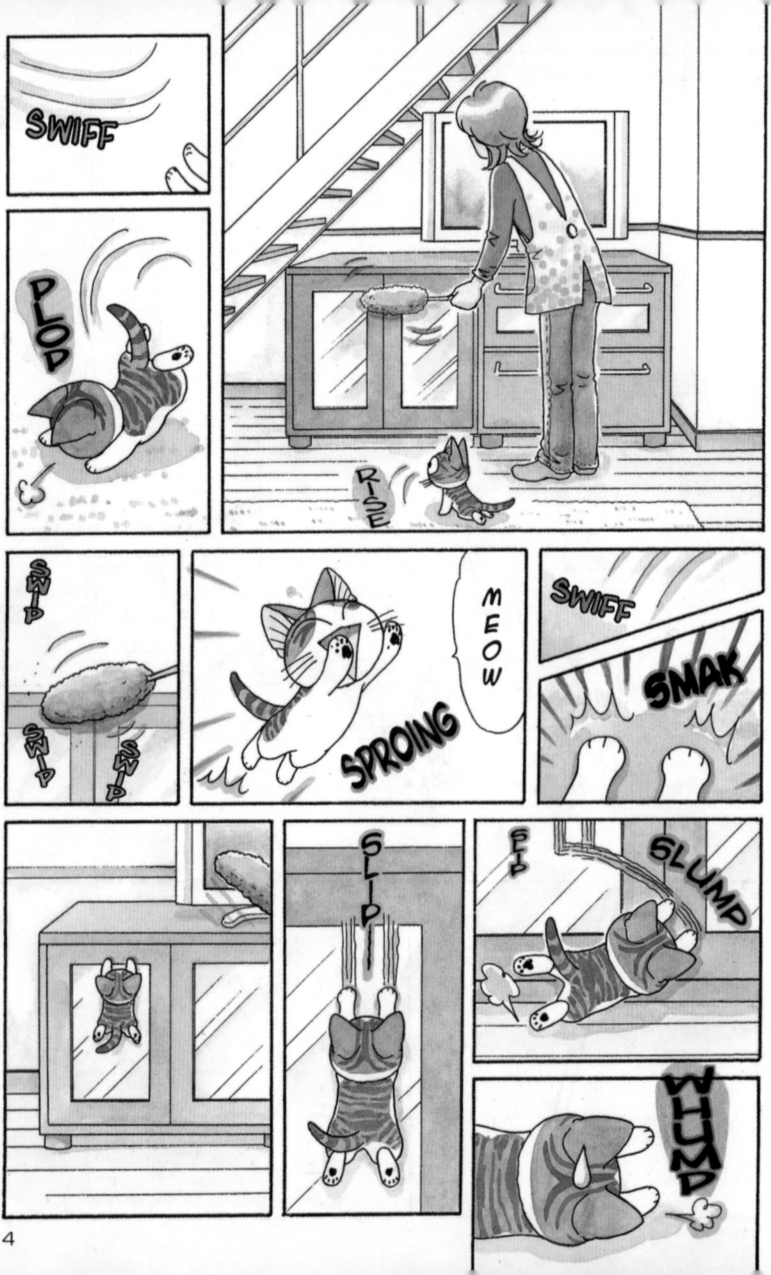
SWIFF
PLOP
RISE
SWIP
SWIP
SWIP
MEOW
SPROING
SWIFF
SMAK
SLID
SLIP
SLUMP
WHUMP

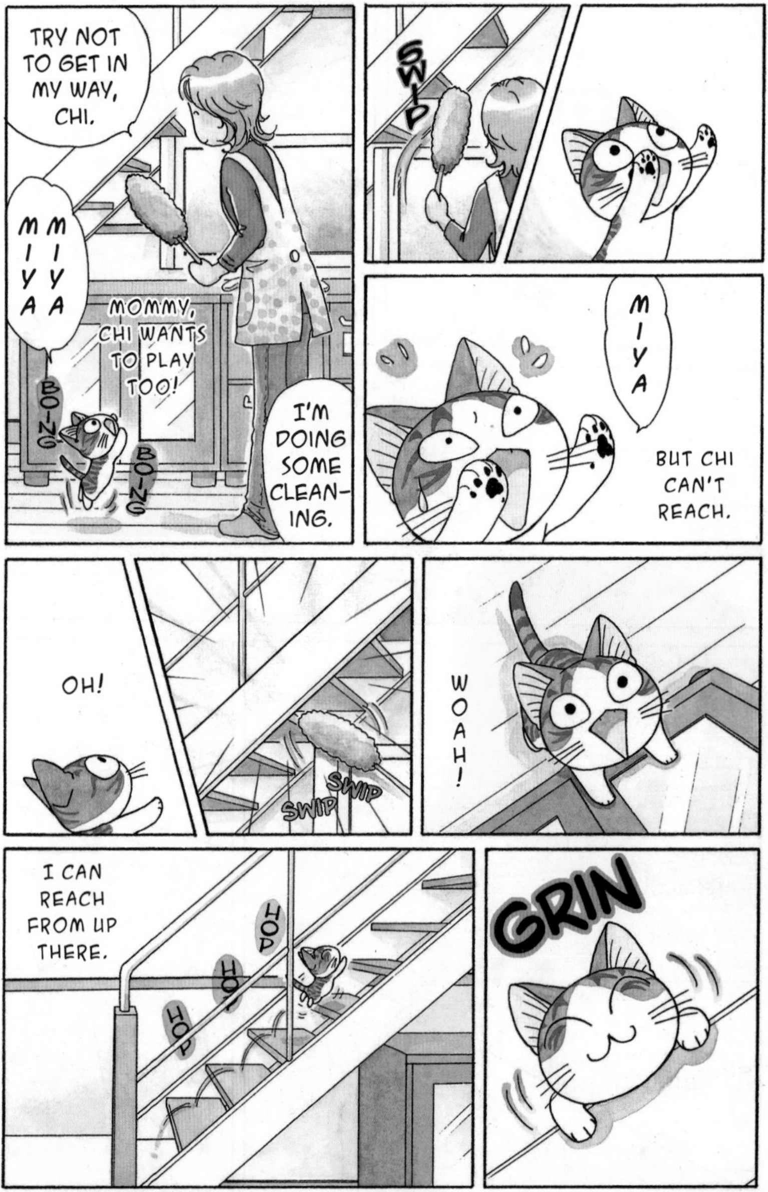
TRY NOT TO GET IN MY WAY, CHI.
MIYA MIYA
MOMMY, CHI WANTS TO PLAY TOO!
BOING
BOING
I'M DOING SOME CLEAN-ING.
SWIP
MIYA
BUT CHI CAN'T REACH.
OH!
SWIP
SWIP
WOAH!
I CAN REACH FROM UP THERE.
HOP
HOP
HOP
GRIN

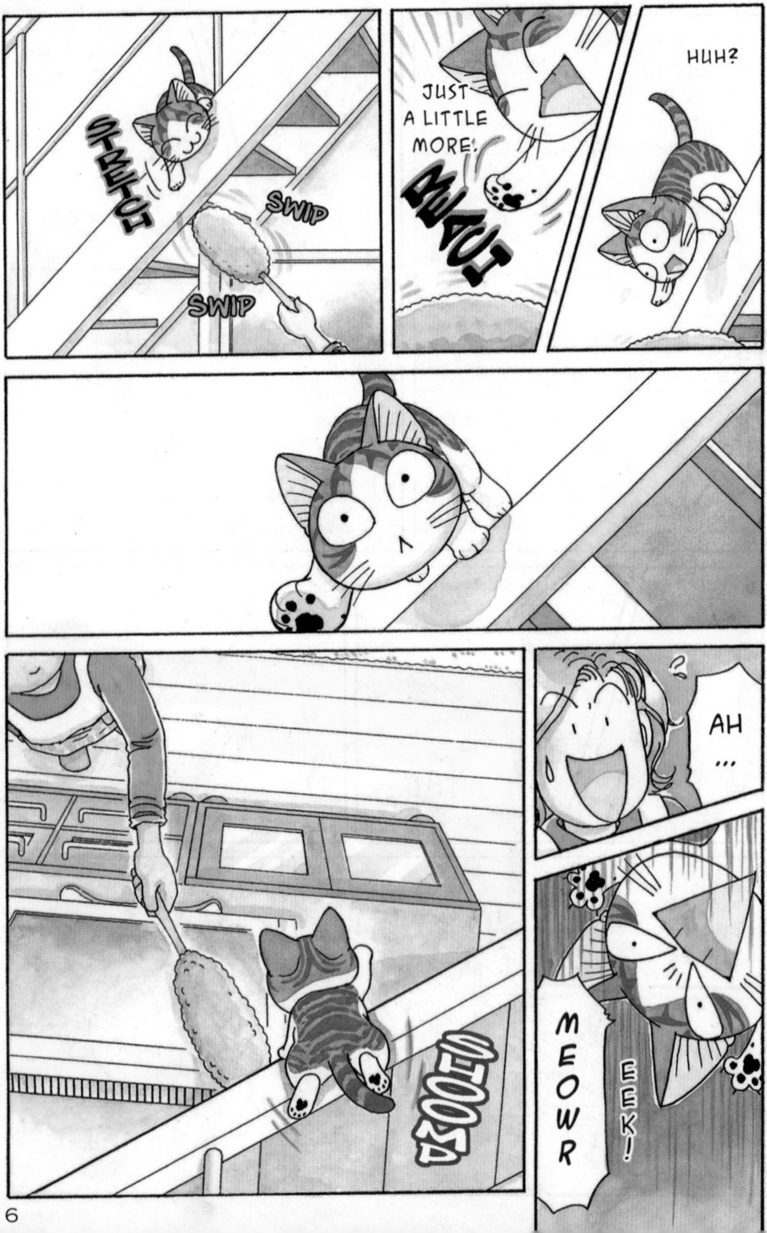
STRETCH
SWIP
SWIP
JUST A LITTLE MORE!
MYAU!
HUH?
AH ...
MEOWR
EEK!
SHOOP

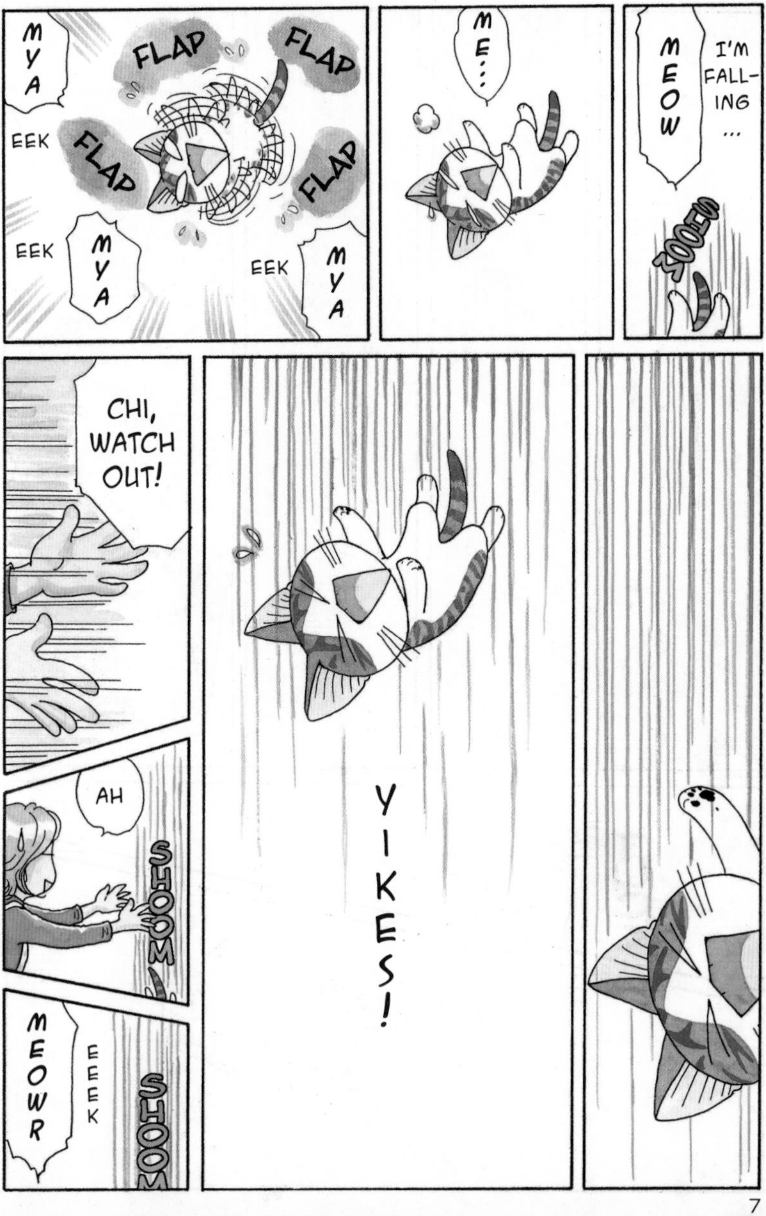
MYA
EEK
FLAP
FLAP
FLAP
FLAP
EEK
MYA
EEK
MYA
ME...
MEOW
I'M FALLING...
SWOOP
CHI, WATCH OUT!
AH
SHOOM
MEOWR
EEEEK
SHOOM
YIKES!

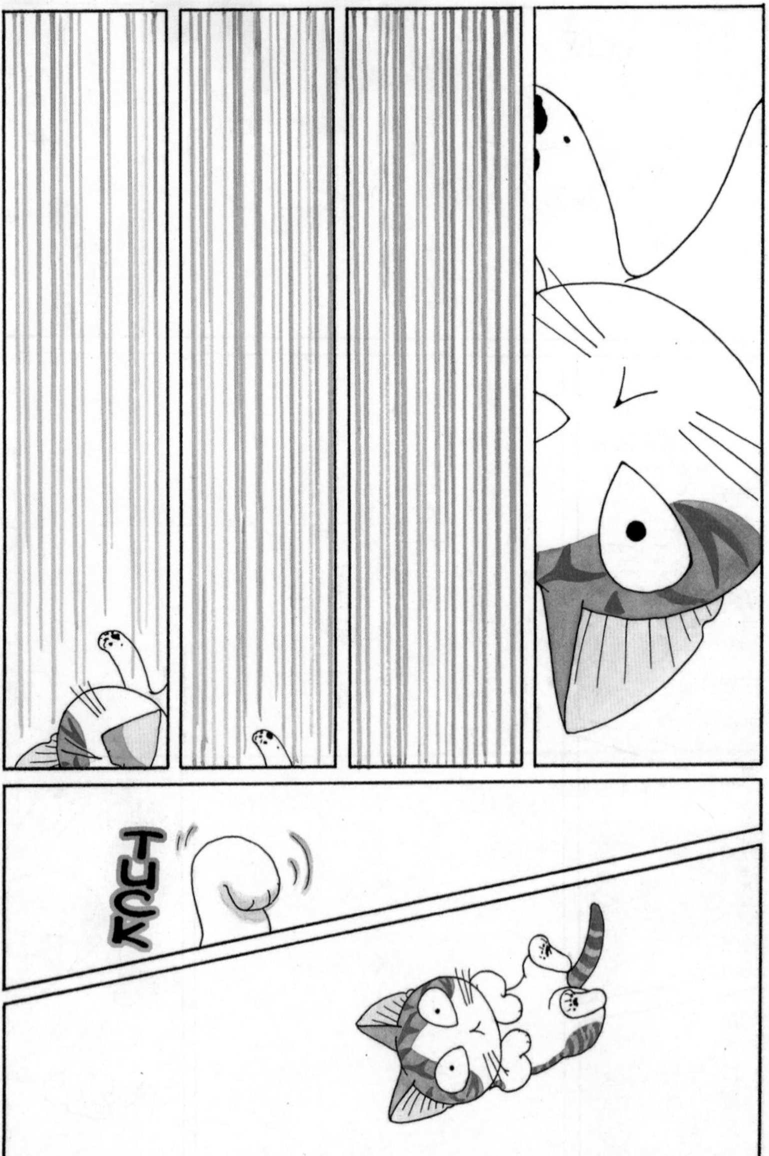
TUCK

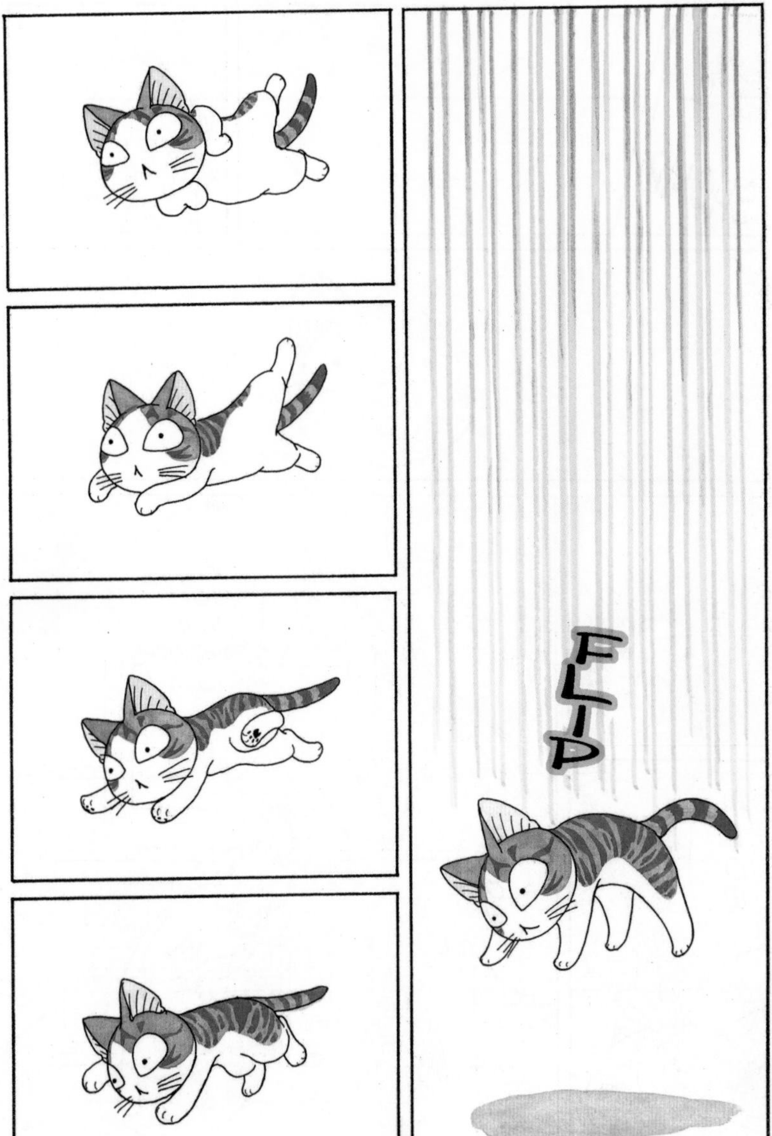
FLIP

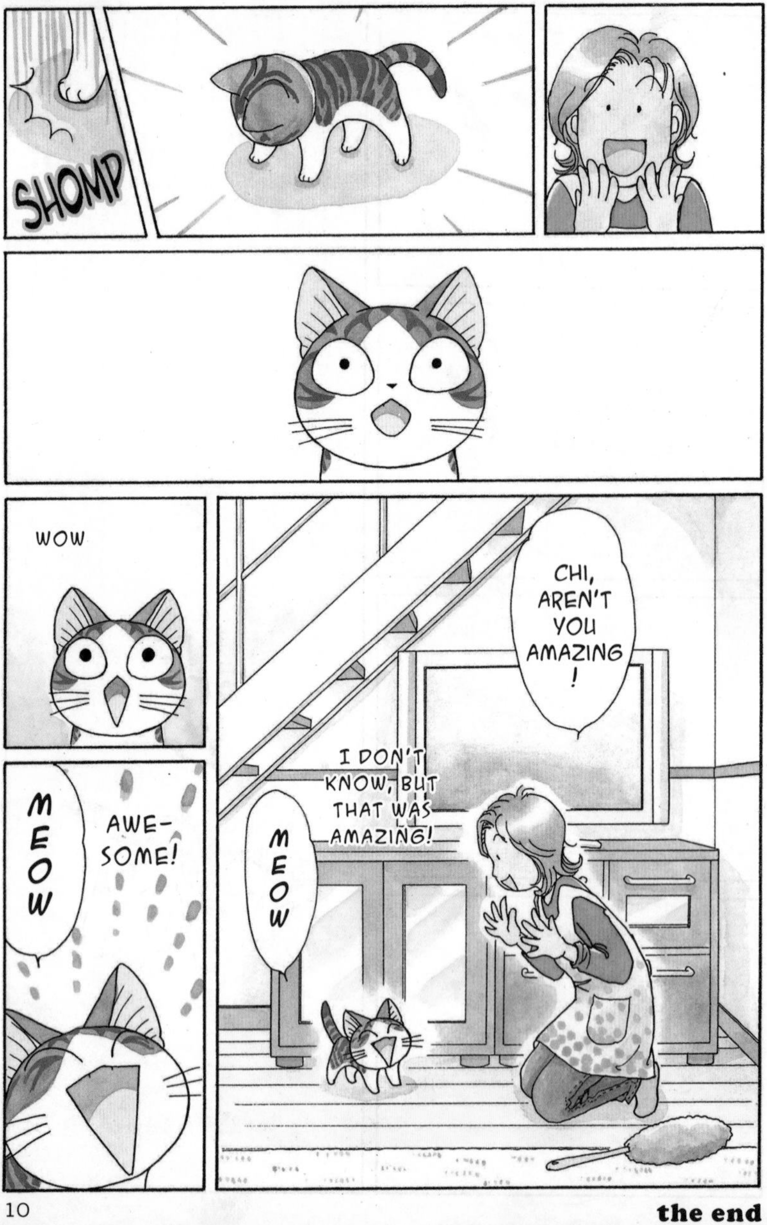
SHOMP
WOW
MEOW
AWE-SOME!
CHI, AREN'T YOU AMAZING!
MEOW
I DON'T KNOW, BUT THAT WAS AMAZING!

the end

homemade 130: a cat anticipates

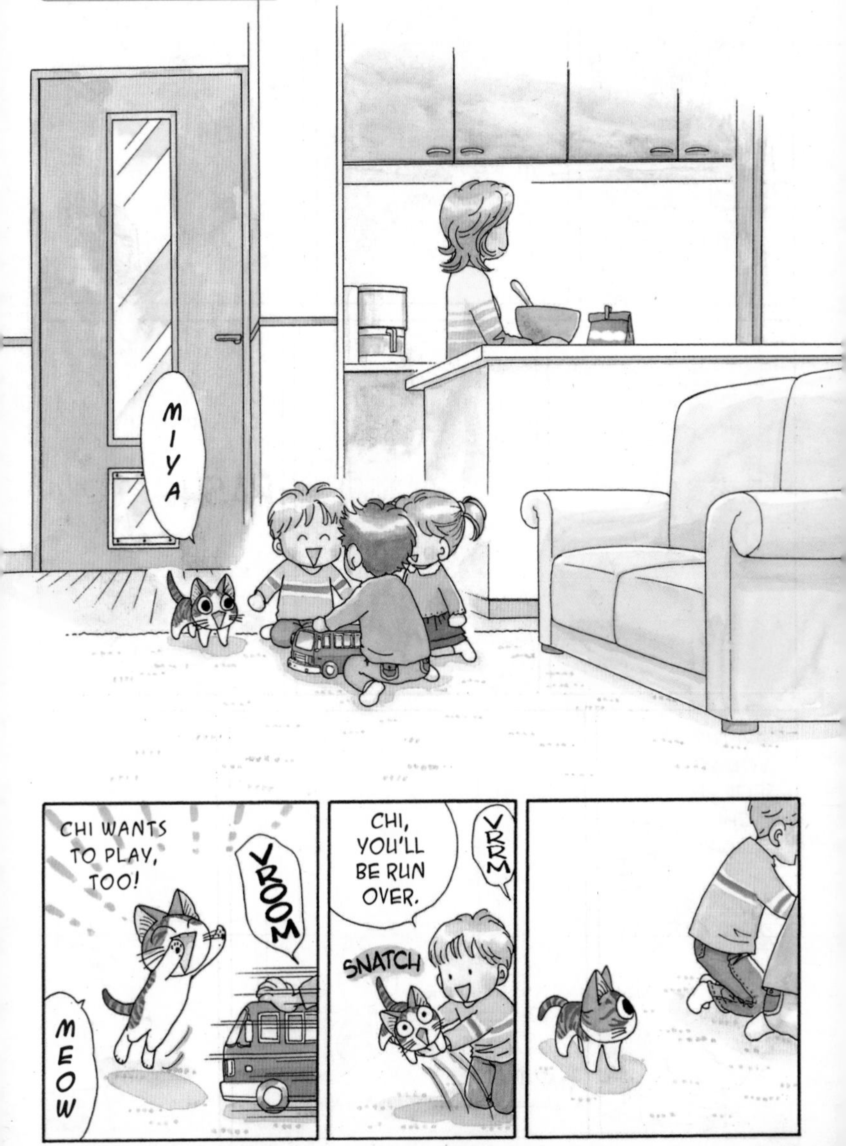
MIYA
CHI WANTS TO PLAY, TOO!
VROOM
MEOW
CHI, YOU'LL BE RUN OVER.
VRRM
SNATCH

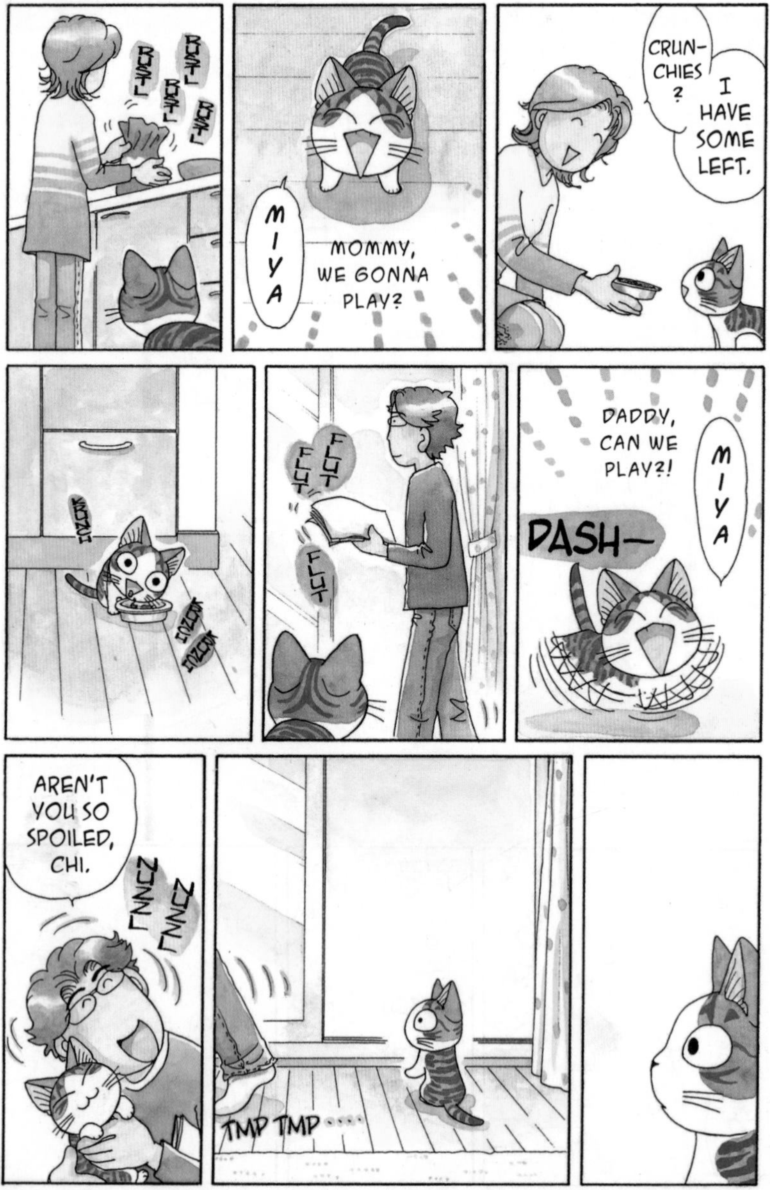
RUSTL RUSTL
RUSTL RUSTL
MIYA
MOMMY, WE GONNA PLAY?
CRUNCHIES?
I HAVE SOME LEFT.
KRONCH
KRONCH KRONCH
FLUT FLUT
FLUT
DADDY, CAN WE PLAY?!
MIYA
DASH—
AREN'T YOU SO SPOILED, CHI.
NUZZL NUZZL
TMP TMP....

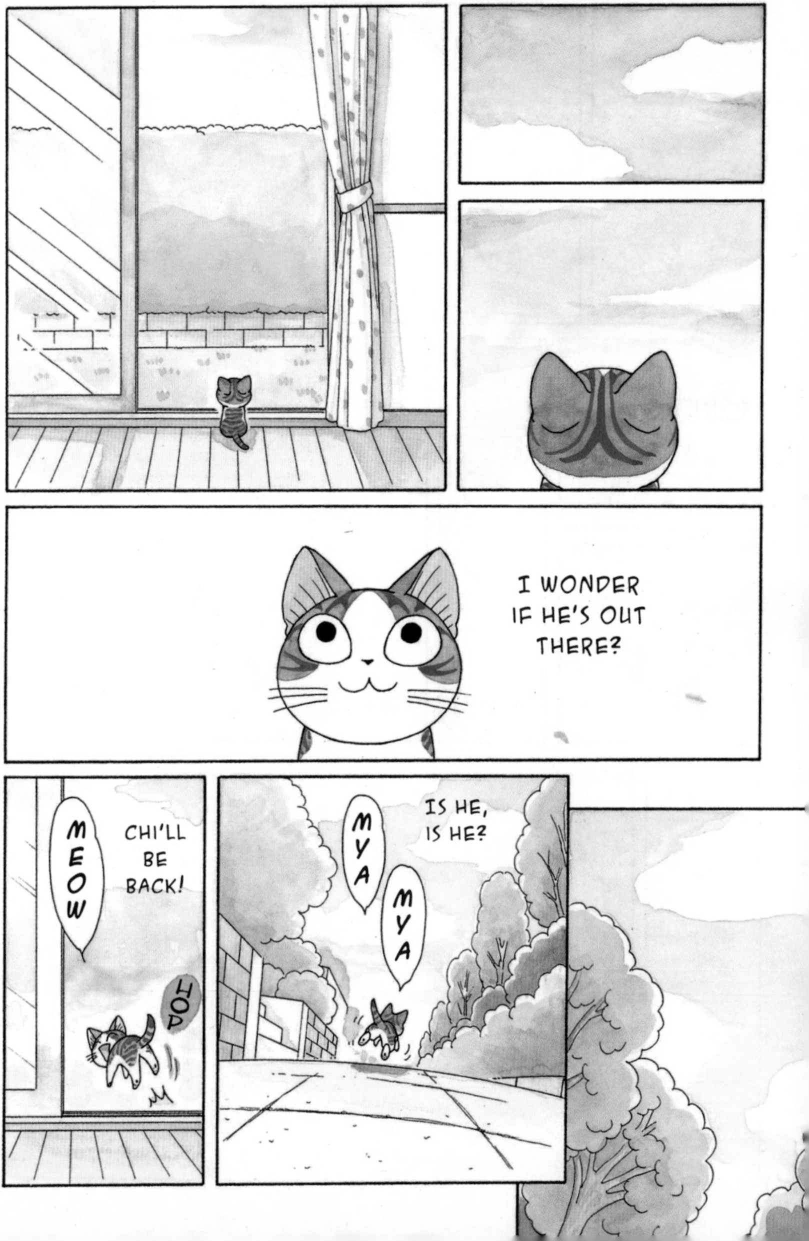
I WONDER IF HE'S OUT THERE?
MEOW
CHI'LL BE BACK!
HOP
MYA
MYA
IS HE, IS HE?

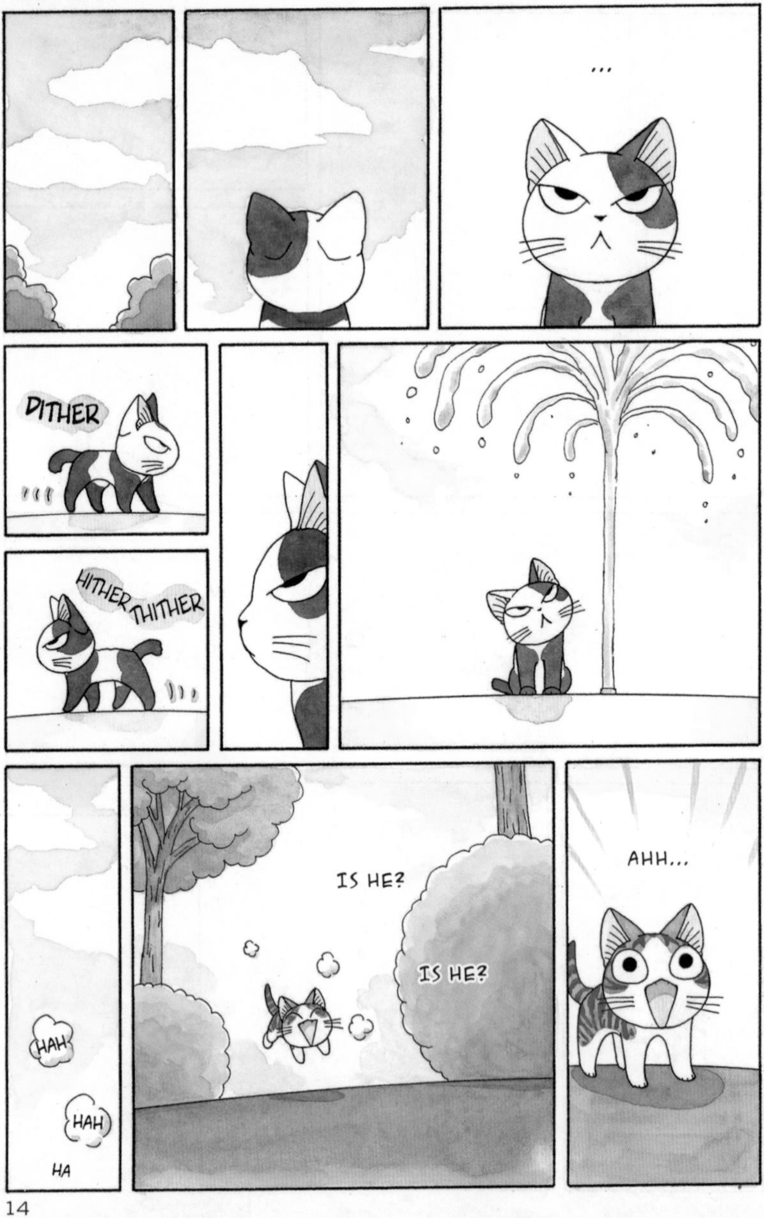
...
DITHER
HITHER THITHER
HAH
HAH
HA
IS HE?
IS HE?
AHH...

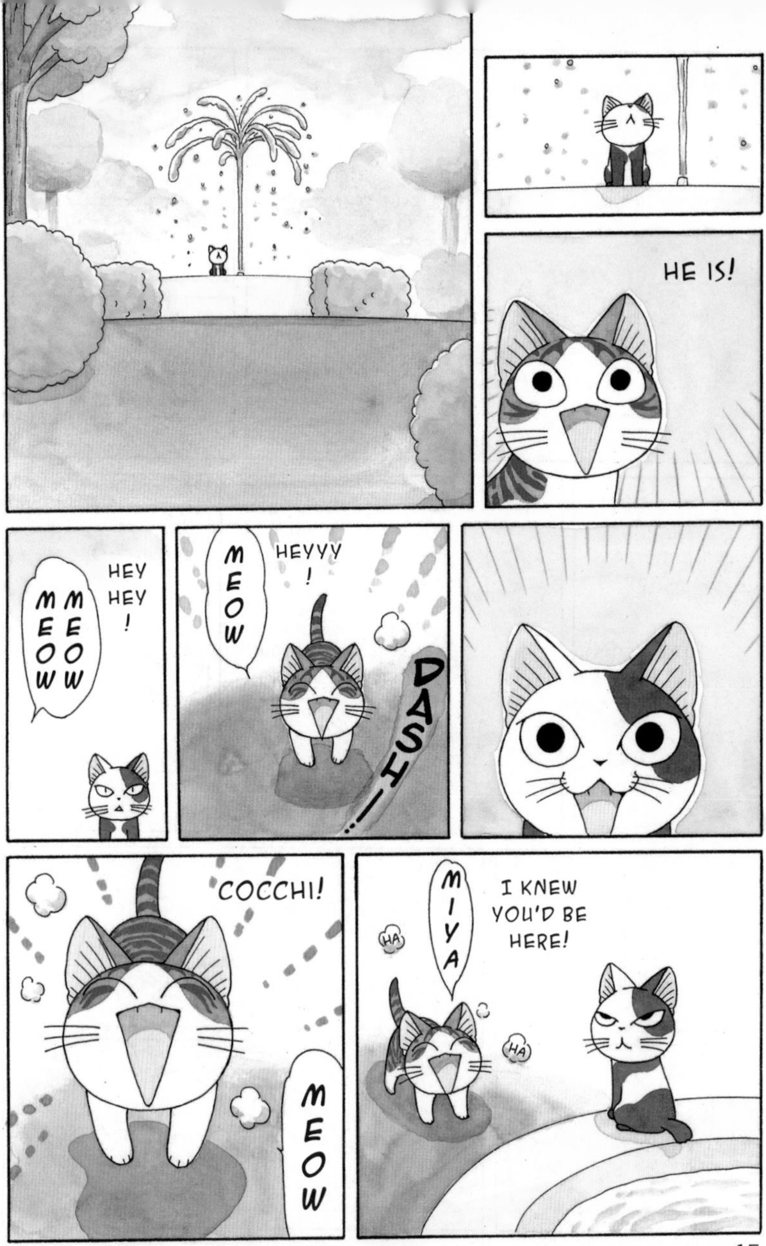
HE IS!
MEOW MEOW
HEY HEY!
MEOW
HEYYY!
DASH!
COCCHI!
MEOW
MIYA
HA
I KNEW YOU'D BE HERE!
HA

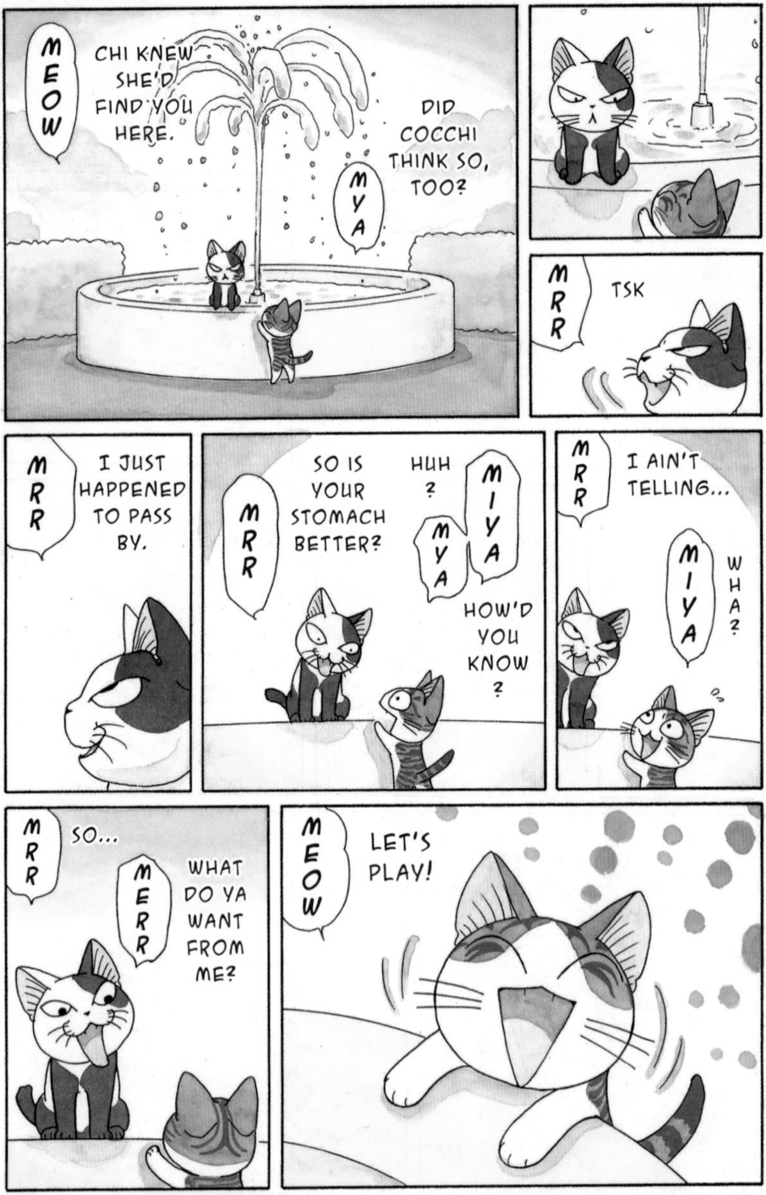

MEOW
CHI KNEW SHE'D FIND YOU HERE.
MYA
DID COCCHI THINK SO, TOO?
MRR
TSK
MRR
I JUST HAPPENED TO PASS BY.
MRR
SO IS YOUR STOMACH BETTER?
MYA
HUH?
MIYA
HOW'D YOU KNOW?
MRR
I AIN'T TELLING...
MIYA
WHA?
MRR
SO...
MERR
WHAT DO YA WANT FROM ME?
MEOW
LET'S PLAY!

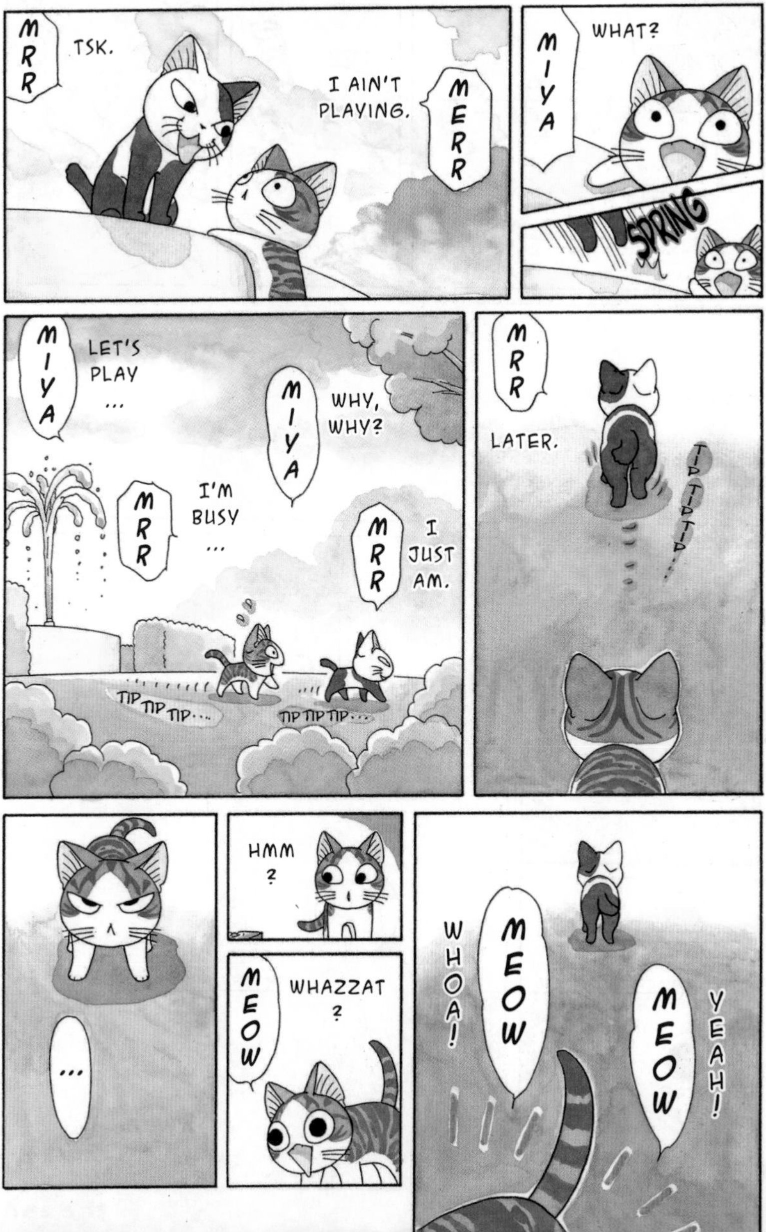
MRR
TSK.
MERR
I AIN'T PLAYING.
MIYA
WHAT?
SPRING
MIYA
LET'S PLAY ...
MIYA
WHY, WHY?
MRR
I'M BUSY ...
MRR
I JUST AM.
TIP TIP TIP....
TIP TIP TIP...
MRR
LATER.
TIP TIP TIP...
...
HMM ?
MEOW
WHAZZAT ?
MEOW
WHOA!
MEOW
YEAH!

MYAMYA

SHR RSTL RSTL RSTL

SHR SHR SHR

RSTL SHR RSTL SMAK SMAK SHR RSTL SMAK WRR WRR WRR

SKFF

HUH?

HEY ?!

MEOW

MRR HEH-HEH!

18

the end

homemade 131: a cat cases

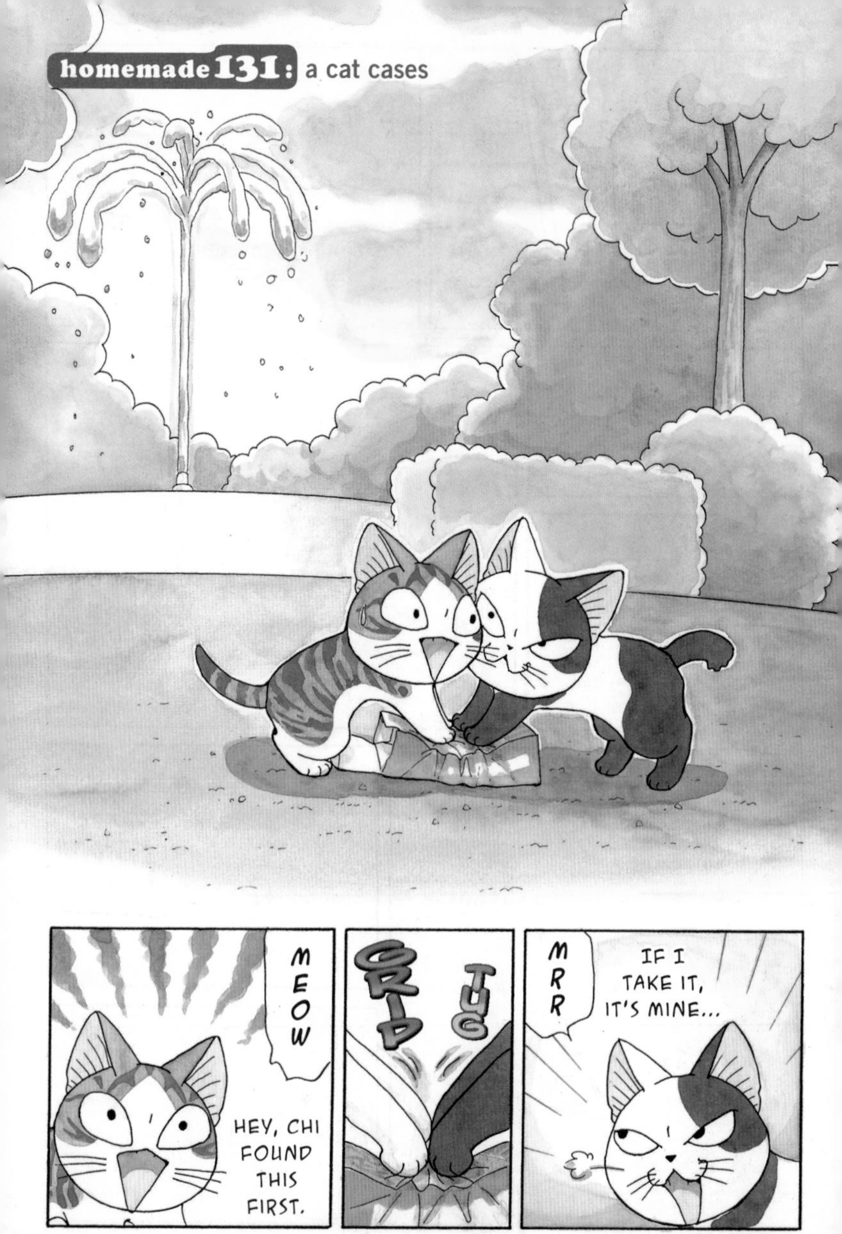
MEOW
HEY, CHI FOUND THIS FIRST.
GRIP
TUG
MRR
IF I TAKE IT, IT'S MINE...

BUT CHI WAS PLAYING WITH IT.

MRR

MEOW

HOW NAIVE.

HUH?

MRR

YOU HAVEN'T CHECKED WHAT'S INSIDE?

!

MYA MYA

C-CHI WAS THINKING TO.

MERR

REALLY?

MEOW

IT MIGHT BE SOMETHING AWESOME.

MEOW

MRR

AWESOME?

YEAH, SOMETHING AWESOME.

MRR

AWESOME... LIKE WHAT?

HUH?

MYA

AWE-
SOME...

LIKE...

MEOW
DO YOU
GET IT,
COCCHI?
HRN
?
MRR

AWESOME,
THAT'S
LIKE...
MRR

WHAT
COULD
IT BE?
MYA
MRR
SUSPI-
CIOUS
...

LET'S
JUST
CHECK
IT OUT.
MRR

21

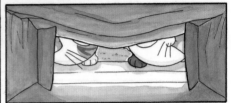

I CAN'T SEE ALL THE WAY IN...

MRR

MEOW

NOPE.

MRR

KURUT

I'M GONNA CHECK.

KURUT

MEOW

CHI'S GOING FIRST.

SHUV

PLUSH

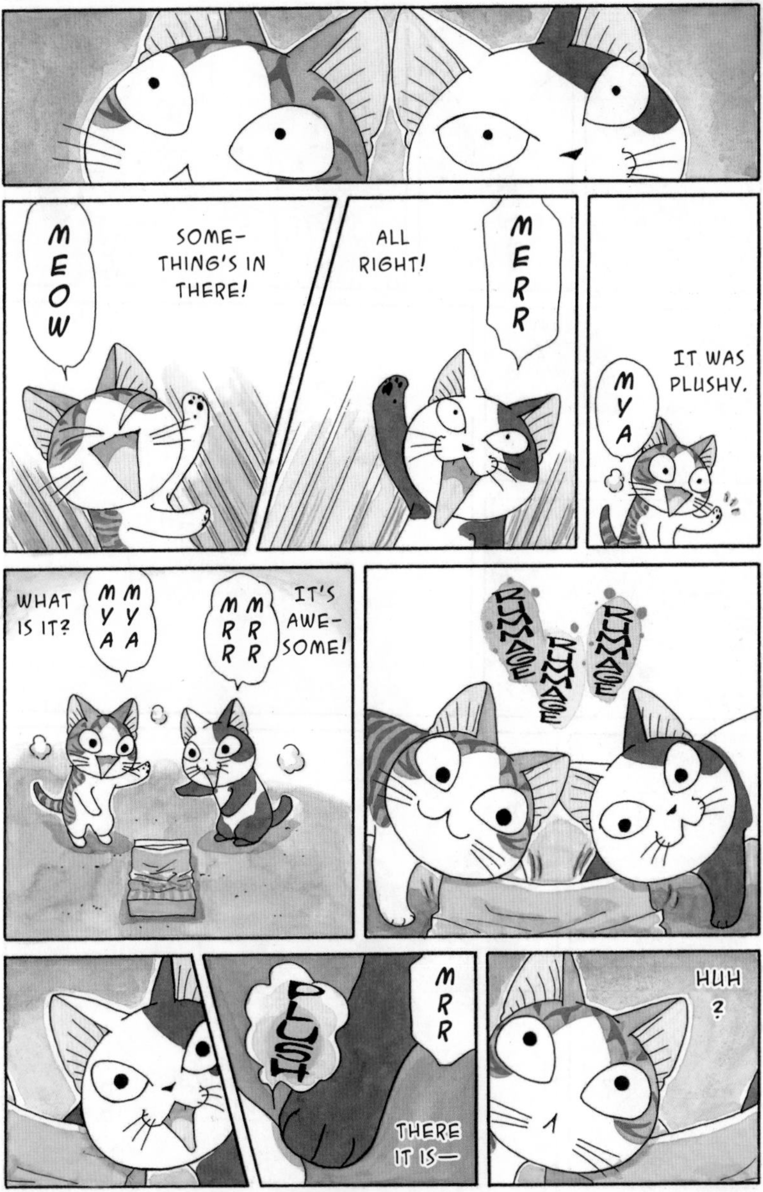
MEOW
SOME-THING'S IN THERE!
ALL RIGHT!
MERR
MYA
IT WAS PLUSHY.
WHAT IS IT?
MYA MYA
MRR MRR
IT'S AWE-SOME!
RUMMAGE
RUMMAGE
RUMMAGE
PLUSH
MRR
THERE IT IS—
HUH?

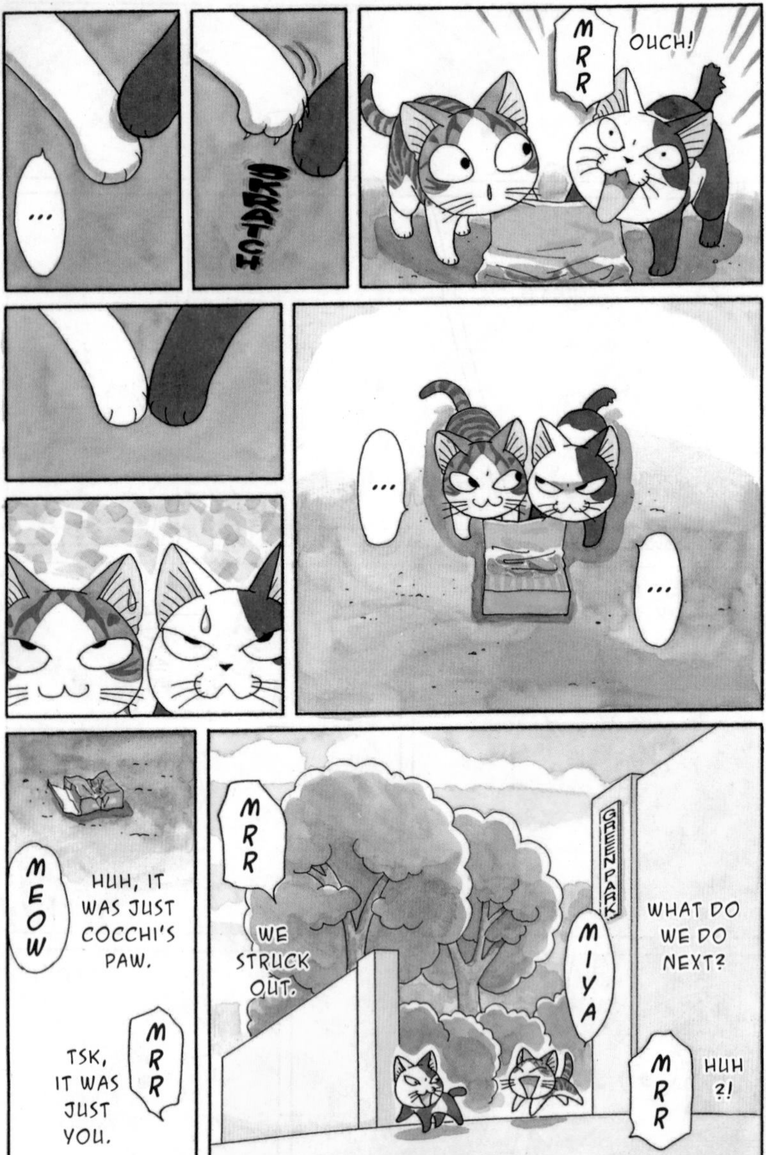
...
SKRATCH
MRR
OUCH!
...
...
MEOW
HUH, IT WAS JUST COCCHI'S PAW.
MRR
TSK, IT WAS JUST YOU.
MRR
WE STRUCK OUT.
GREENPARK
MIYA
WHAT DO WE DO NEXT?
MRR
HUH?!

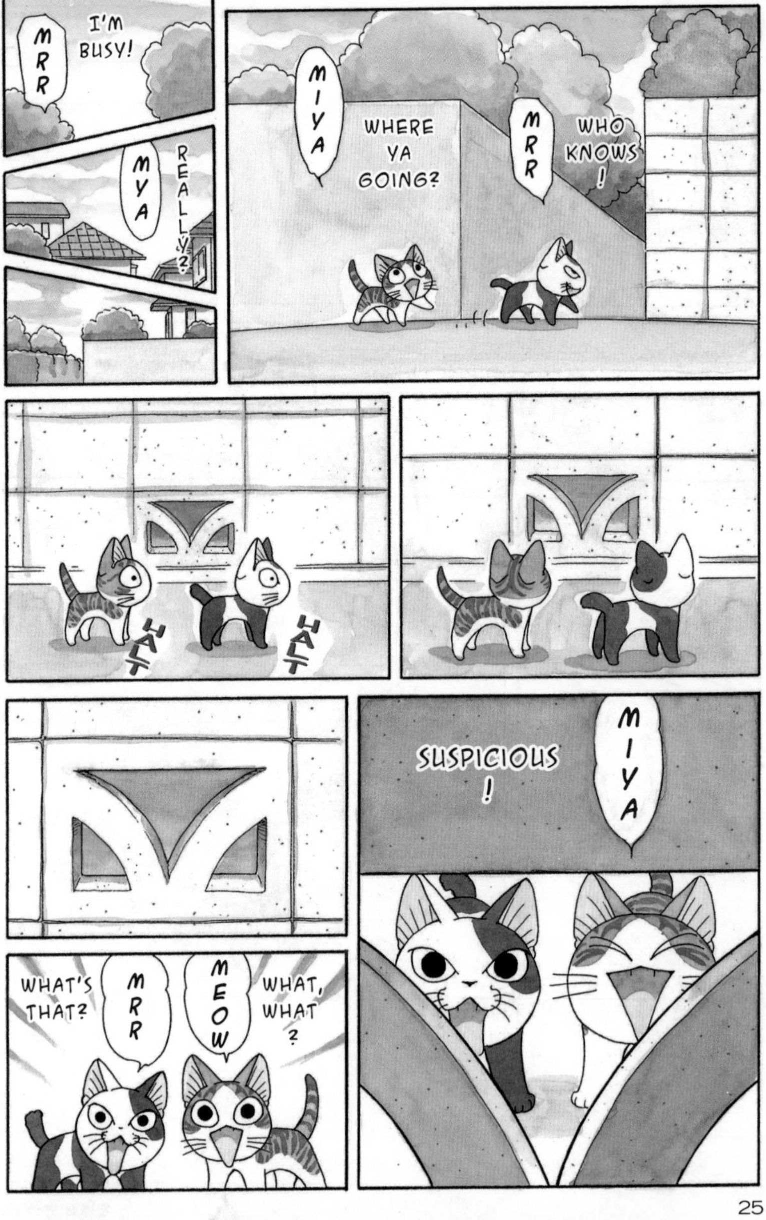
MRR
I'M BUSY!
MYA
REALLY?
MIYA
WHERE YA GOING?
MRR
WHO KNOWS!
HALT
HALT
SUSPICIOUS!
MIYA
WHAT'S THAT?
MRR
MEOW
WHAT, WHAT?

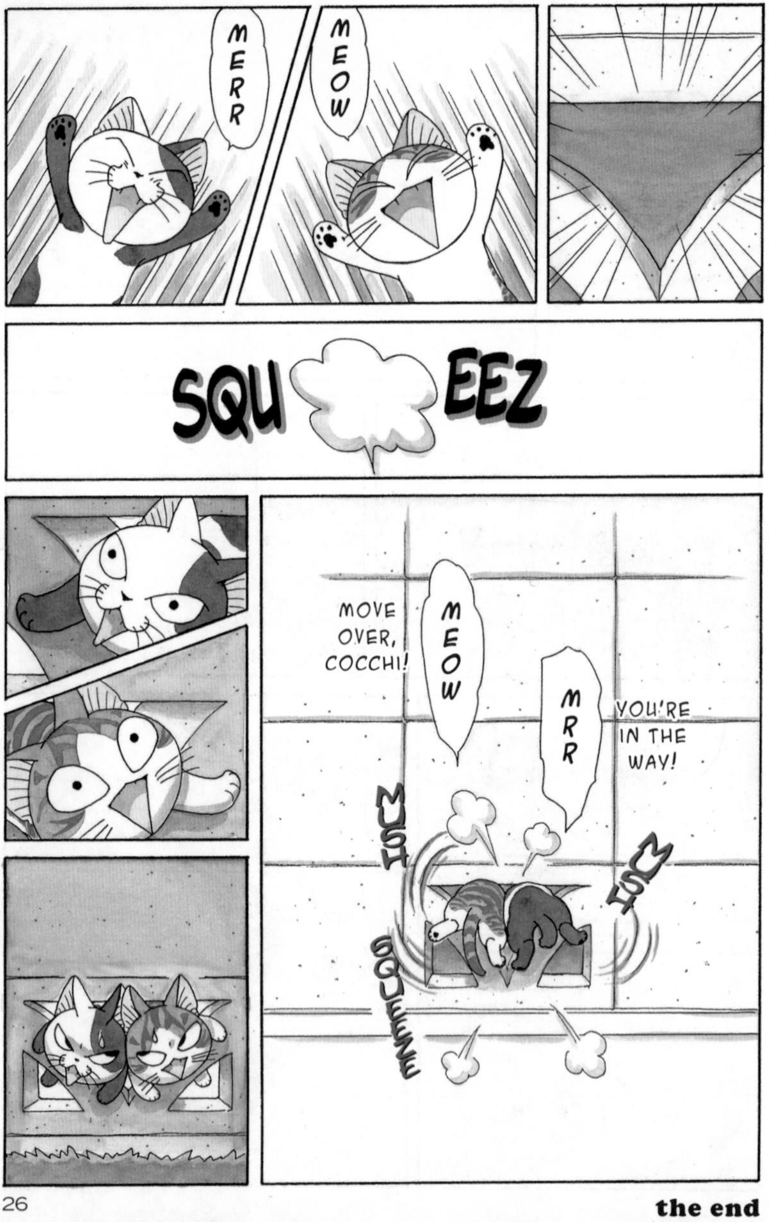

MERR
MEOW
SQU EEZ
MOVE OVER, COCCHI!
MEOW
MRR
YOU'RE IN THE WAY!
MUSH
MUSH

the end

homemade 132: a cat is wowed

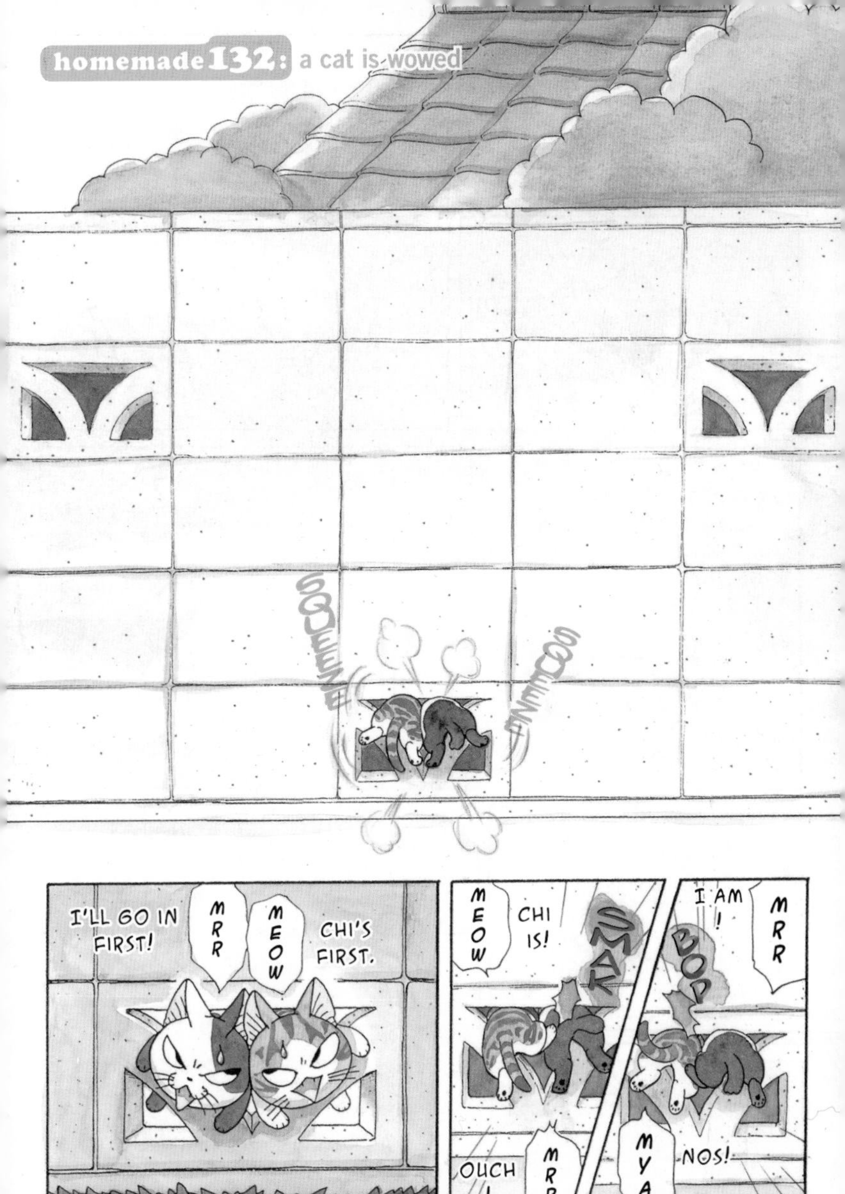
SQUEEEE
SQUEEEE
I'LL GO IN FIRST!
MRR
MEOW
CHI'S FIRST.
MEOW
CHI IS!
SMAK
OUCH!
MRR
I AM!
MRR
BOP
MYA
NOS!

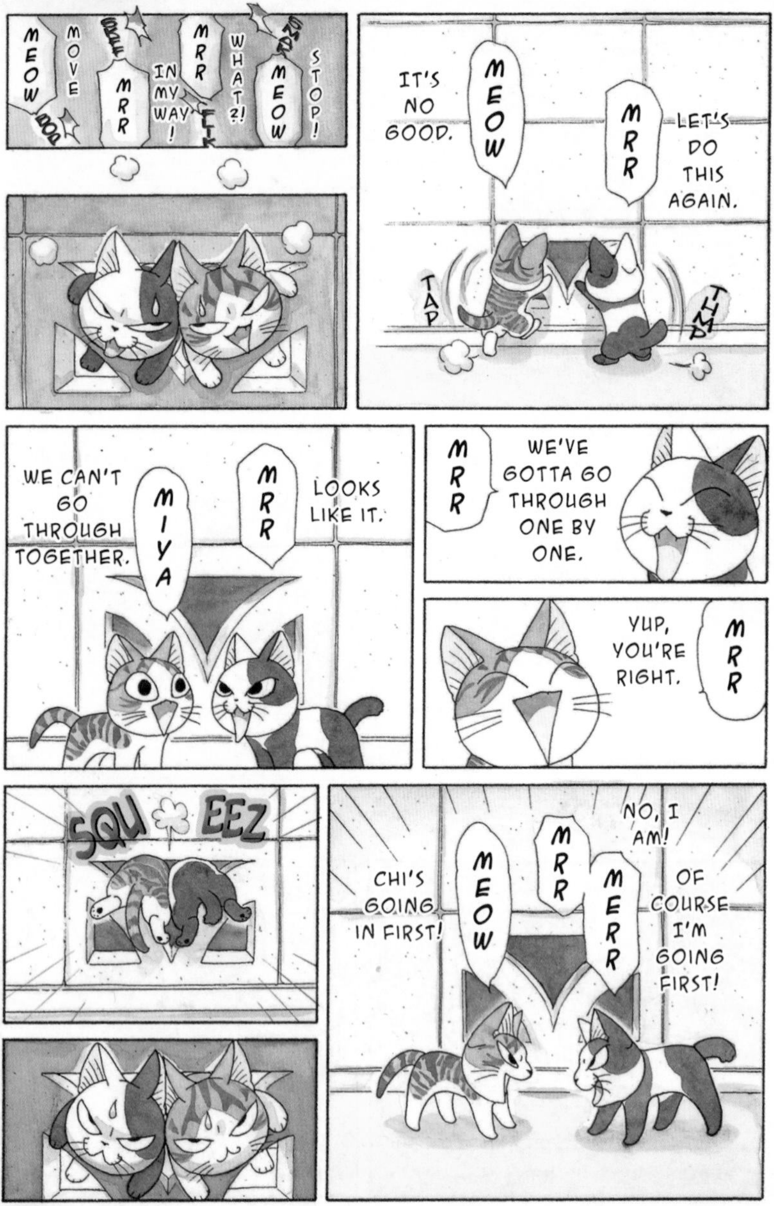
MEOW
MOVE
MRR
IN MY WAY!
MRR
FLIK
WHAT?!
MEOW
STOP!
IT'S NO GOOD.
MEOW
MRR
LET'S DO THIS AGAIN.
TAP
THMP
WE CAN'T GO THROUGH TOGETHER.
MIYA
MRR
LOOKS LIKE IT.
MRR
WE'VE GOTTA GO THROUGH ONE BY ONE.
YUP, YOU'RE RIGHT.
MRR
SQU EEZ
CHI'S GOING IN FIRST!
MEOW
MRR
NO, I AM!
MERR
OF COURSE I'M GOING FIRST!

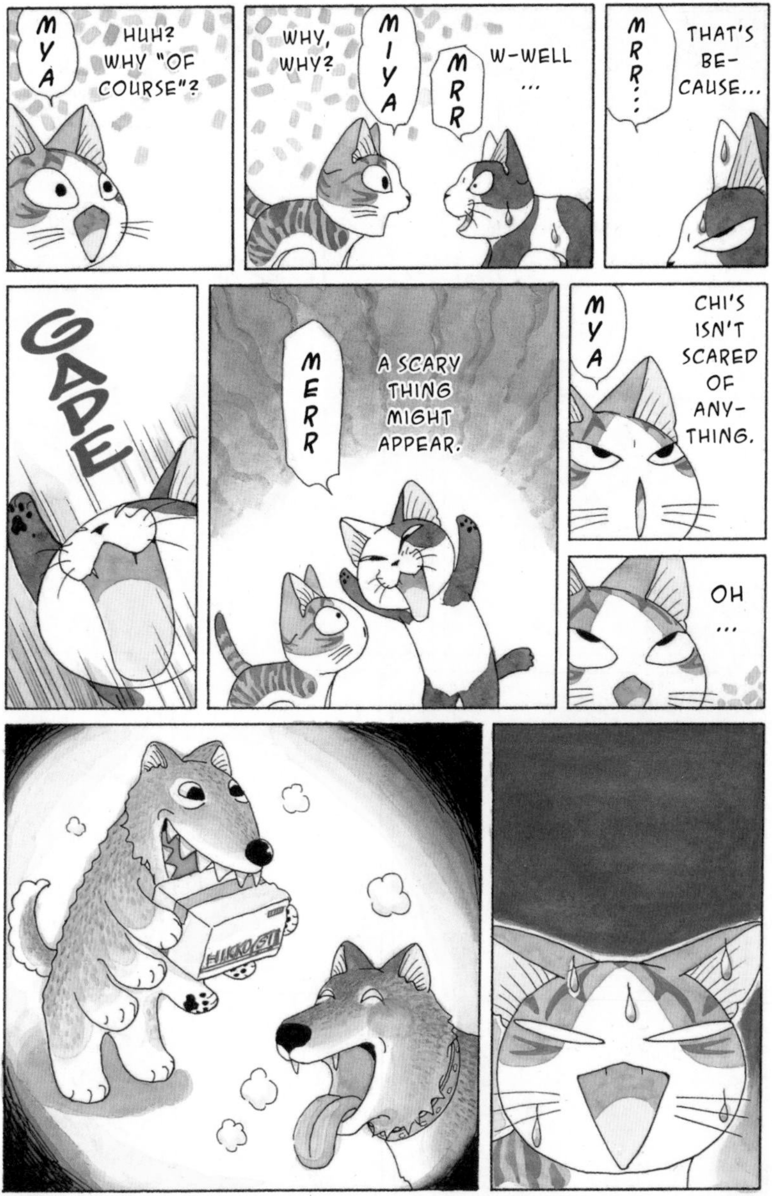
MYA
HUH? WHY "OF COURSE"?
WHY, WHY?
MIYA
MRR
W-WELL ...
MRR...
THAT'S BE-CAUSE...
GADE
MERR
A SCARY THING MIGHT APPEAR.
MYA
CHI'S ISN'T SCARED OF ANY-THING.
OH ...

...

HEH
HEH

MRR

I'LL
GO ON
AHEAD
THEN.

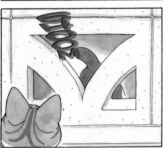

MIYA

COCCHI,
ARE YOU
OKAY?

COME
ON
OVER.

MRR

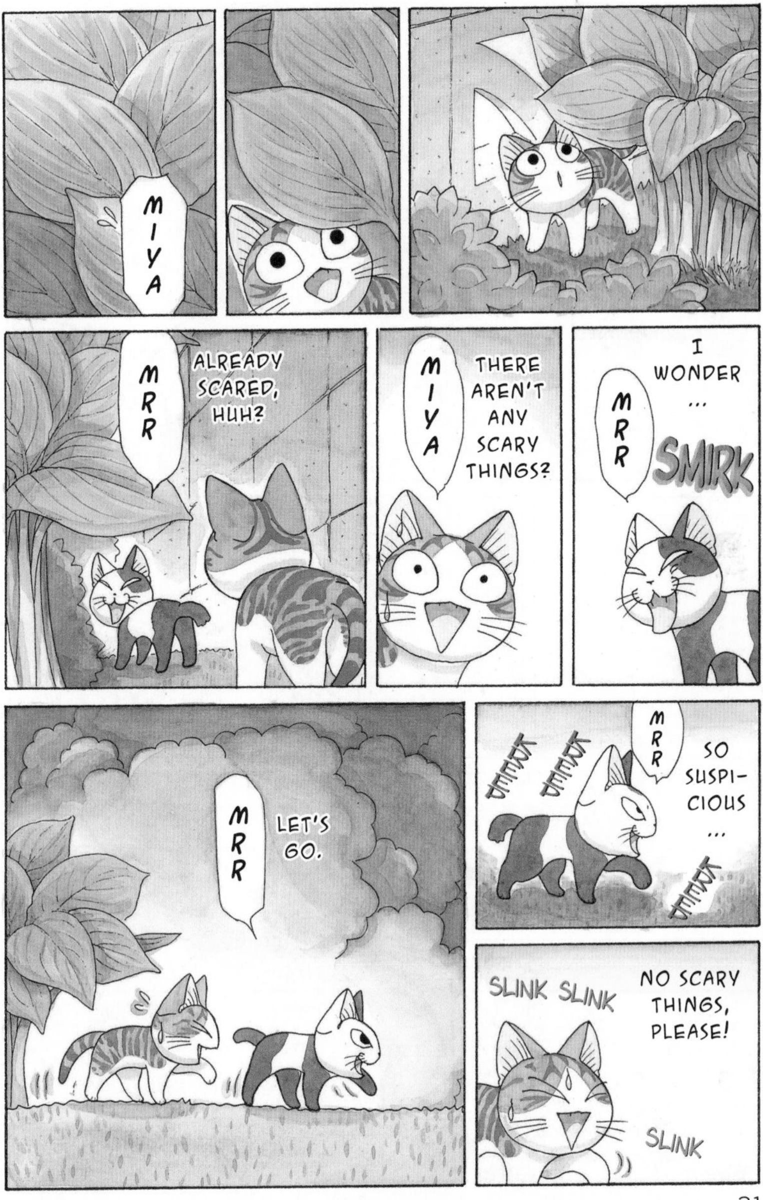
MIYA
MRR
ALREADY SCARED, HUH?
MIYA
THERE AREN'T ANY SCARY THINGS?
MRR
I WONDER ...
SMIRK
MRR
LET'S GO.
MRR
SO SUSPICIOUS ...
SLINK SLINK
NO SCARY THINGS, PLEASE!
SLINK

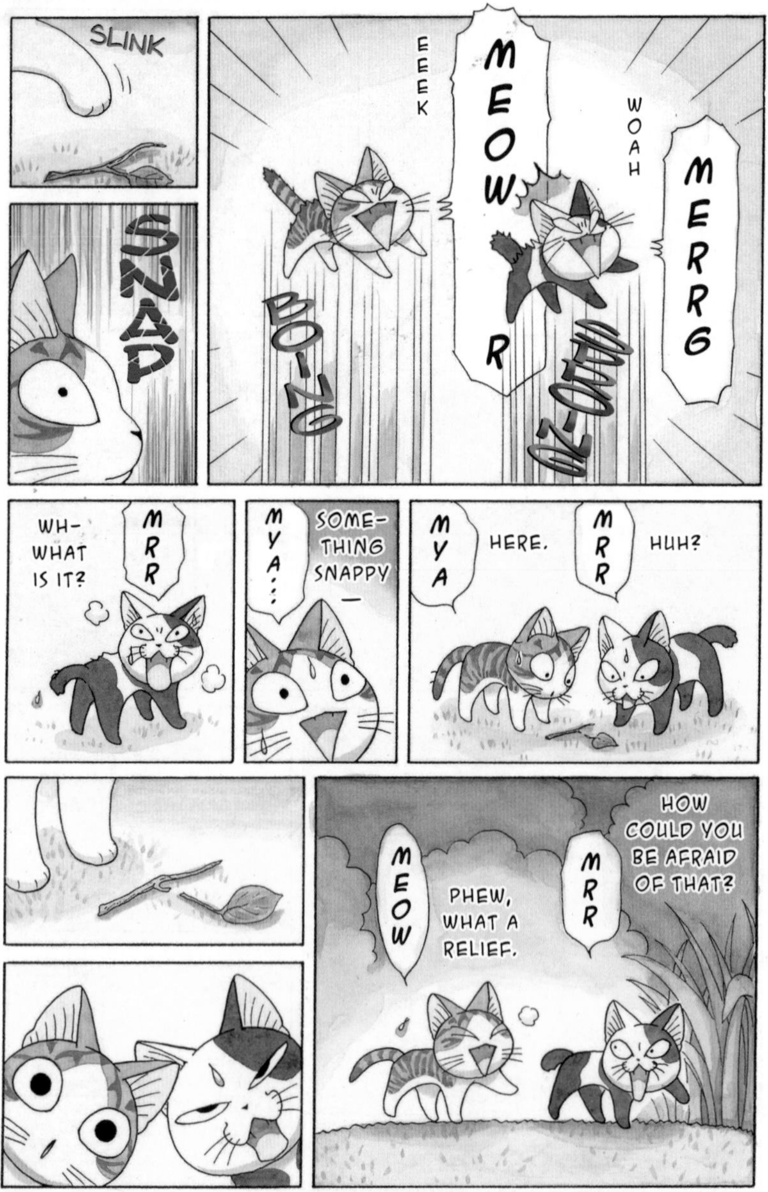
SLINK
SNAP
EEEK
MEOWR
BOING
WOAH
MERRG
BOING
MRR
WH-WHAT IS IT?
MYA...
SOMETHING SNAPPY—
MYA
HERE.
MRR
HUH?
MEOW
PHEW, WHAT A RELIEF.
MRR
HOW COULD YOU BE AFRAID OF THAT?

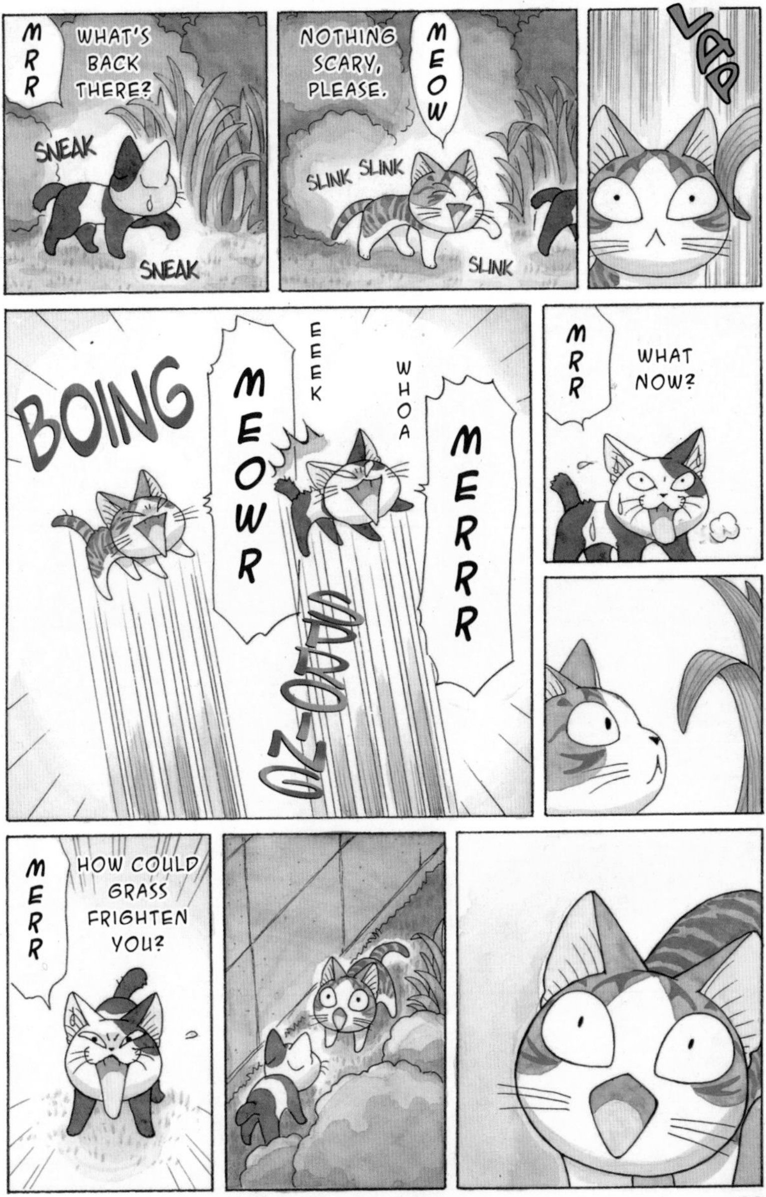
MRR
WHAT'S BACK THERE?
SNEAK
SNEAK
NOTHING SCARY, PLEASE.
MEOW
SLINK SLINK
SLINK
VAP
BOING
MEOWR
EEEK
WHOA
MERRRR
SPRO-ING
MRR
WHAT NOW?
MERR
HOW COULD GRASS FRIGHTEN YOU?

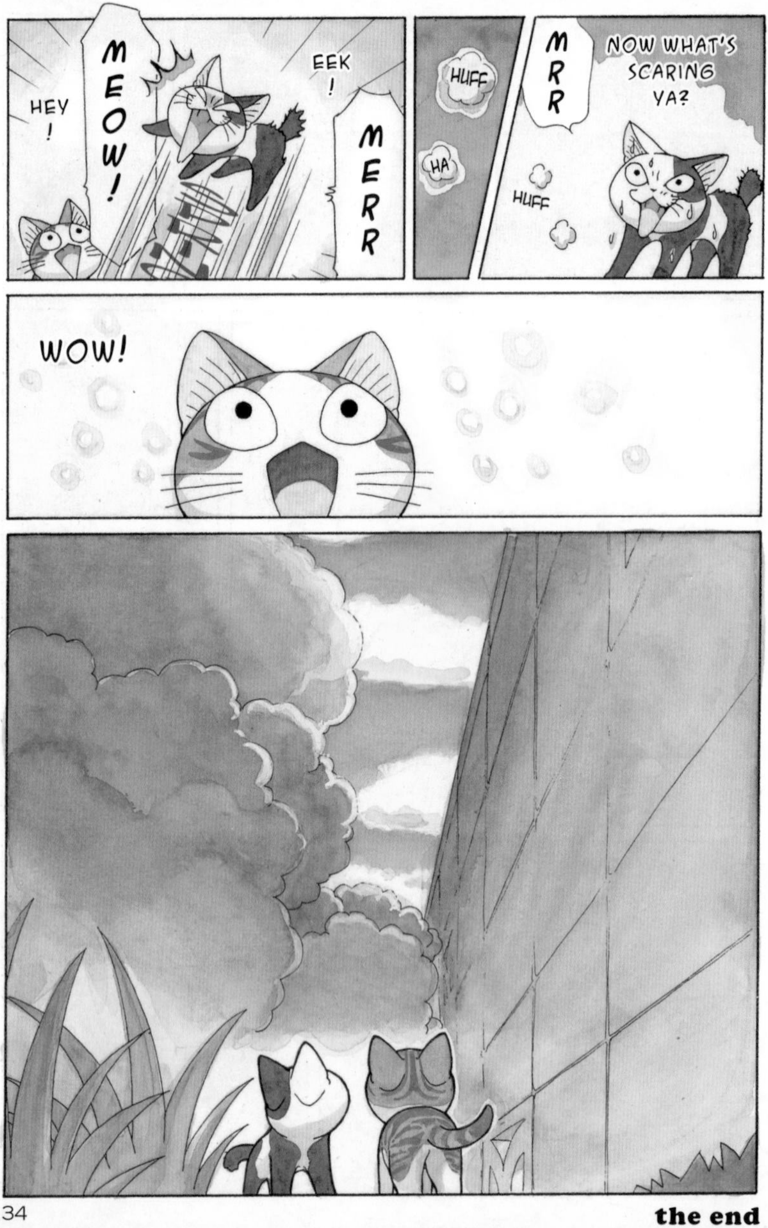
NOW WHAT'S SCARING YA?
MRR
HUFF
HUFF
HA
EEK!
MERR
MEOW!
HEY!
WOW!

the end

homemade 133: a cat has a blast

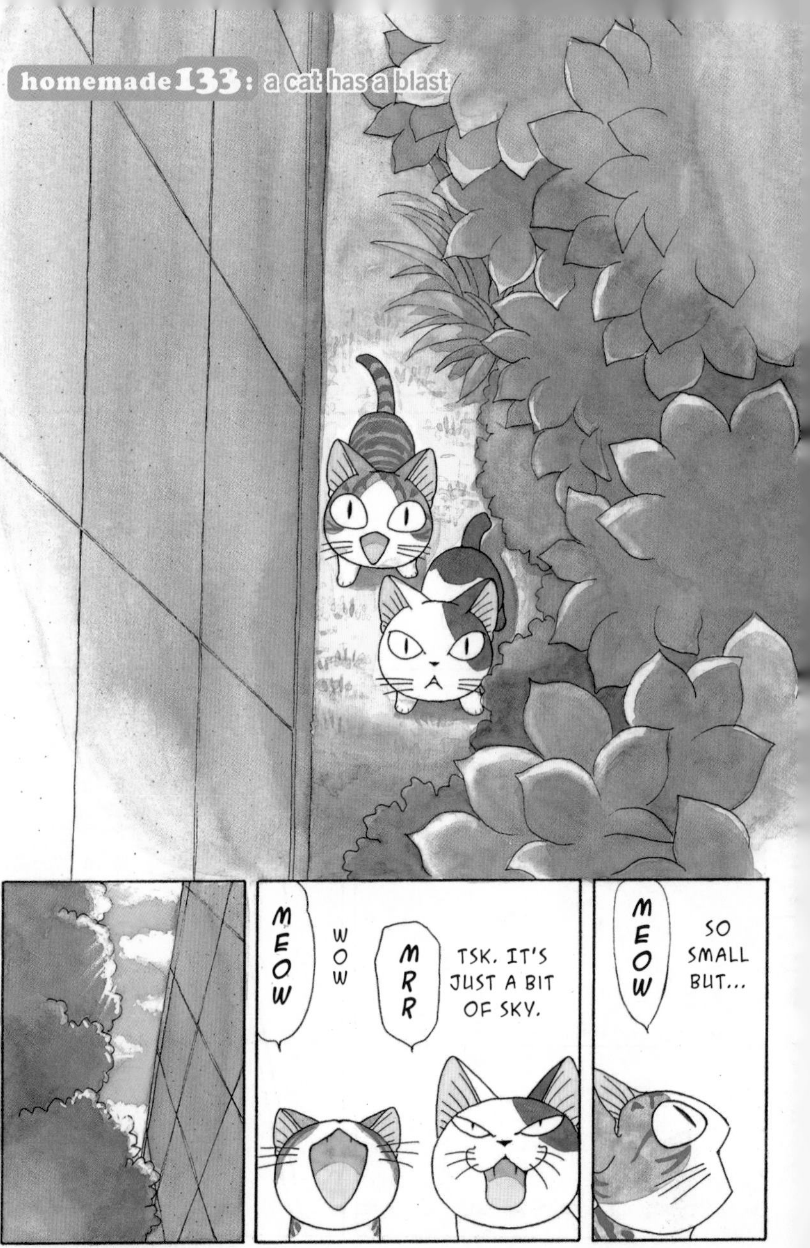

MEOW
WOW
MRR
TSK. IT'S JUST A BIT OF SKY.
MEOW
SO SMALL BUT...

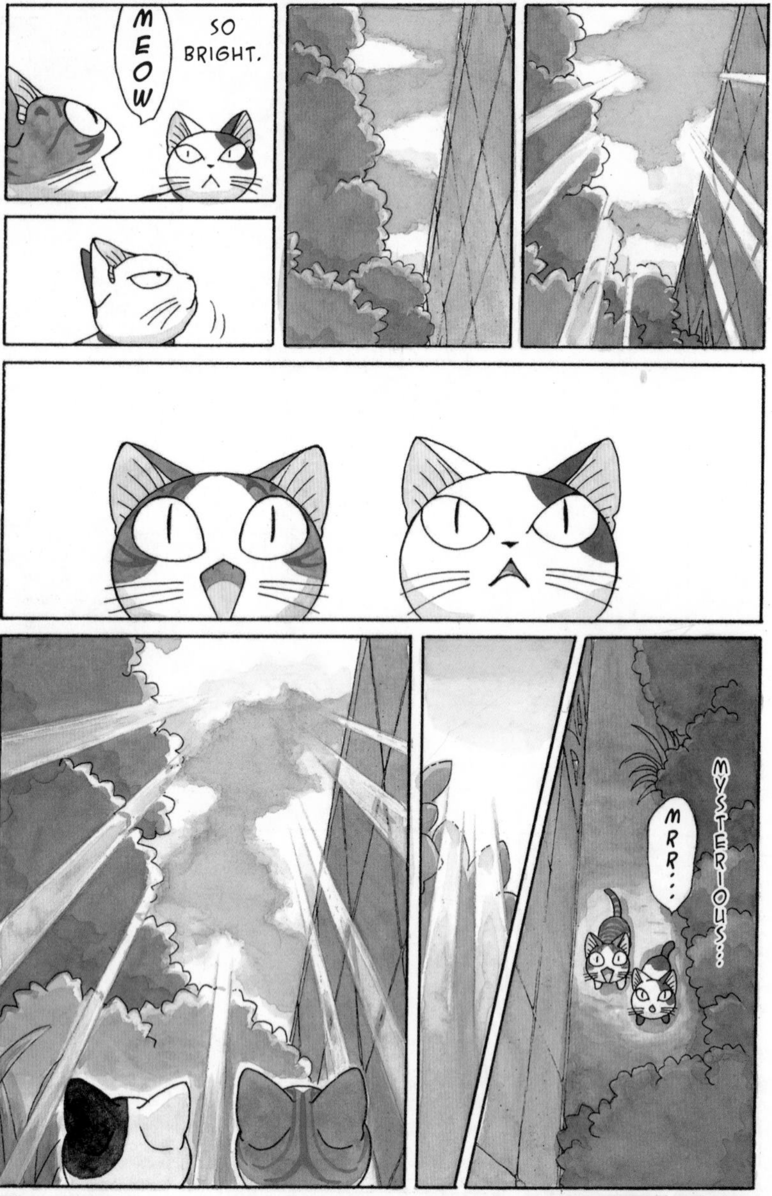
MEOW
SO BRIGHT.
MRR...
MYSTERIOUS...

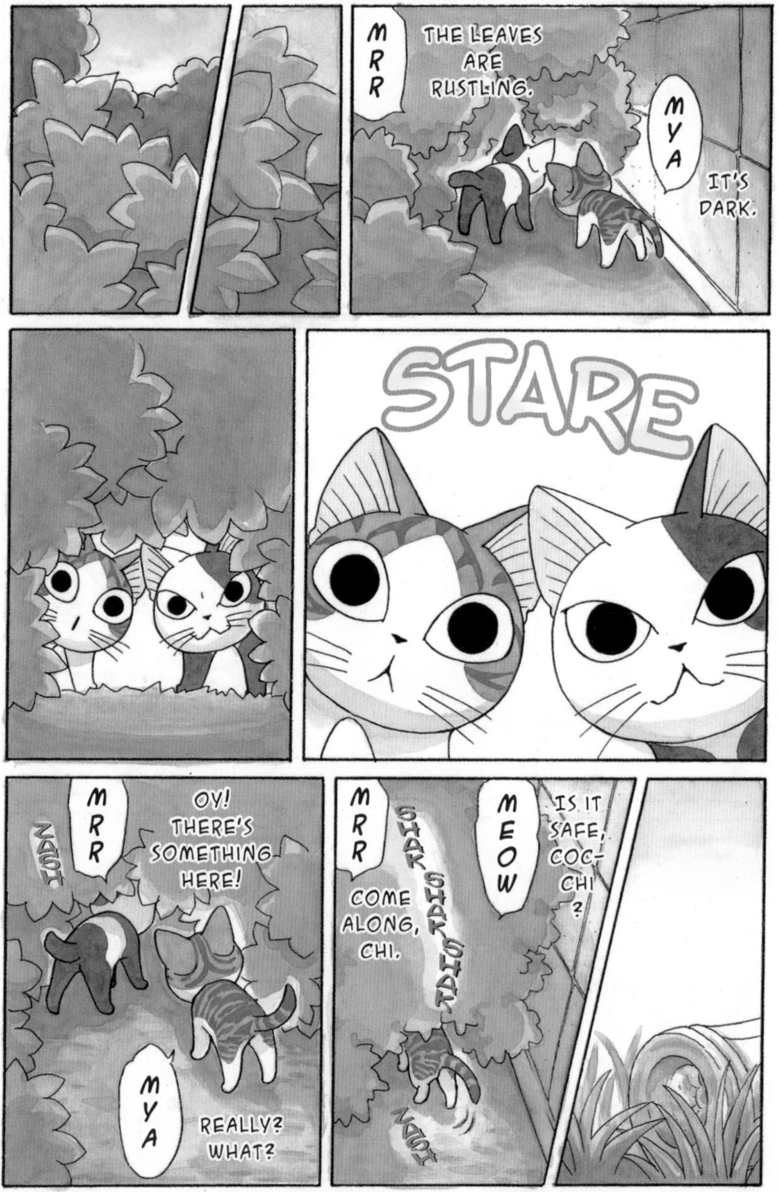
MRR
THE LEAVES ARE RUSTLING.
MYA
IT'S DARK.
STARE
MRR
OY! THERE'S SOMETHING HERE!
ZASH
MYA
REALLY? WHAT?
MRR
SHAK SHAK SHAK SHAK
COME ALONG, CHI.
MEOW
IS IT SAFE, COC-CHI?
ZASH

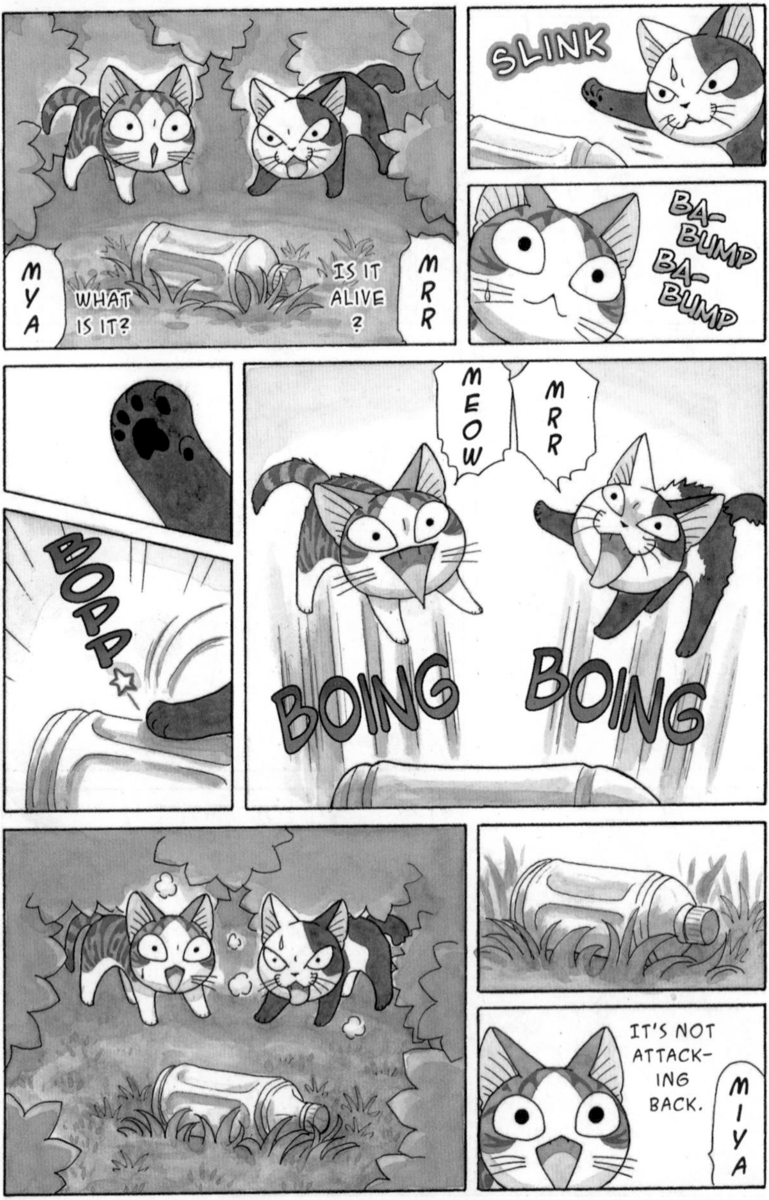
MYA
WHAT IS IT?
IS IT ALIVE?
MRR
SLINK
BA-BUMP BA-BUMP
BOPP
MEOW
MRR
BOING BOING
IT'S NOT ATTACK-ING BACK.
MIYA

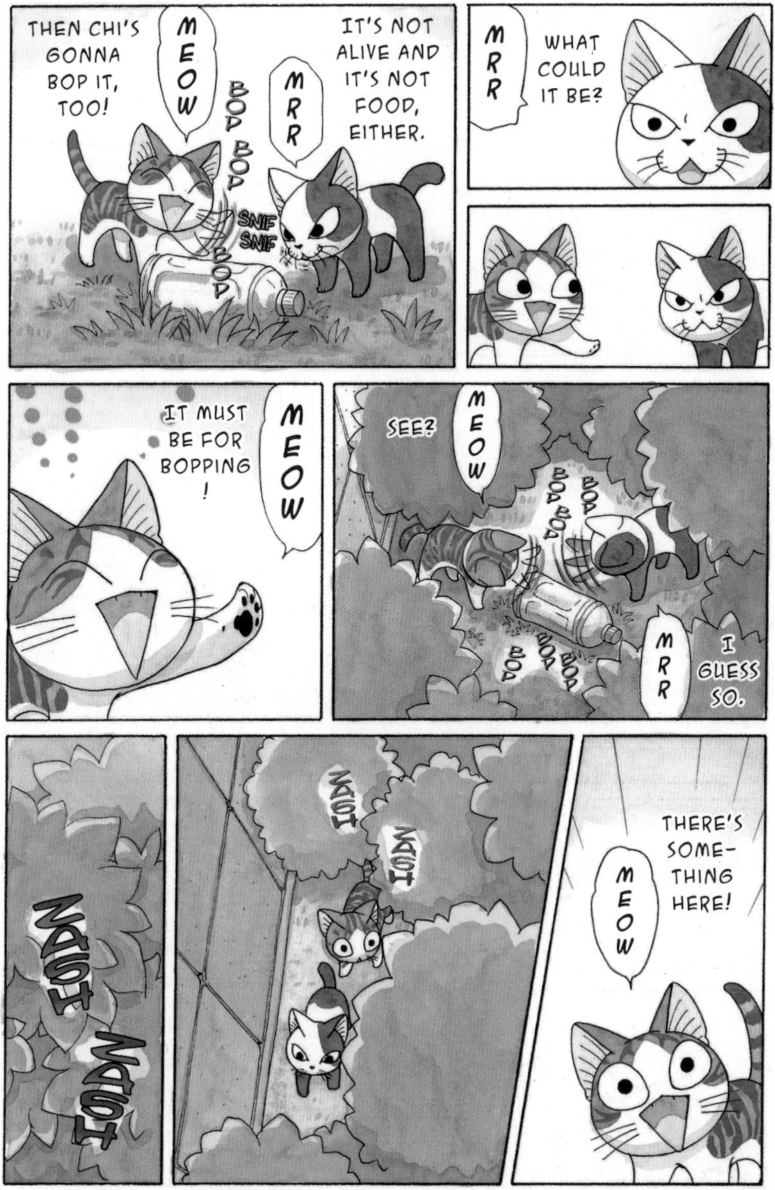
THEN CHI'S GONNA BOP IT, TOO!
MEOW
BOP BOP BOP
MRR
IT'S NOT ALIVE AND IT'S NOT FOOD, EITHER.
SNIF SNIF
BOP BOP
MRR
WHAT COULD IT BE?
IT MUST BE FOR BOPPING!
MEOW
SEE?
MEOW
BOP BOP BOP BOP
BOP BOP BOP
MRR
I GUESS SO.
HOSH HOSH
HOSH HOSH
MEOW
THERE'S SOME-THING HERE!

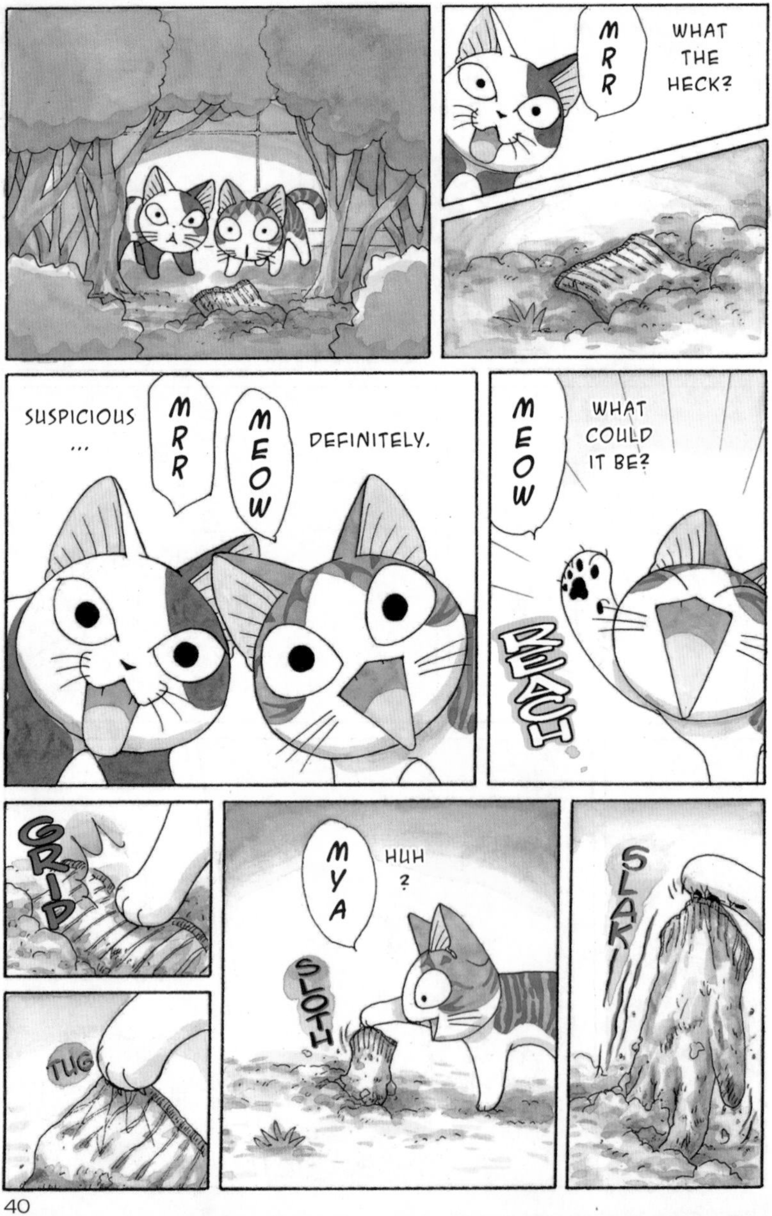
MRR
WHAT THE HECK?
SUSPICIOUS ...
MRR
MEOW
DEFINITELY.
MEOW
WHAT COULD IT BE?
REACH
GRIP
TUG
MYA
HUH ?
SLOTH
SLAK!

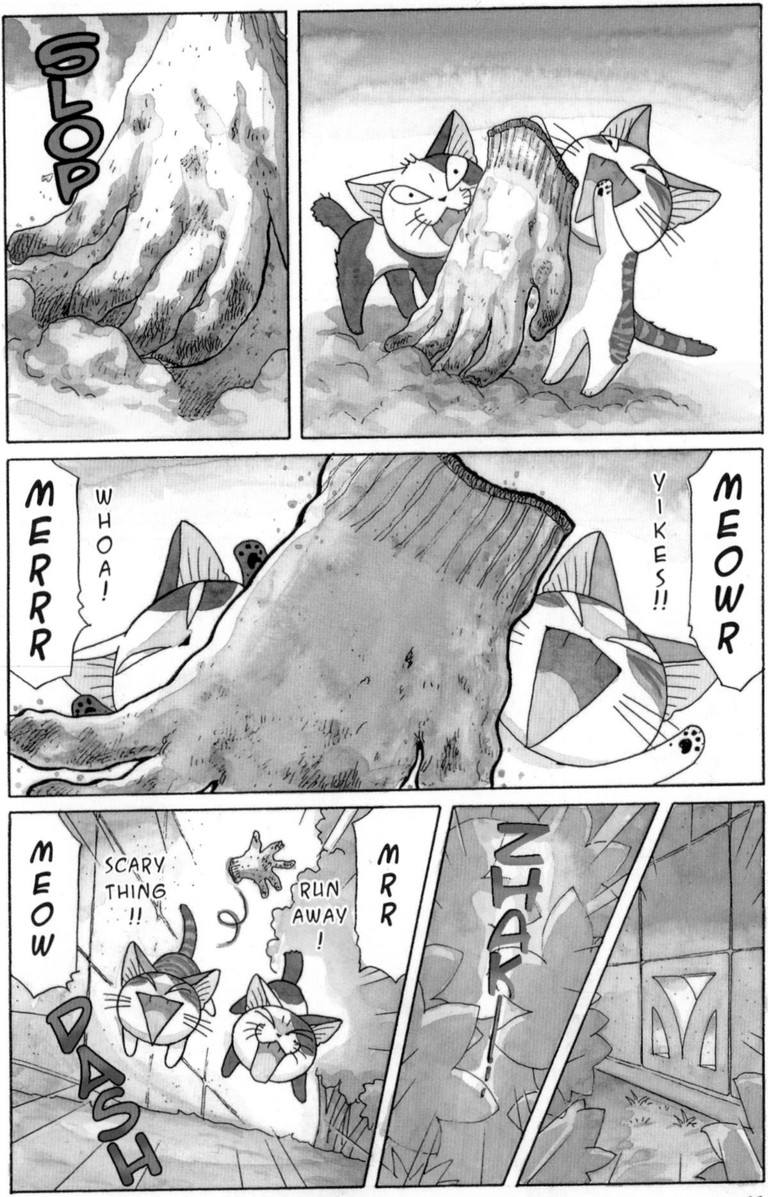
SLOP
MERRRR
WHOA!
YIKES!!
MEOWR
MEOW
SCARY THING!!
RUN AWAY!
MRR
DASH
ZHAK!!

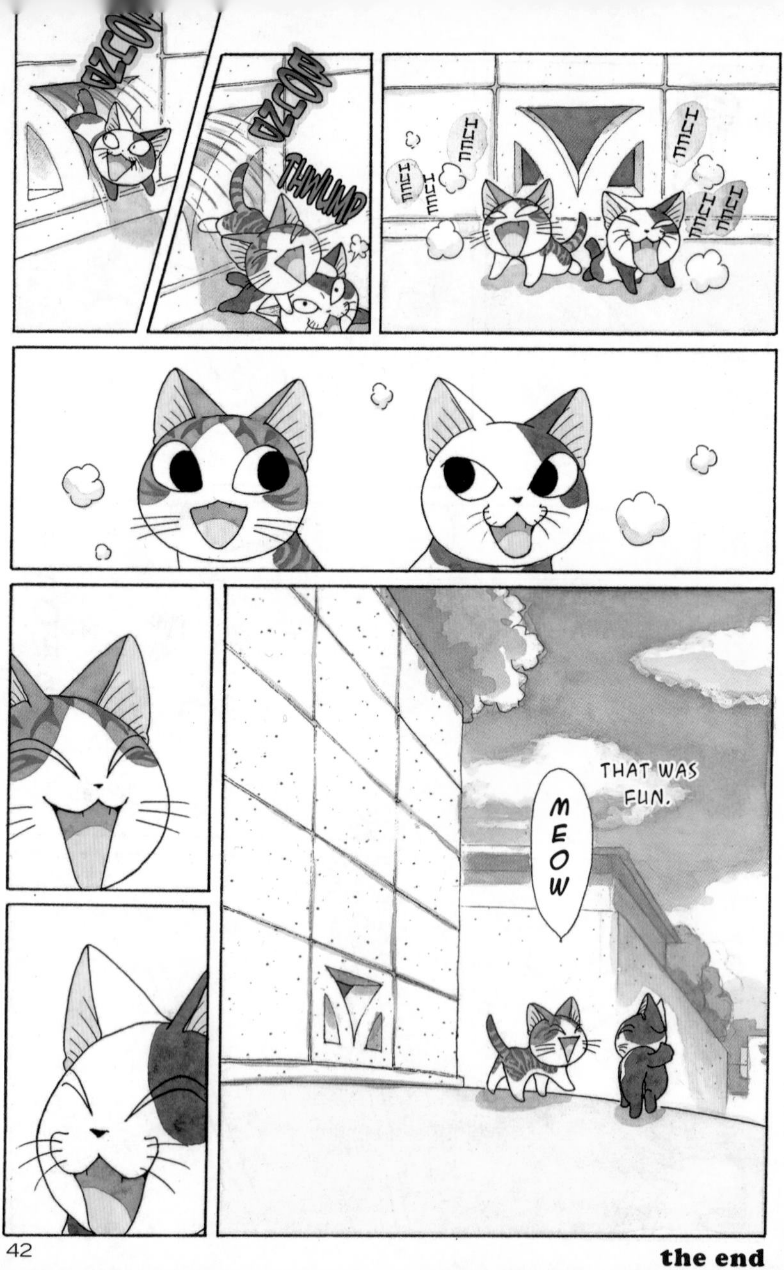
DZCO
DZCOM
THWUMP
HUFF HUFF
HUFF HUFF
HUFF HUFF
HUFF
MEOW
THAT WAS FUN.

the end

homemade 134: a cat is pursued

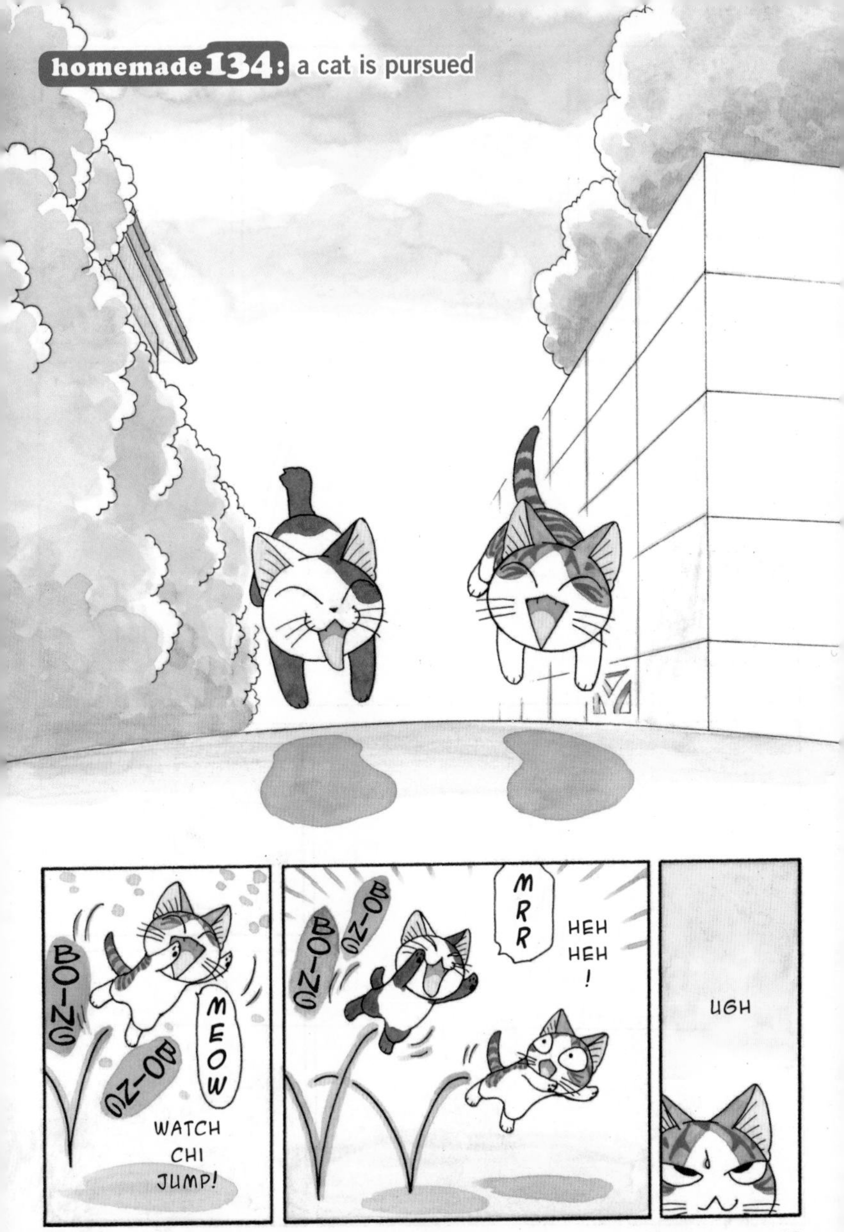
BO-ING
BO-ING
MEOW
WATCH CHI JUMP!
BO-ING
BO-ING
MRR
HEH HEH!
UGH

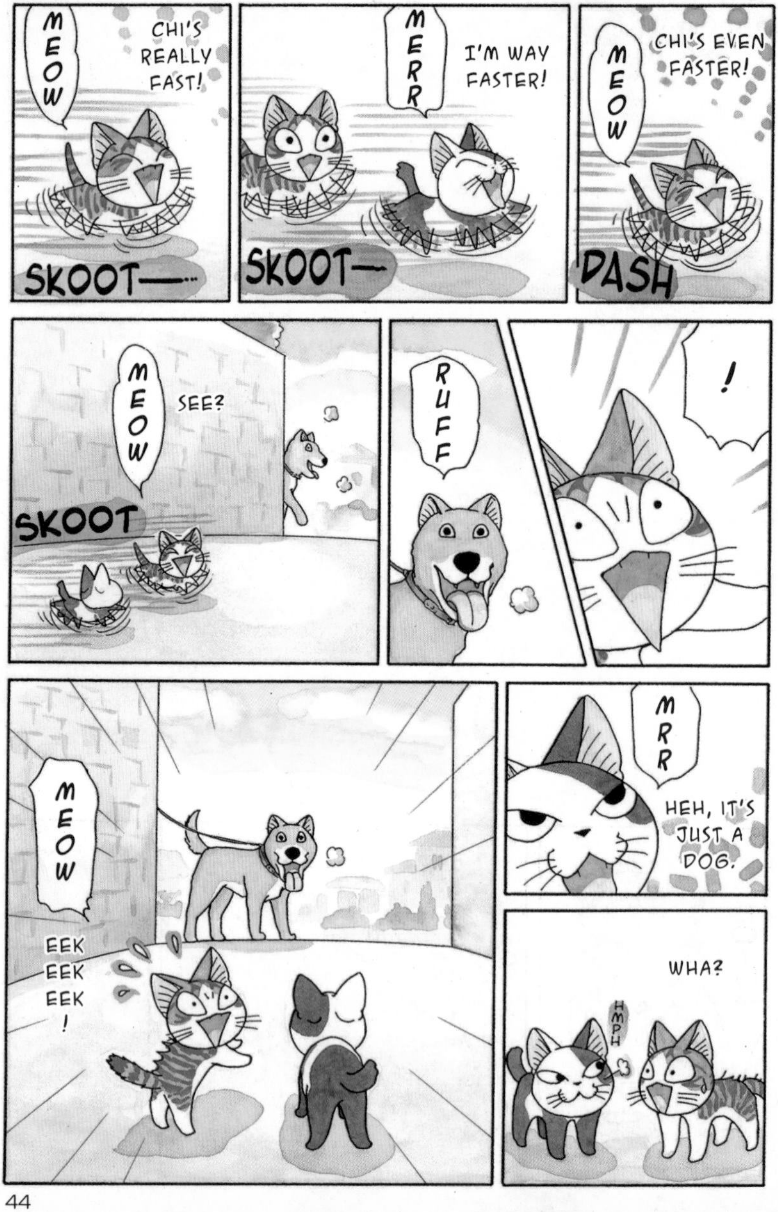
MEOW
CHI'S REALLY FAST!
SKOOT—...
MERR
I'M WAY FASTER!
SKOOT—
MEOW
CHI'S EVEN FASTER!
DASH
MEOW
SEE?
SKOOT
RUFF
!
MEOW
EEK EEK EEK !
MRR
HEH, IT'S JUST A DOG.
HMPH
WHA?

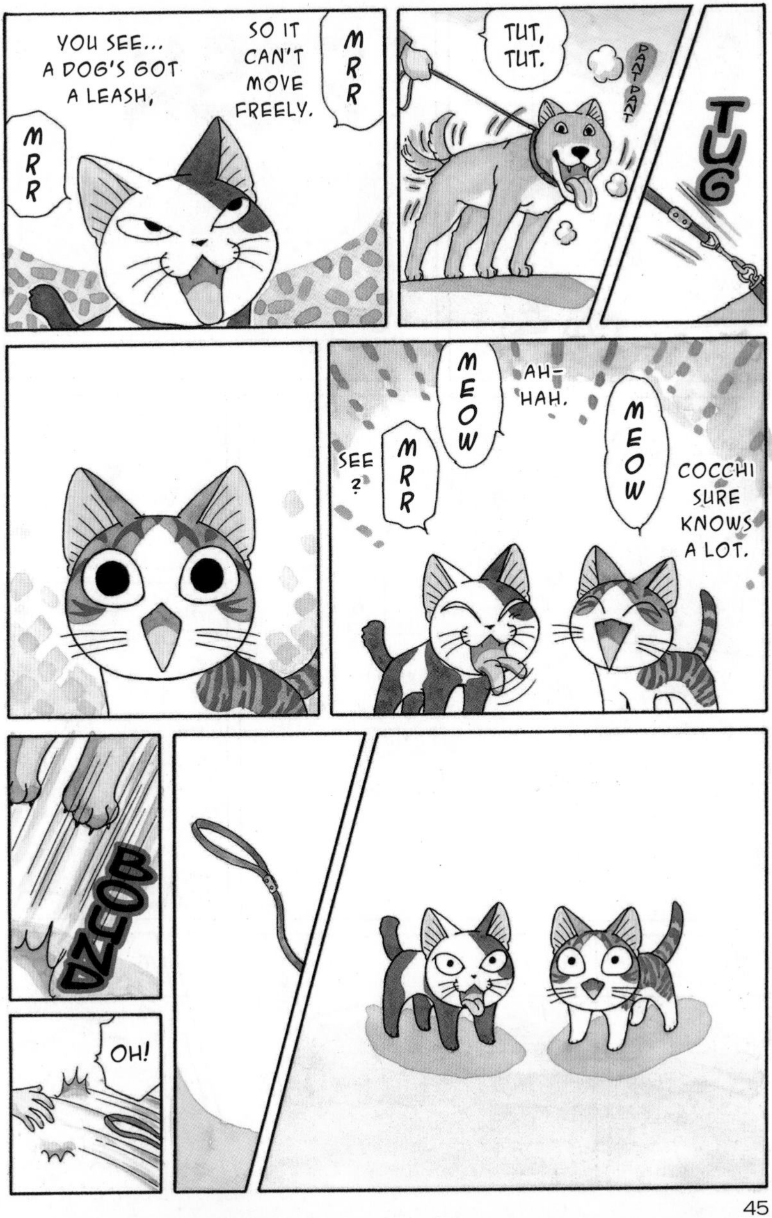
YOU SEE... A DOG'S GOT A LEASH,
MRR
SO IT CAN'T MOVE FREELY.
MRR
TUT, TUT.
PANT PANT
TUG
MEOW
AH-HAH.
SEE?
MRR
MEOW
COCCHI SURE KNOWS A LOT.
BOUND
OH!

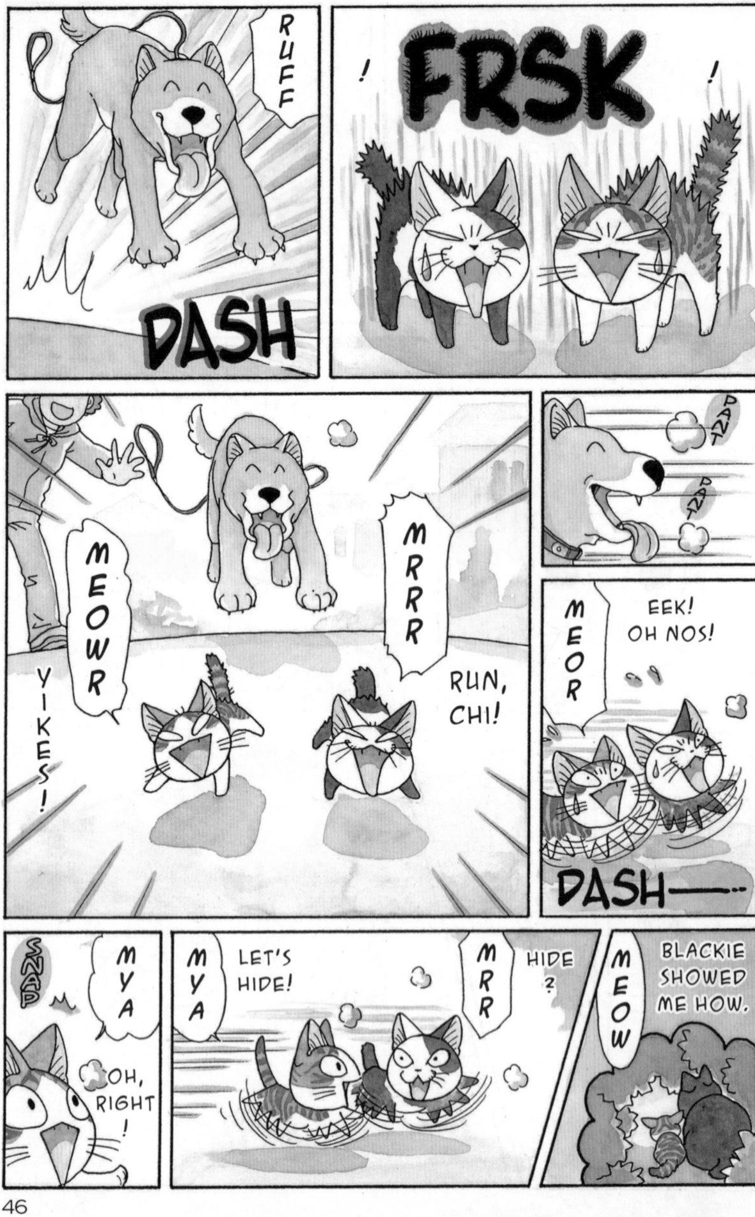
RUFF
DASH
!
FRSK
!
MEOWR
YIKES!
MRRR
RUN, CHI!
PANT
PANT
MEOR
EEK! OH NOS!
DASH——
SNAP
MYA
OH, RIGHT!
MYA
LET'S HIDE!
MRR
HIDE?
MEOW
BLACKIE SHOWED ME HOW.

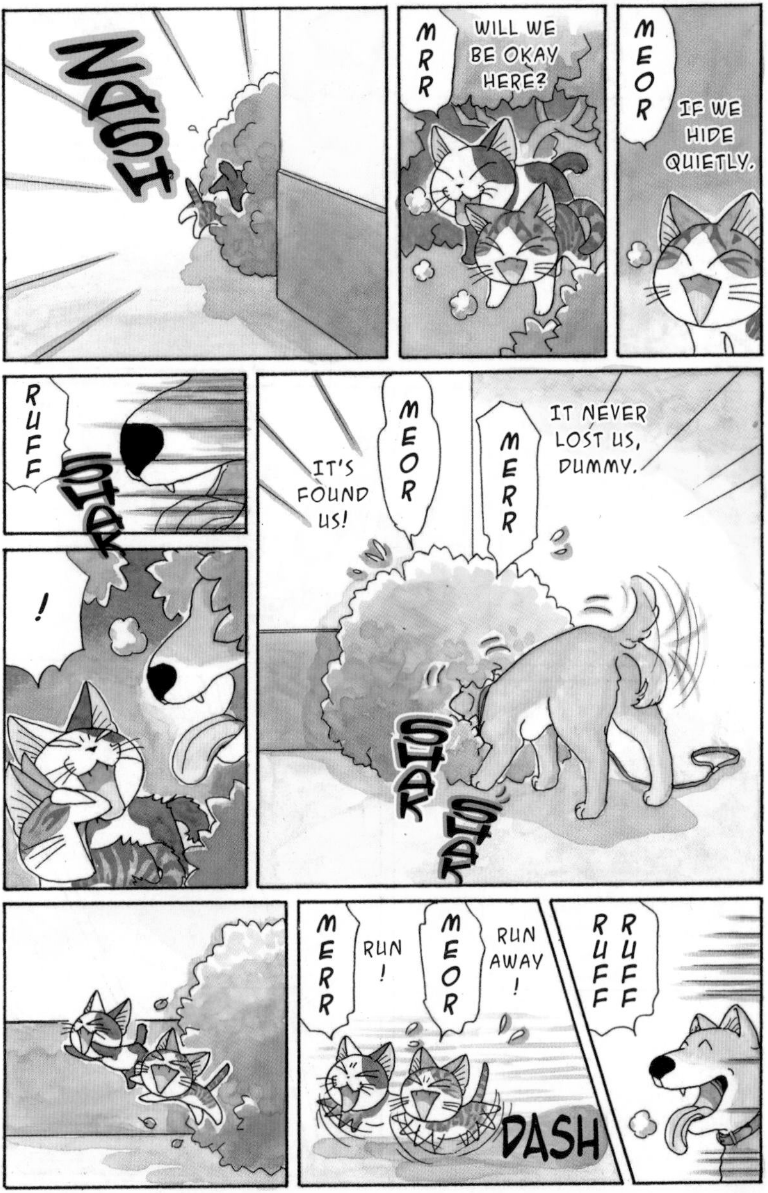
DASH
MRR
WILL WE BE OKAY HERE?
MEOR
IF WE HIDE QUIETLY.
RUFF
SHAR
!
IT'S FOUND US!
MEOR
MERR
IT NEVER LOST US, DUMMY.
SHAR
SHAR
MERR
RUN!
MEOR
RUN AWAY!
DASH
RUFF
RUFF

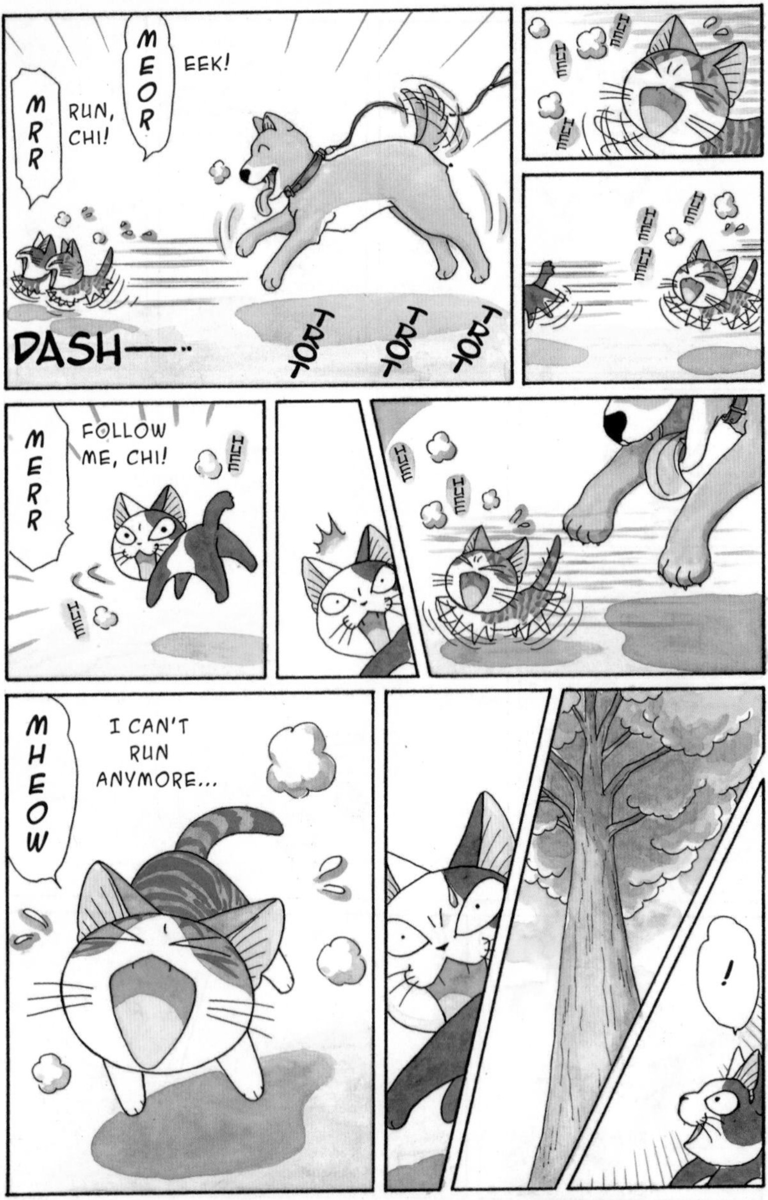
MRR
RUN, CHI!
MEOR
EEK!
DASH—..
TROT
TROT
TROT
HUE
HUE
HUE
HUE
HUE
HUE
MERR
FOLLOW ME, CHI!
HUE
HUE
HUE
HUE
MHEOW
I CAN'T RUN ANYMORE...
!

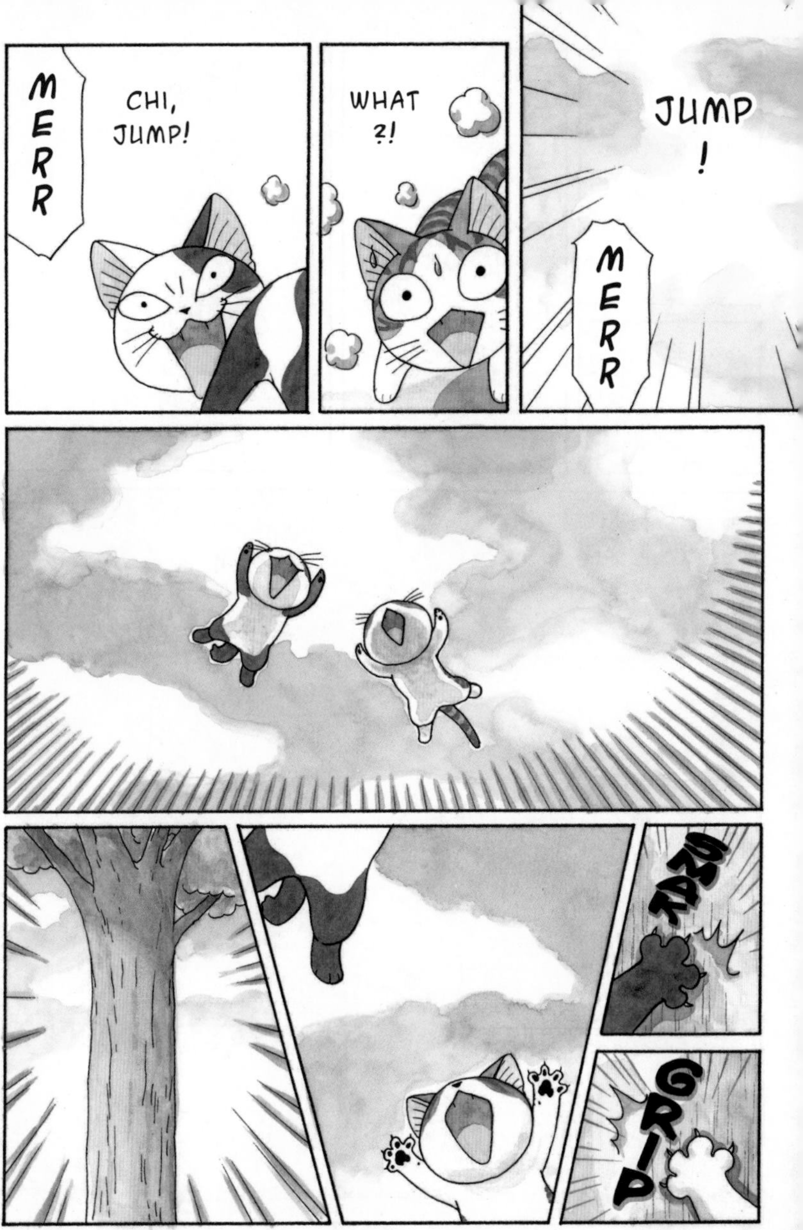
MERR
CHI, JUMP!
WHAT ?!
JUMP !
MERR
SMAK
GRIP

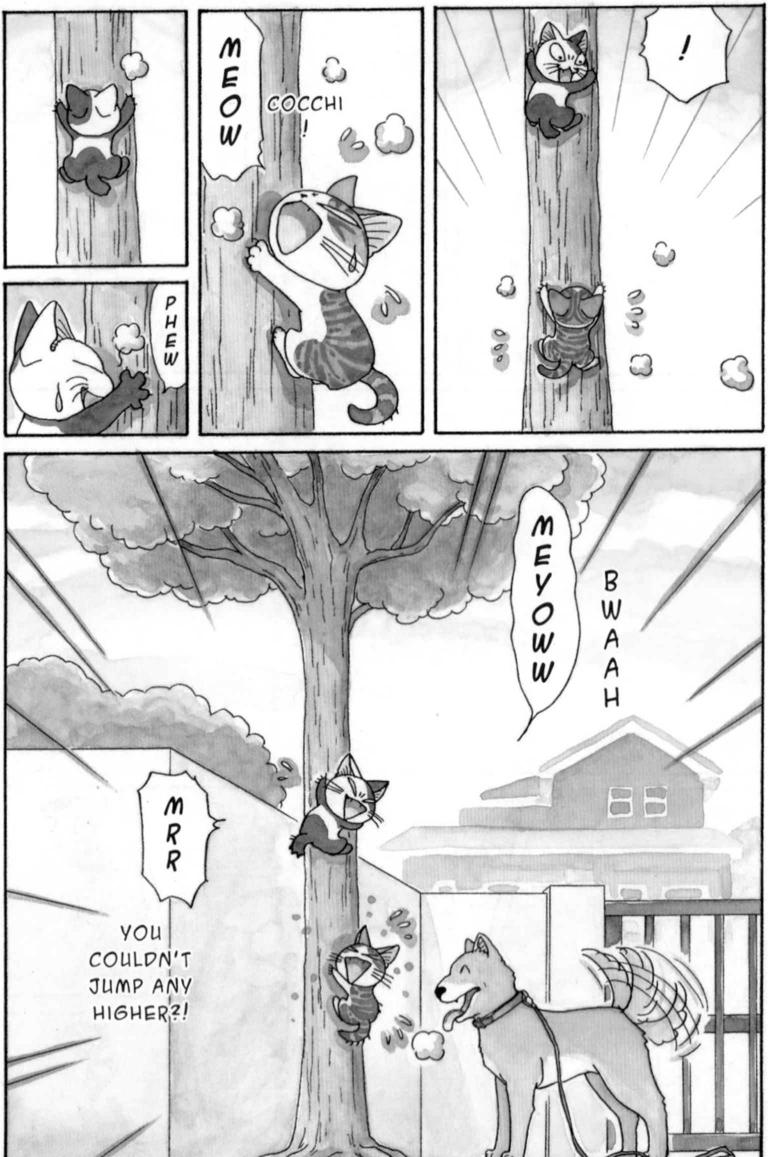
!
MEOW
COCCHI!
PHEW
MEYOWW
BWAAH
MRR
YOU COULDN'T JUMP ANY HIGHER?!

the end

homemade 135: a cat is hemmed

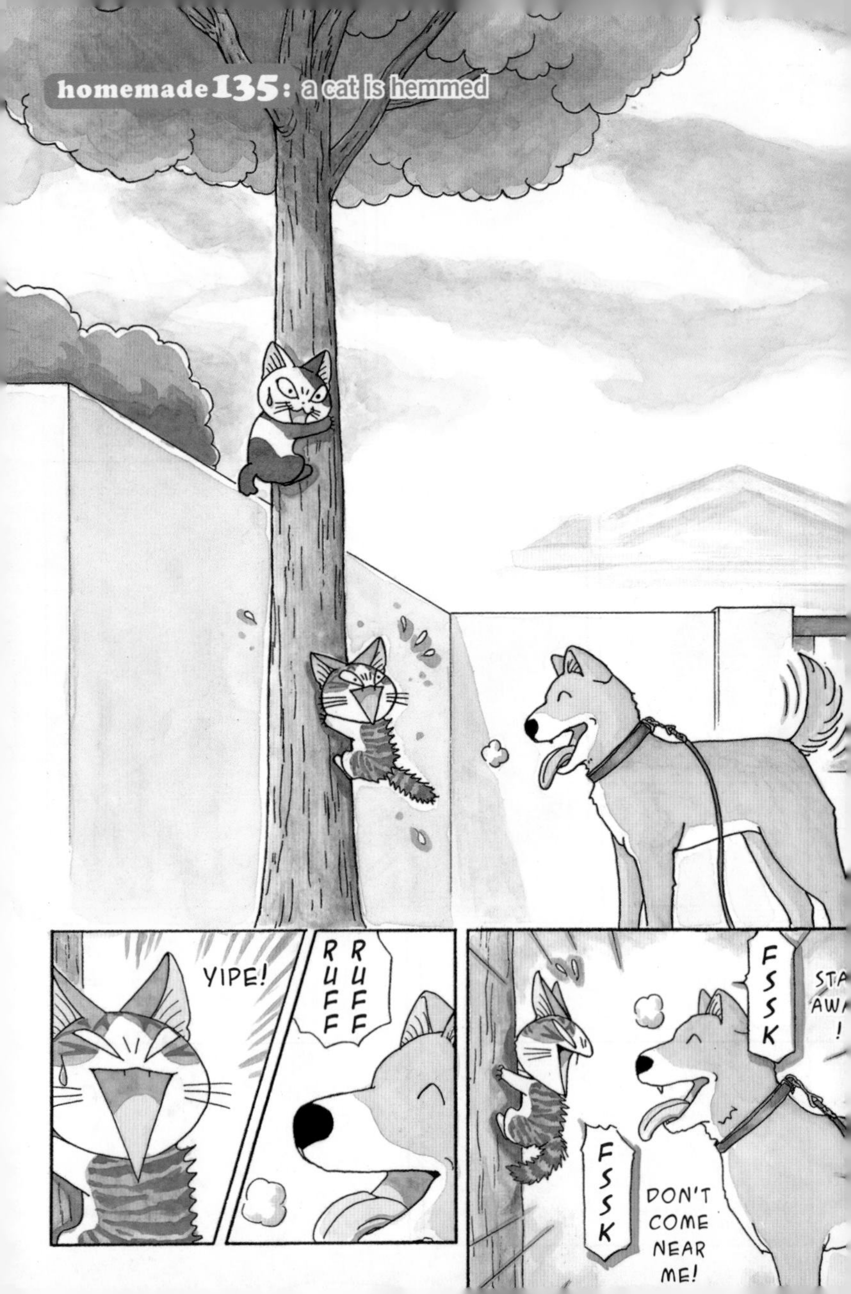
YIPE!
RUFF RUFF
FSSK
STA AWA !
FSSK
DON'T COME NEAR ME!

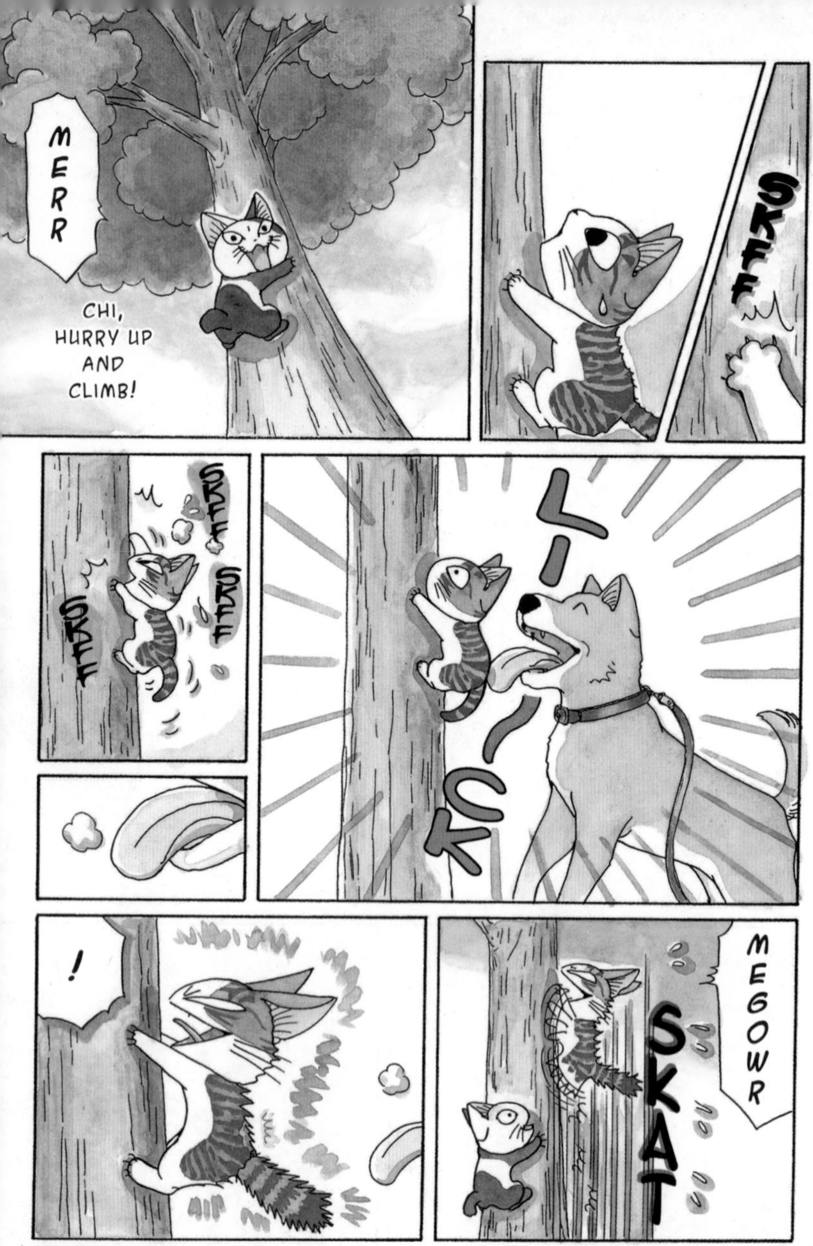
MERR
CHI, HURRY UP AND CLIMB!
SKFF
SKFF
SKFF
SKFF
LICK
!
MEGOWR
SKAT

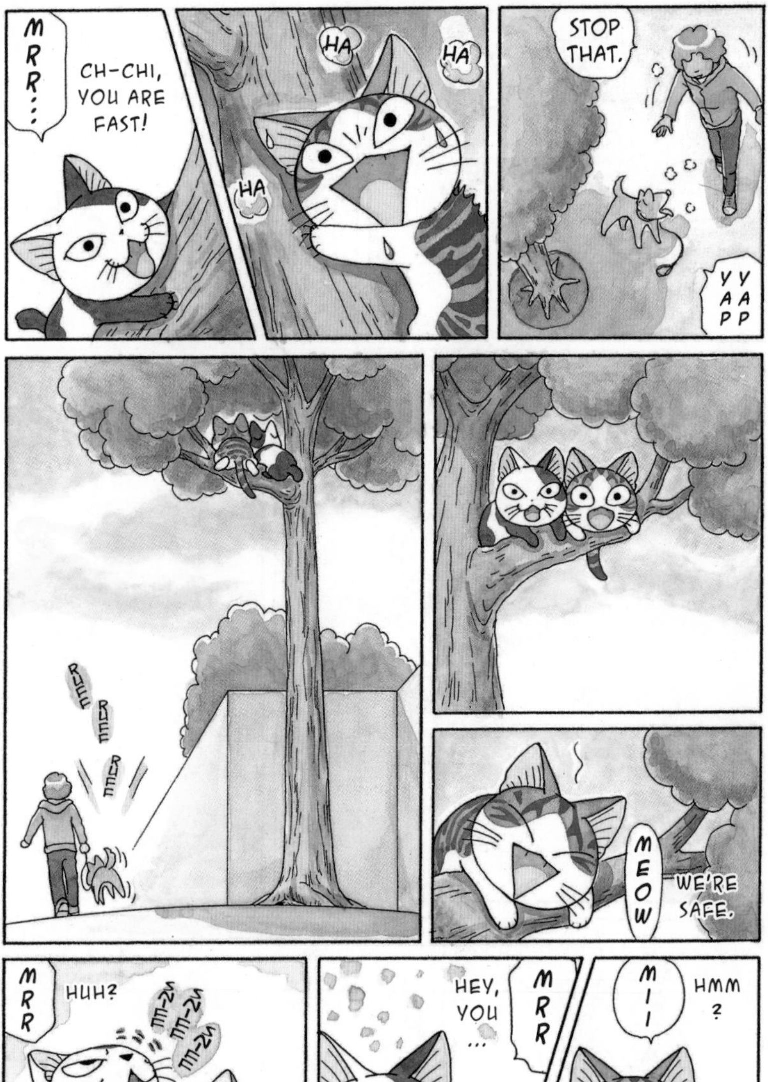
MRR...
CH-CHI, YOU ARE FAST!
HA
HA
HA
STOP THAT.
YAP YAP
RUFF
RUFF
RUFF
MEOW
WE'RE SAFE.
MRR
HUH?
SNIFF
SNIFF
SNIFF
HEY, YOU ...
MRR
MII
HMM ?

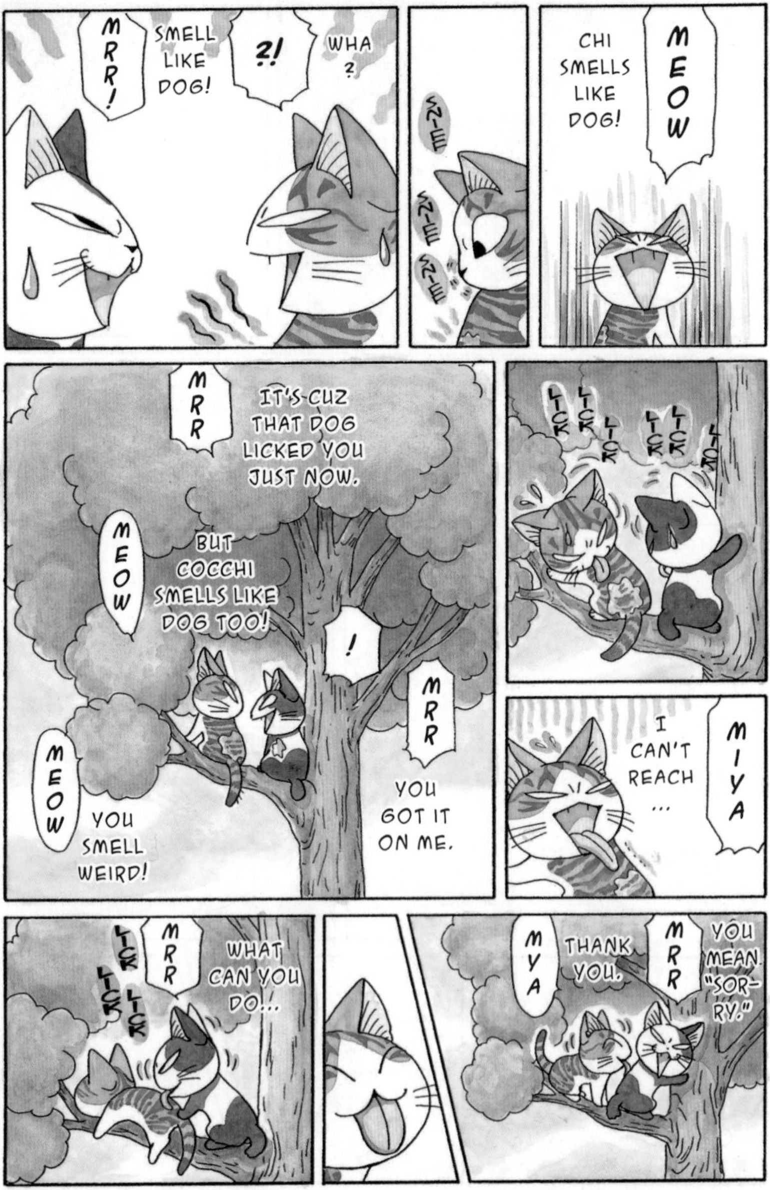
MRR!
SMELL LIKE DOG!
?!
WHA?
SNIFF
SNIFF
SNIFF
MEOW
CHI SMELLS LIKE DOG!
MRR
IT'S CUZ THAT DOG LICKED YOU JUST NOW.
MEOW
BUT COCCHI SMELLS LIKE DOG TOO!
!
MRR
YOU GOT IT ON ME.
MEOW
YOU SMELL WEIRD!
LICK LICK LICK LICK LICK LICK
MIYA
I CAN'T REACH...
LICK LICK LICK
MRR
WHAT CAN YOU DO...
MYA
THANK YOU.
MRR
YOU MEAN "SORRY."

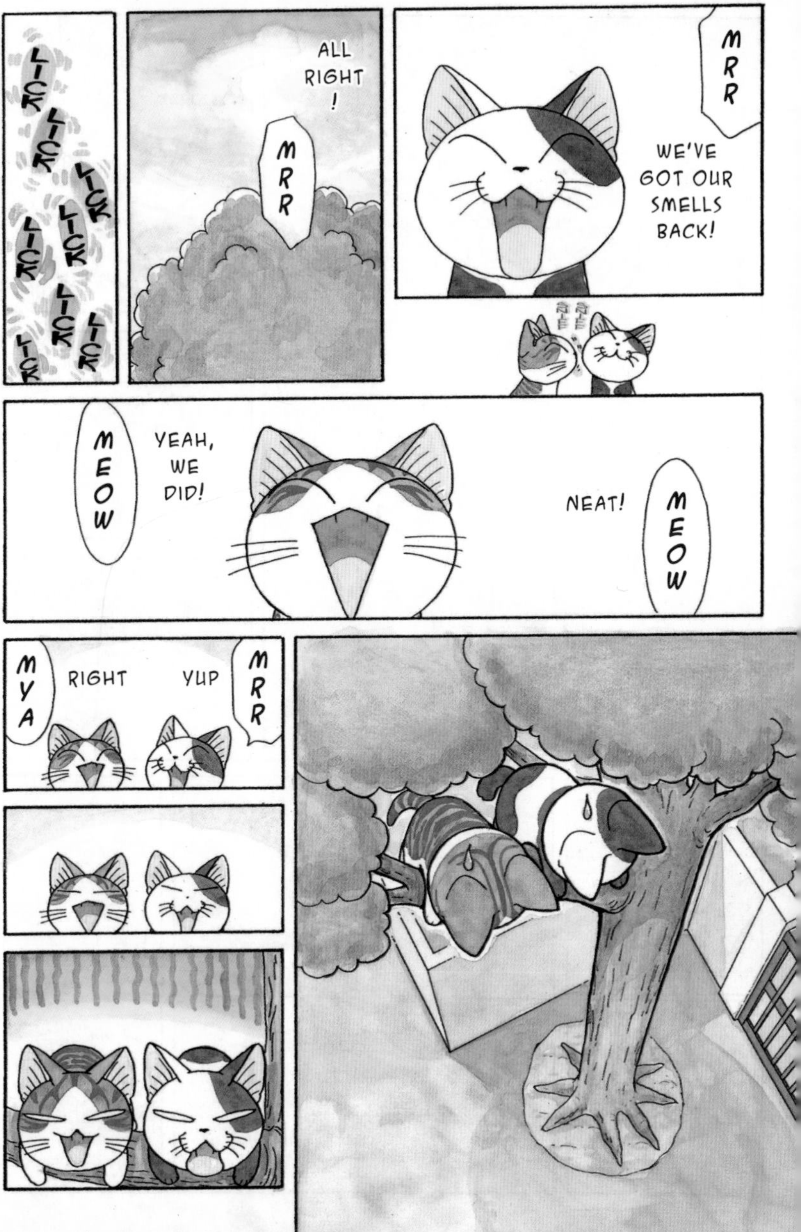
LICK LICK LICK LICK LICK LICK LICK LICK LICK
ALL RIGHT!
MRR
MRR
WE'VE GOT OUR SMELLS BACK!
MEOW
YEAH, WE DID!
NEAT!
MEOW
MYA
RIGHT
YUP
MRR

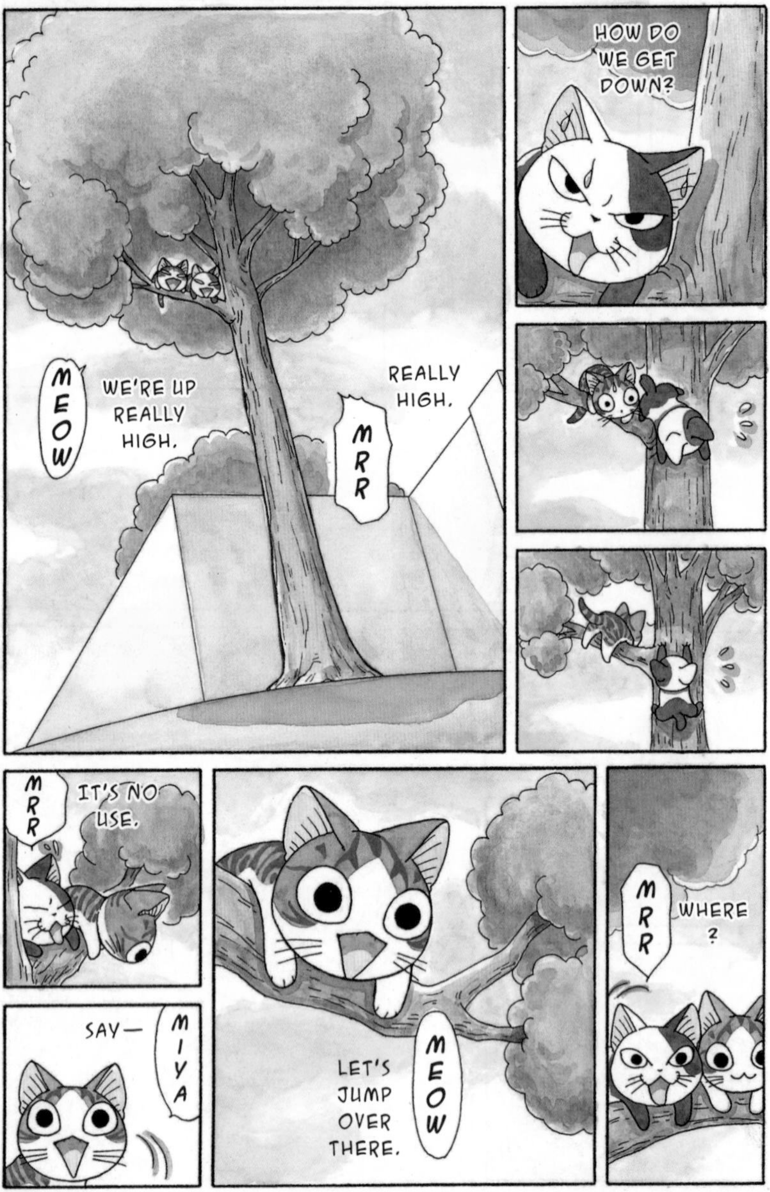
MEOW
WE'RE UP REALLY HIGH.
MRR
REALLY HIGH.
HOW DO WE GET DOWN?
MRR
IT'S NO USE.
SAY—
MIYA
LET'S JUMP OVER THERE.
MEOW
MRR
WHERE?

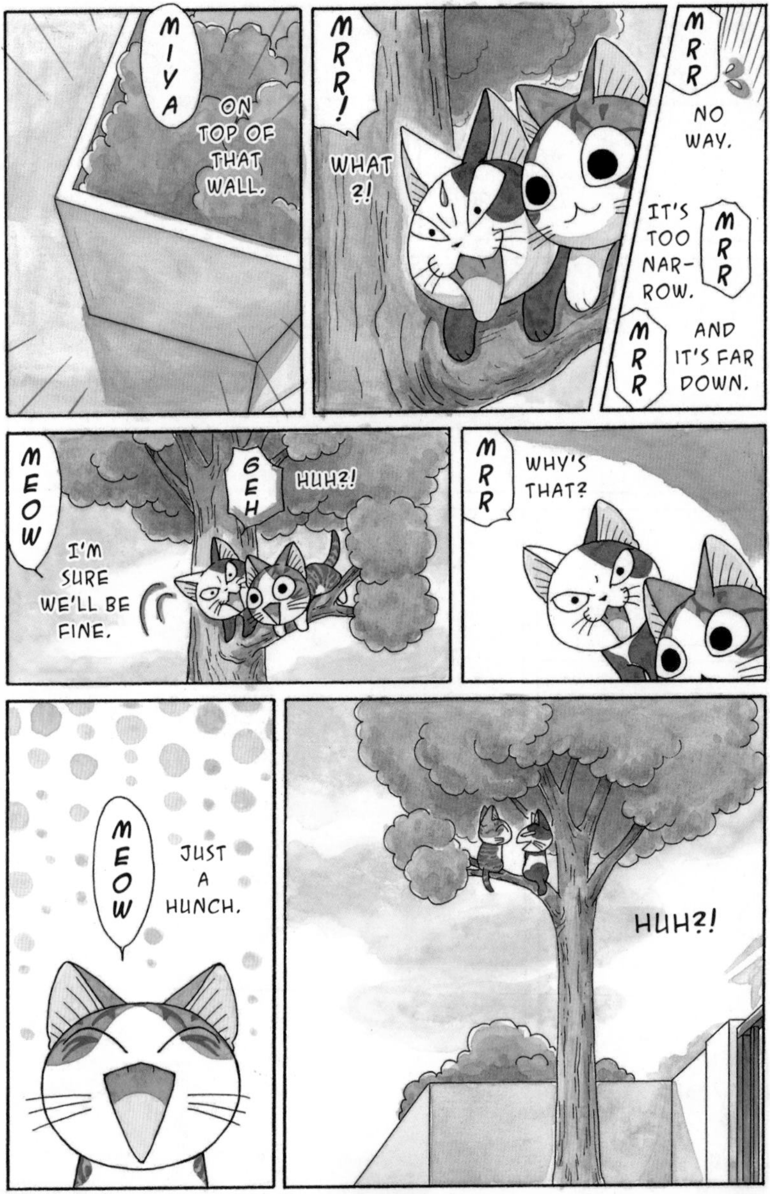
MIYA
ON TOP OF THAT WALL.
MRR!
WHAT ?!
MRR
NO WAY.
IT'S TOO NAR-ROW.
MRR
MRR
AND IT'S FAR DOWN.
MEOW
I'M SURE WE'LL BE FINE.
GEH
HUH?!
MRR
WHY'S THAT?
MEOW
JUST A HUNCH.
HUH?!

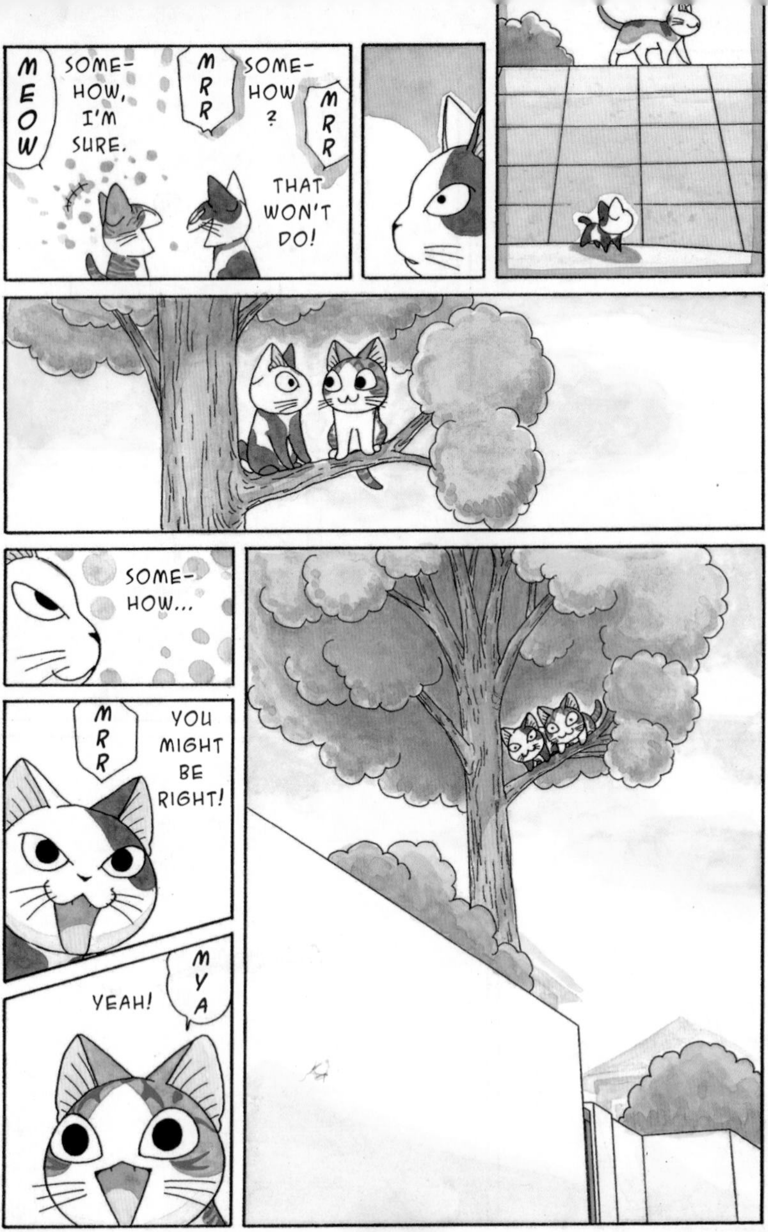
MEOW
SOME-HOW, I'M SURE.
MRR
SOME-HOW?
MRR
THAT WON'T DO!
SOME-HOW...
MRR
YOU MIGHT BE RIGHT!
YEAH!
MYA

the end

homemade 136: a cat leaps

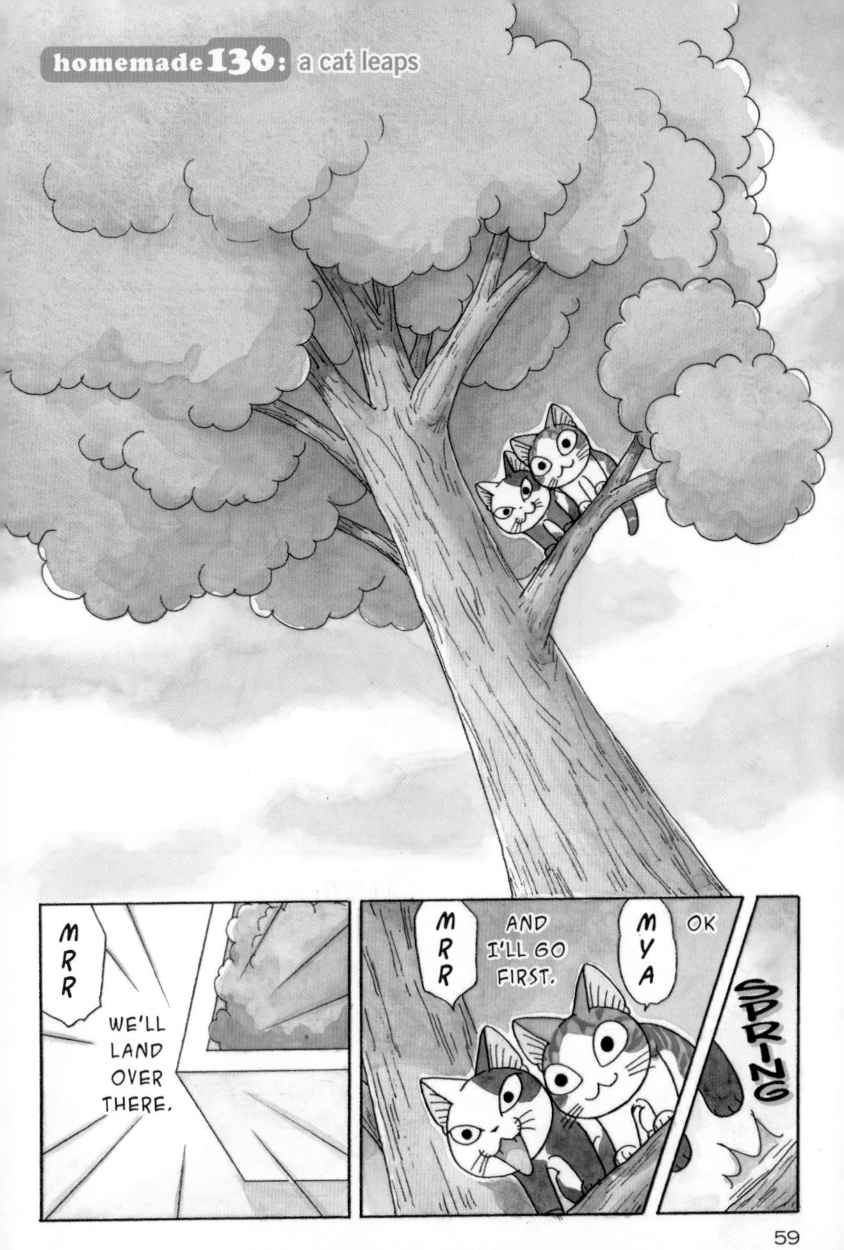
MRR
WE'LL LAND OVER THERE.
MRR
AND I'LL GO FIRST.
MYA
OK
SPRING

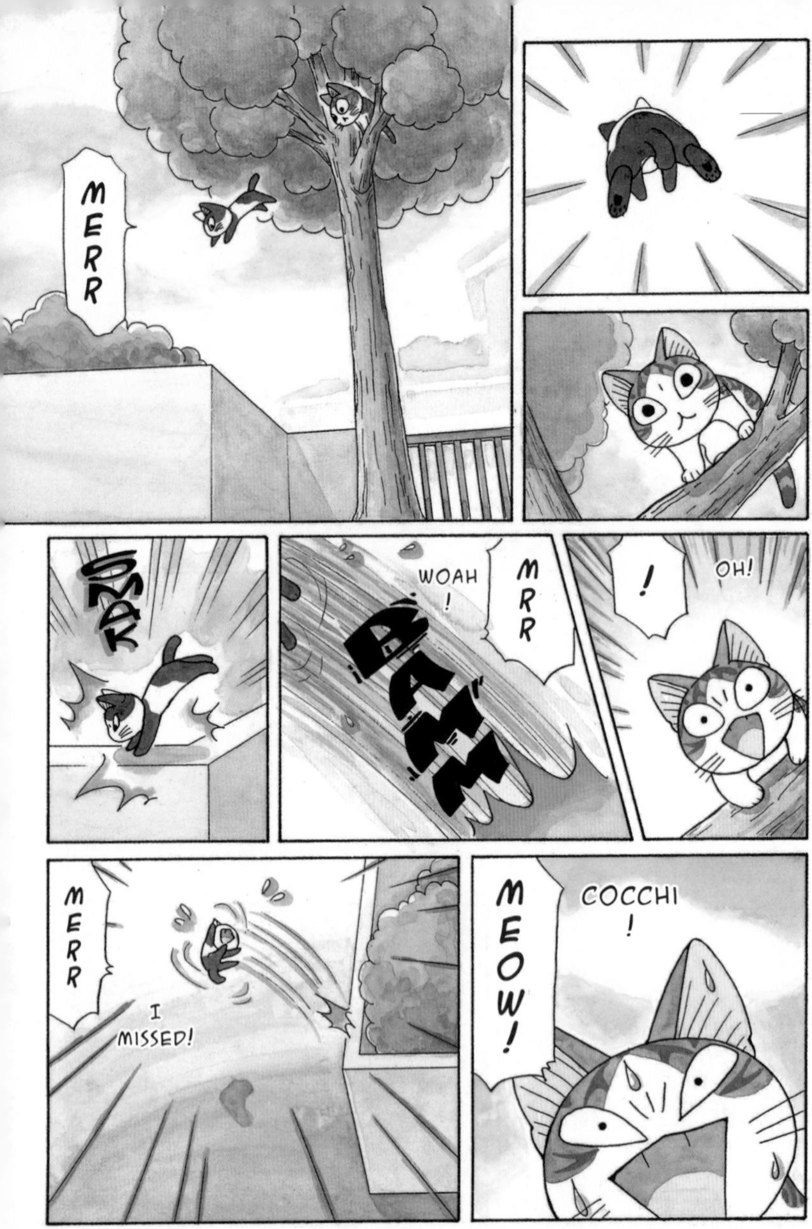
MERR
SMAK
WOAH!
MRR
BAM
!
OH!
MERR
I MISSED!
MEOW!
COCCHI!

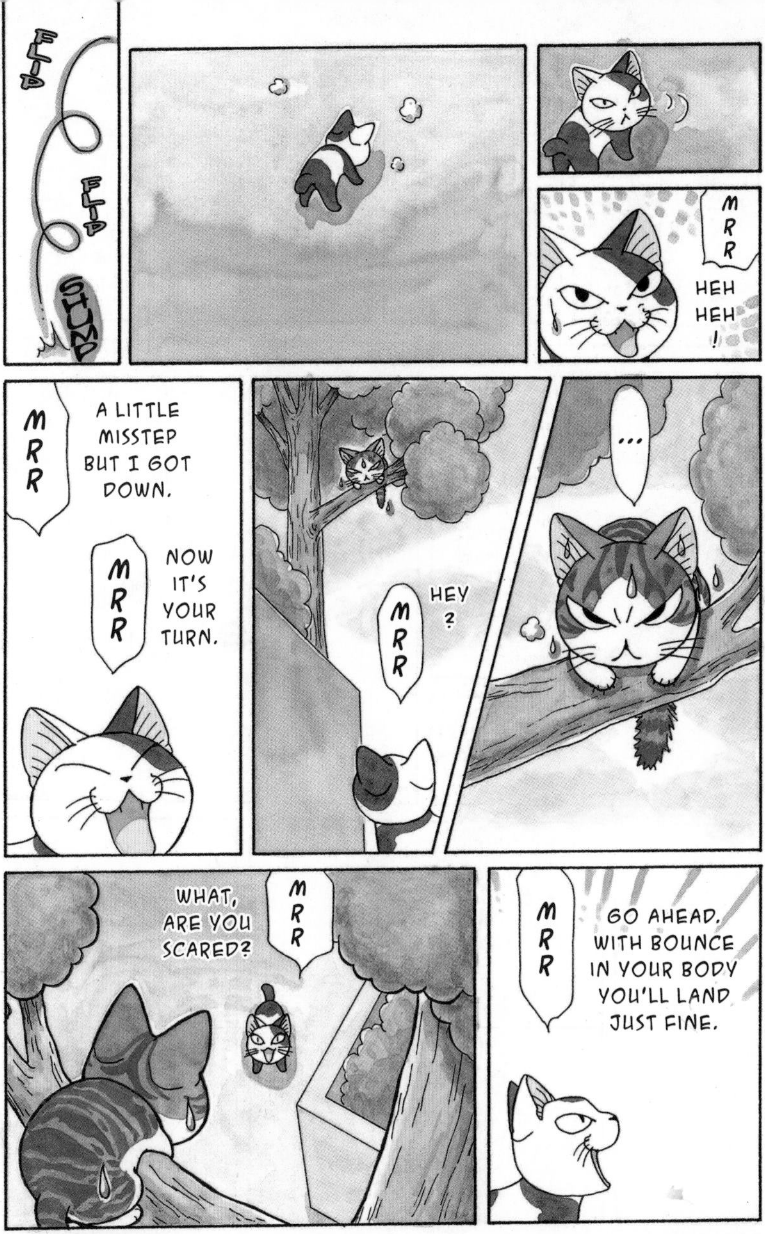
FLIP
FLIP
SHUMP
MRR
HEH HEH!
MRR
A LITTLE MISSTEP BUT I GOT DOWN.
MRR
NOW IT'S YOUR TURN.
MRR
HEY?
...
WHAT, ARE YOU SCARED?
MRR
MRR
GO AHEAD. WITH BOUNCE IN YOUR BODY YOU'LL LAND JUST FINE.

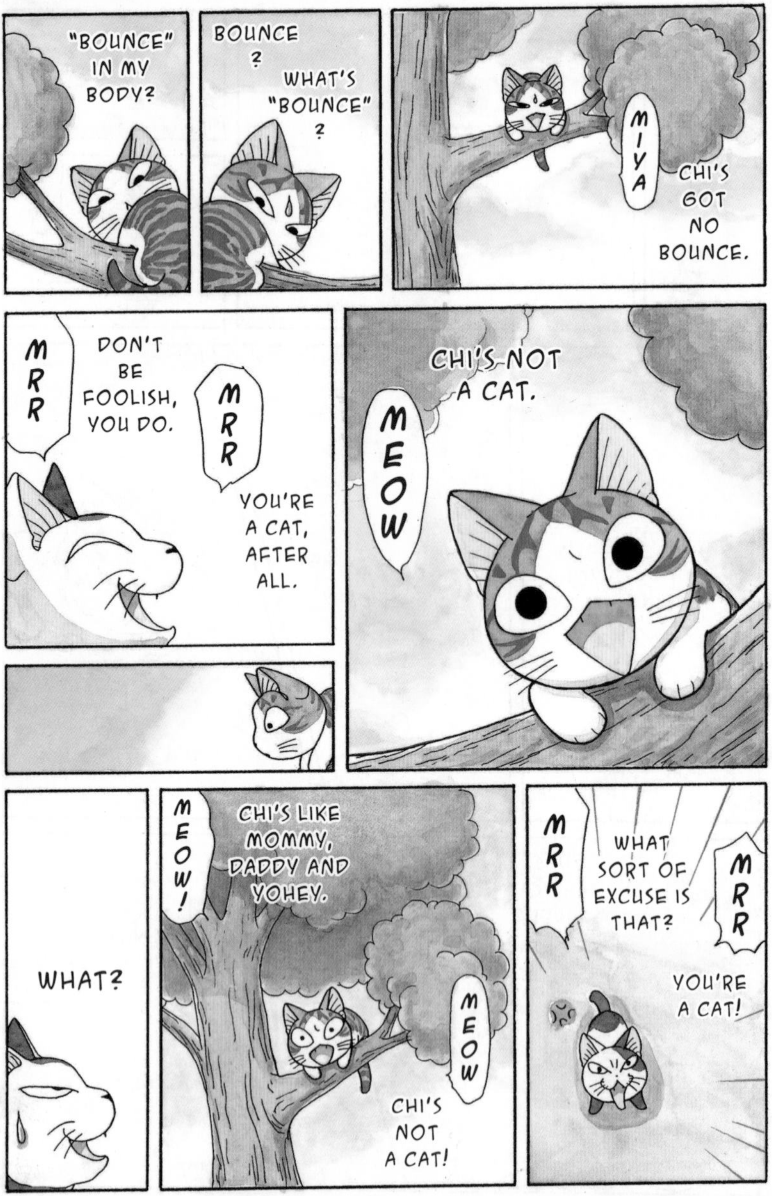
"BOUNCE" IN MY BODY?
BOUNCE?
WHAT'S "BOUNCE"?
MIYA
CHI'S GOT NO BOUNCE.
MRR
DON'T BE FOOLISH, YOU DO.
MRR
YOU'RE A CAT, AFTER ALL.
CHI'S NOT A CAT.
MEOW
WHAT?
MEOW!
CHI'S LIKE MOMMY, DADDY AND YOHEY.
MEOW
CHI'S NOT A CAT!
MRR
WHAT SORT OF EXCUSE IS THAT?
MRR
YOU'RE A CAT!

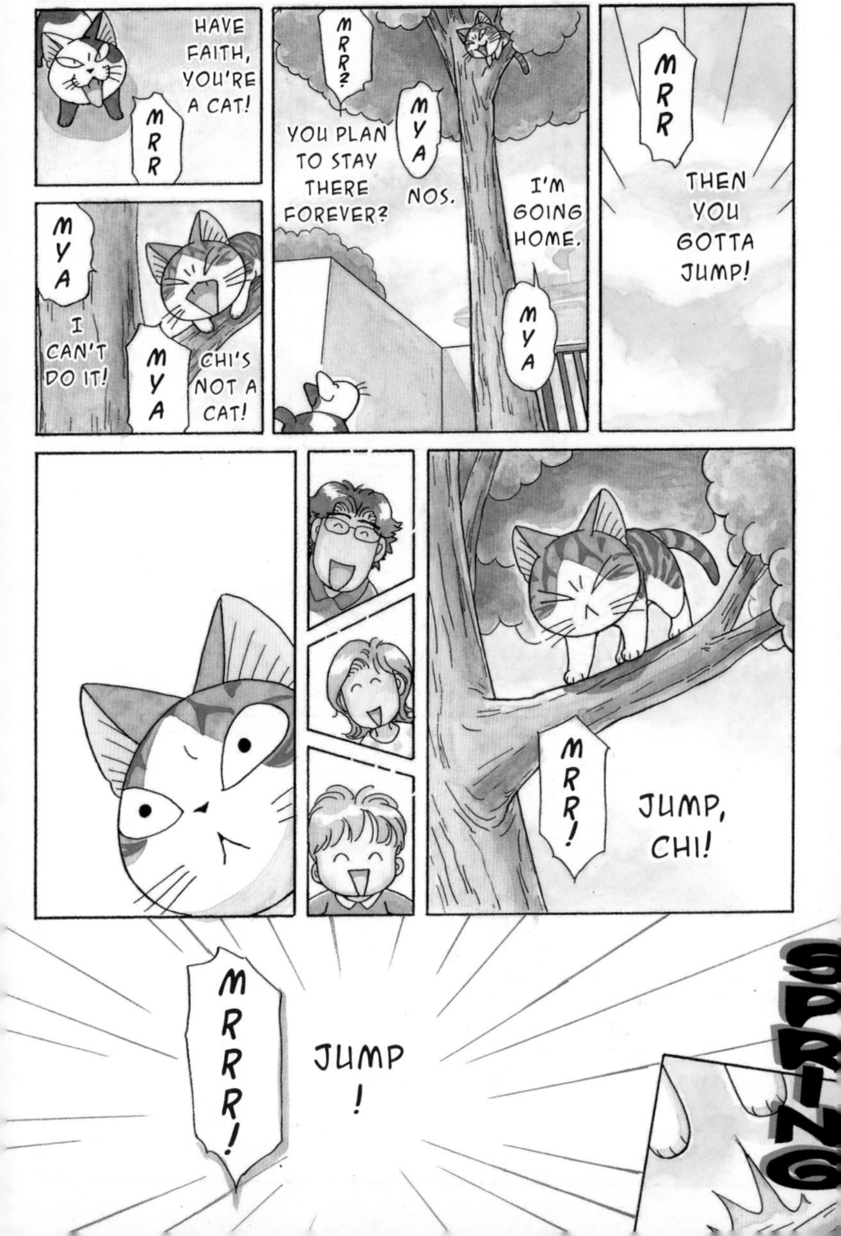
HAVE FAITH, YOU'RE A CAT!
MRR
MYA
I CAN'T DO IT!
MYA
CHI'S NOT A CAT!
MRR?
YOU PLAN TO STAY THERE FOREVER?
MYA
NOS.
I'M GOING HOME.
MYA
MRR
THEN YOU GOTTA JUMP!
MRR!
JUMP, CHI!
MRRRR!
JUMP!
SPRING

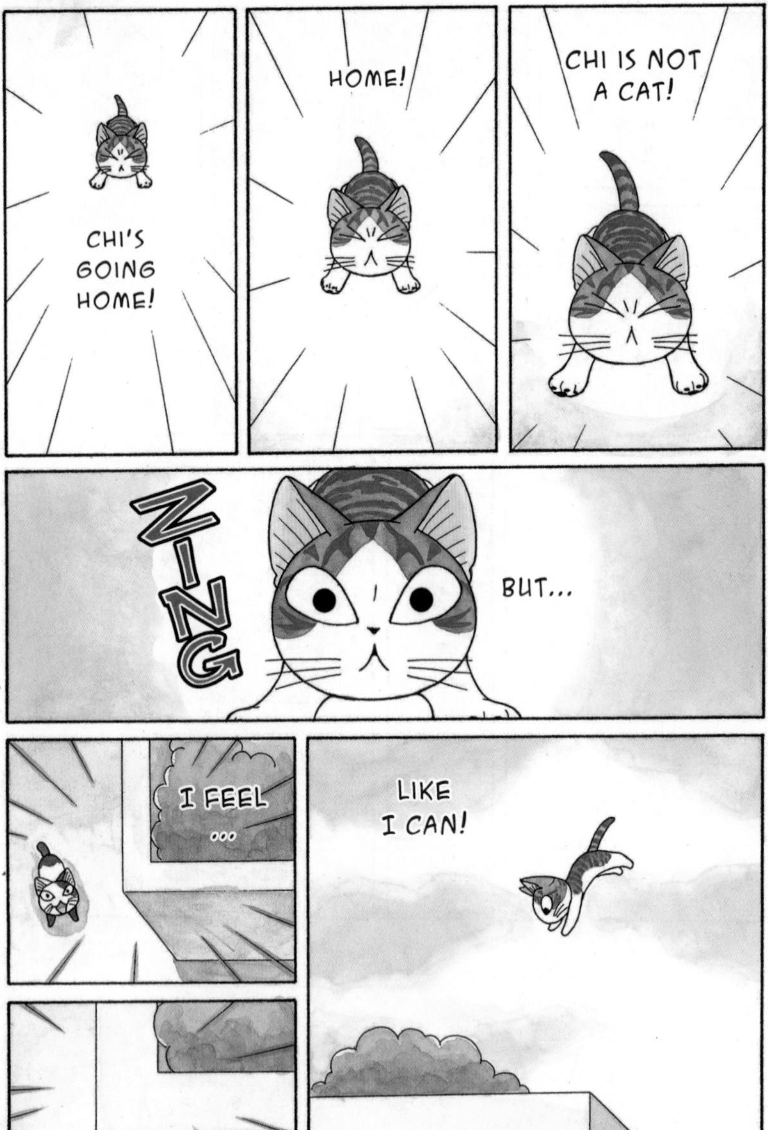
CHI'S GOING HOME!
HOME!
CHI IS NOT A CAT!
ZING
BUT...
I FEEL ...
LIKE I CAN!

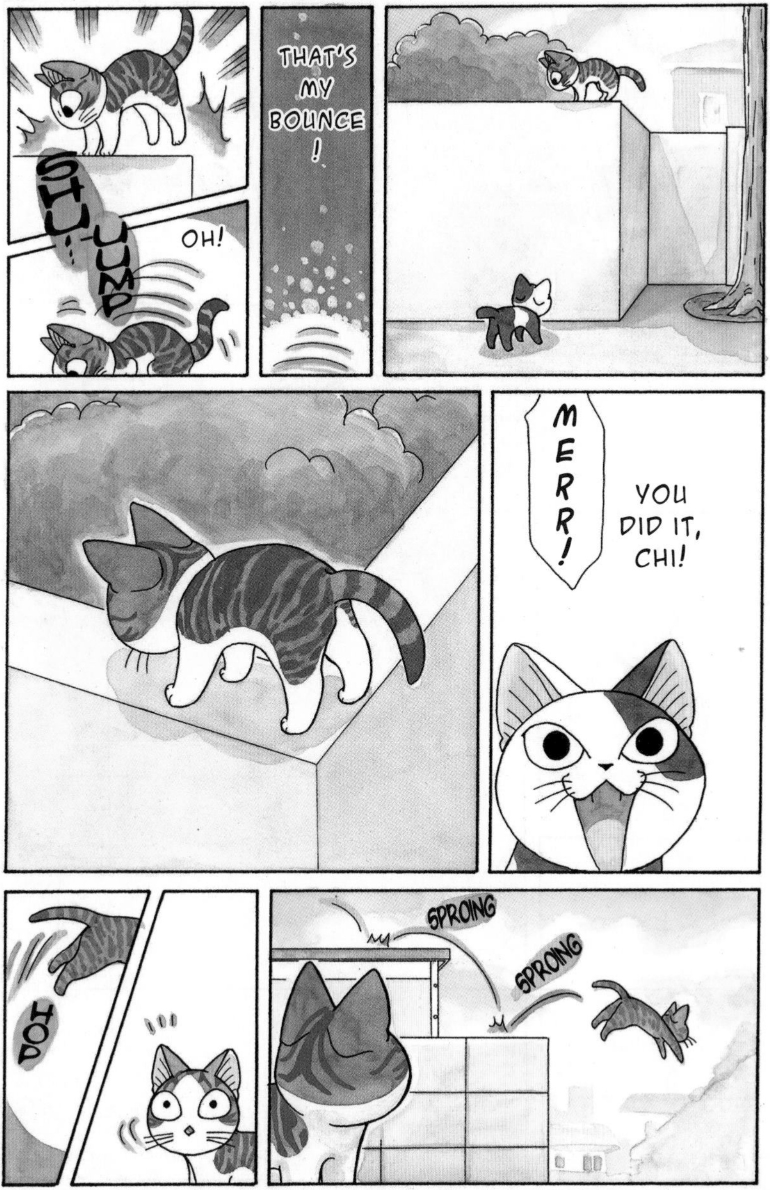
SHU-UUMP
OH!
THAT'S MY BOUNCE!
MERR!
YOU DID IT, CHI!
HOP
SPROING
SPROING

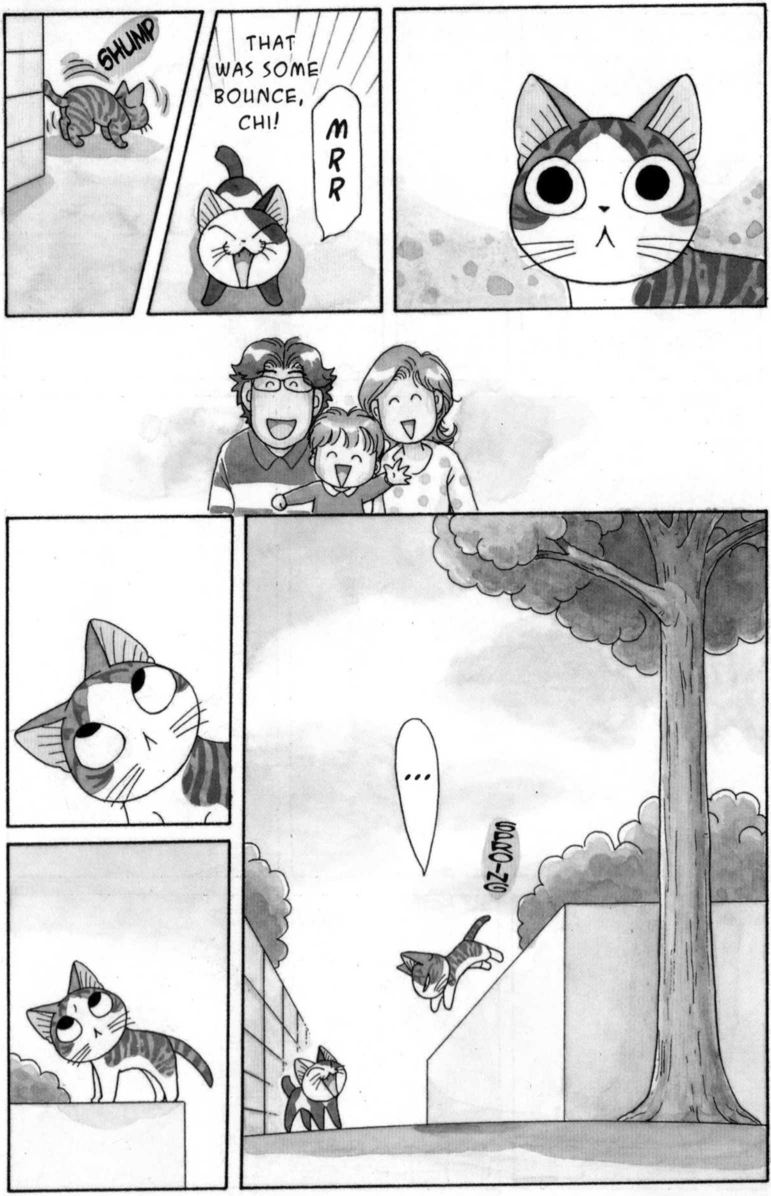
SHUMP
THAT WAS SOME BOUNCE, CHI!
MRR
...
SPROING

the end

homemade 137: a cat returns

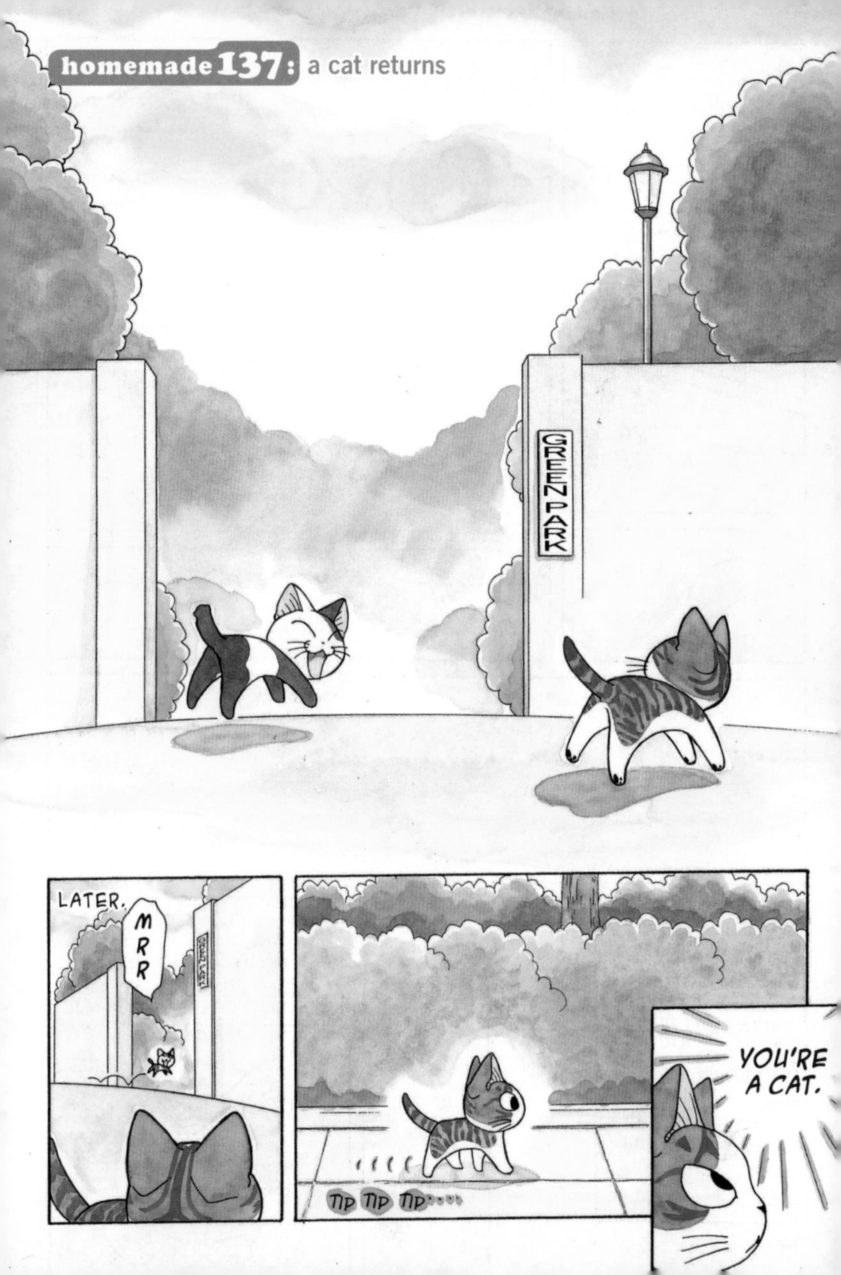
GREEN PARK
LATER.
MRR
TIP TIP TIP...
YOU'RE A CAT.

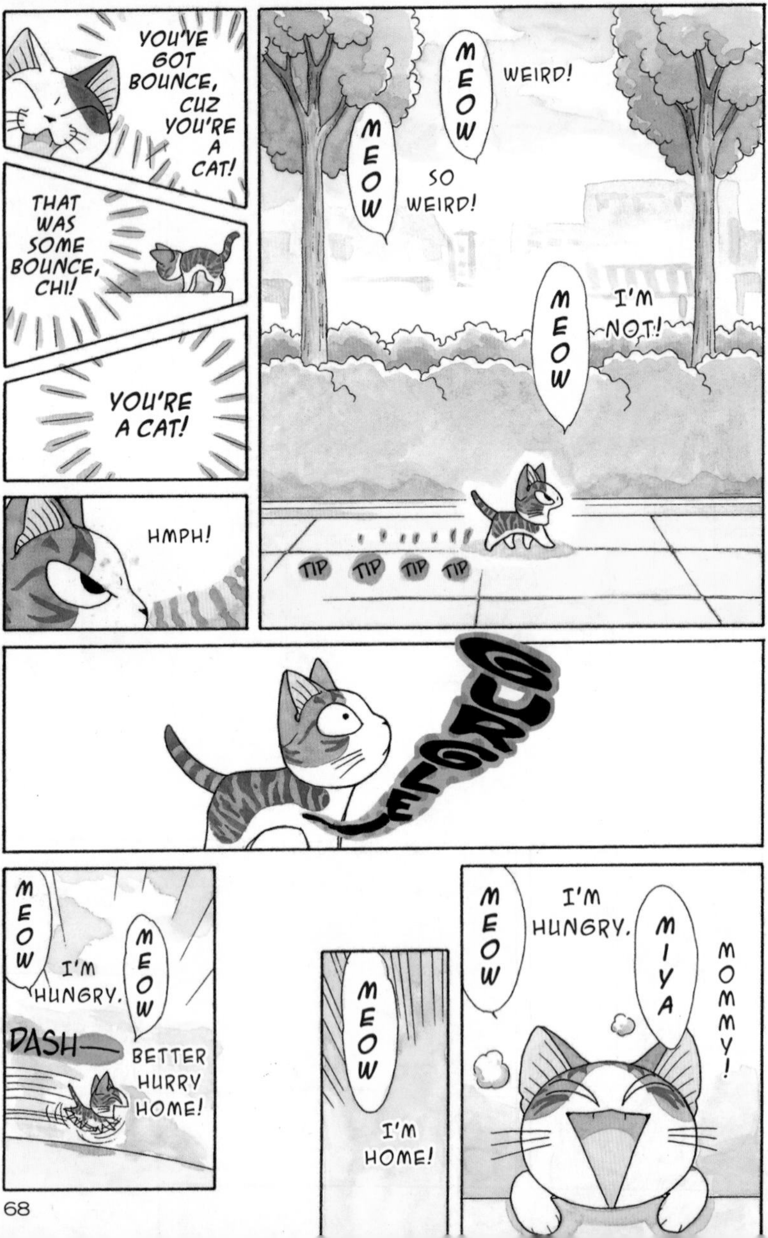
YOU'VE GOT BOUNCE, CUZ YOU'RE A CAT!
THAT WAS SOME BOUNCE, CHI!
YOU'RE A CAT!
HMPH!
MEOW
WEIRD!
MEOW
SO WEIRD!
MEOW
I'M NOT!
TIP TIP TIP TIP
GURGLE
MEOW
I'M HUNGRY.
MEOW
DASH
BETTER HURRY HOME!
MEOW
I'M HOME!
MEOW
I'M HUNGRY.
MIYA
MOMMY!

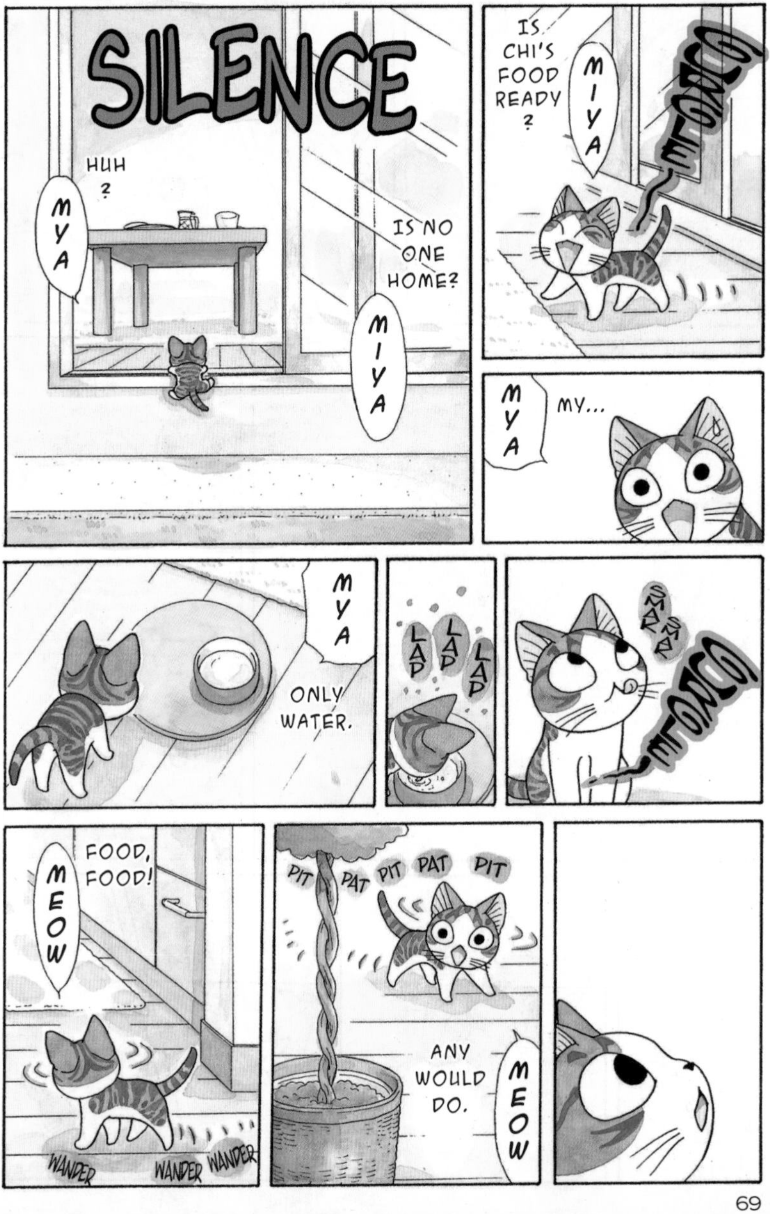
SILENCE
MYA
HUH?
MIYA
IS NO ONE HOME?
MIYA
IS CHI'S FOOD READY?
MYA
MY...
MYA
ONLY WATER.
LAP
LAP
LAP
SMAK
SMAK
MEOW
FOOD, FOOD!
WANDER
WANDER
WANDER
PIT
PAT
PIT
PAT
PIT
MEOW
ANY WOULD DO.

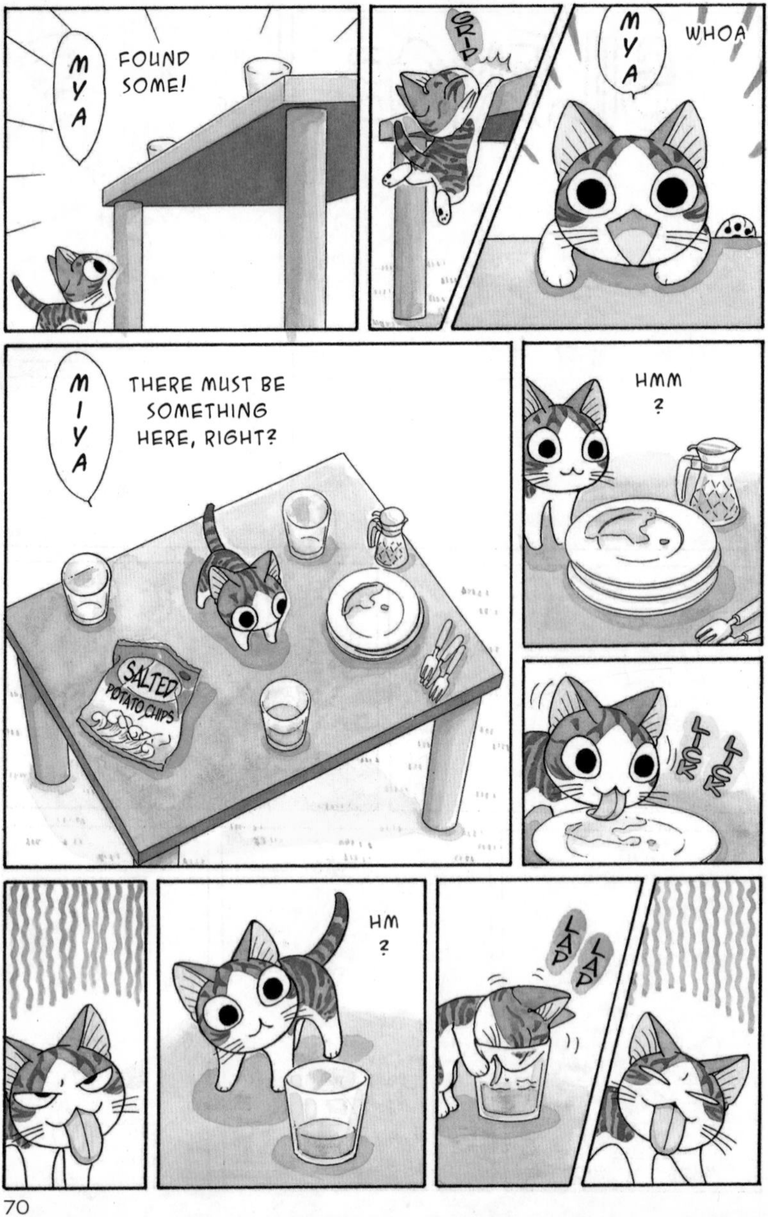
MYA
FOUND SOME!
GRIP
MYA
WHOA
MIYA
THERE MUST BE SOMETHING HERE, RIGHT?
SALTED POTATO CHIPS
HMM ?
LICK LICK
HM ?
LAP LAP

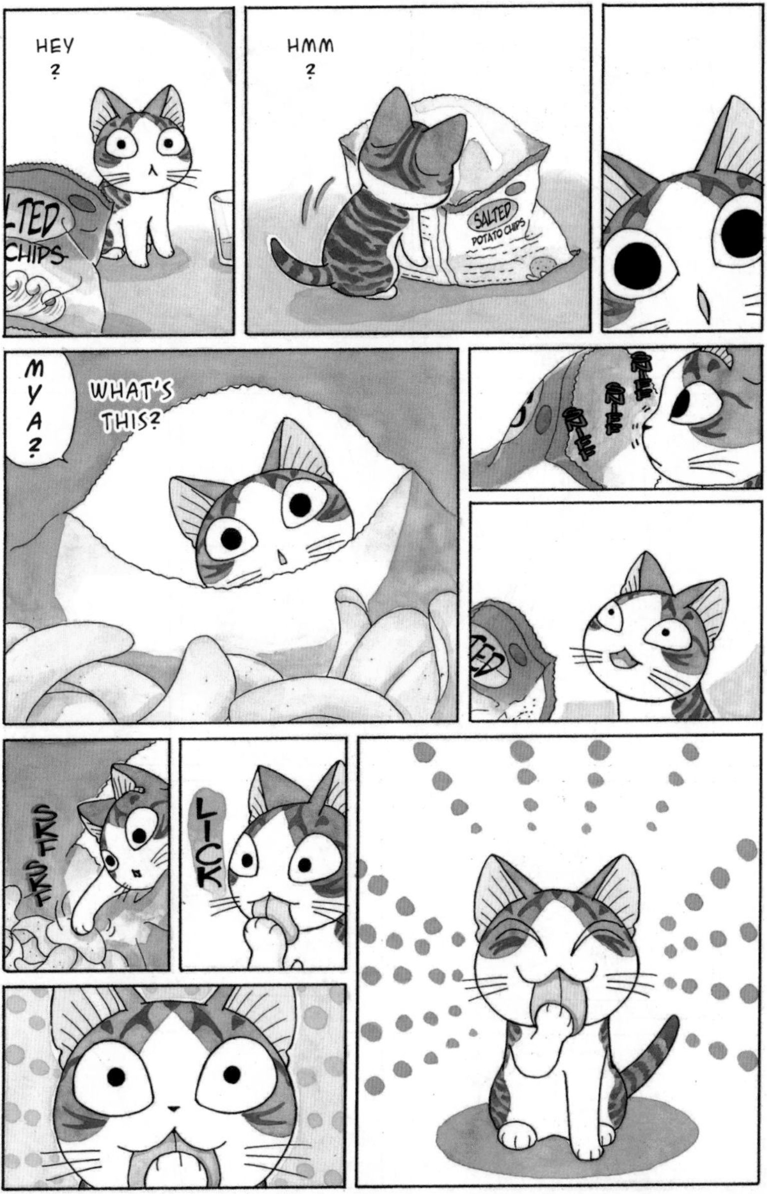
HEY
?
HMM
?
MYA?
WHAT'S THIS?
SNIFF
SNIFF
SNIFF
SKF SKF
LICK

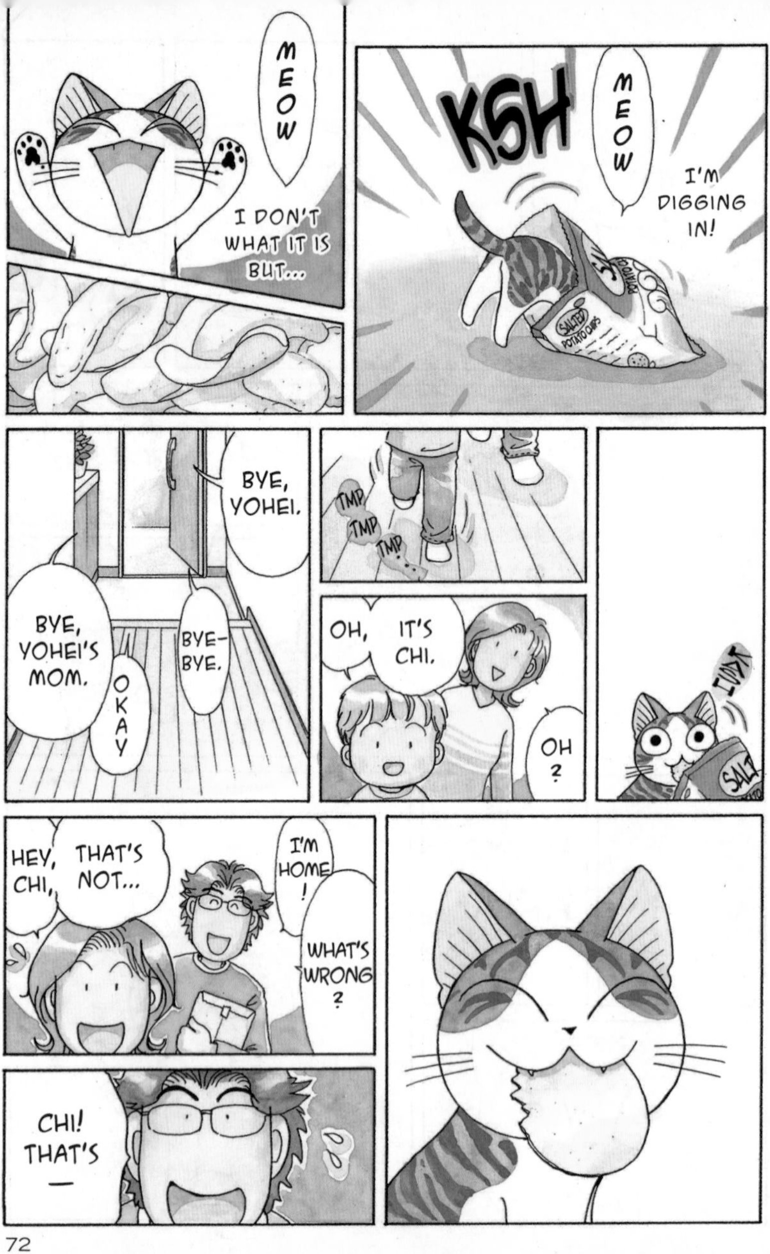
MEOW
I DON'T WHAT IT IS BUT...
KSH
MEOW
I'M DIGGING IN!
SALTED POTATO CHIPS
BYE, YOHEI.
BYE, YOHEI'S MOM.
OKAY
BYE-BYE.
TMP TMP TMP
OH, IT'S CHI.
OH?
HEY, CHI, THAT'S NOT...
I'M HOME!
WHAT'S WRONG?
CHI! THAT'S —

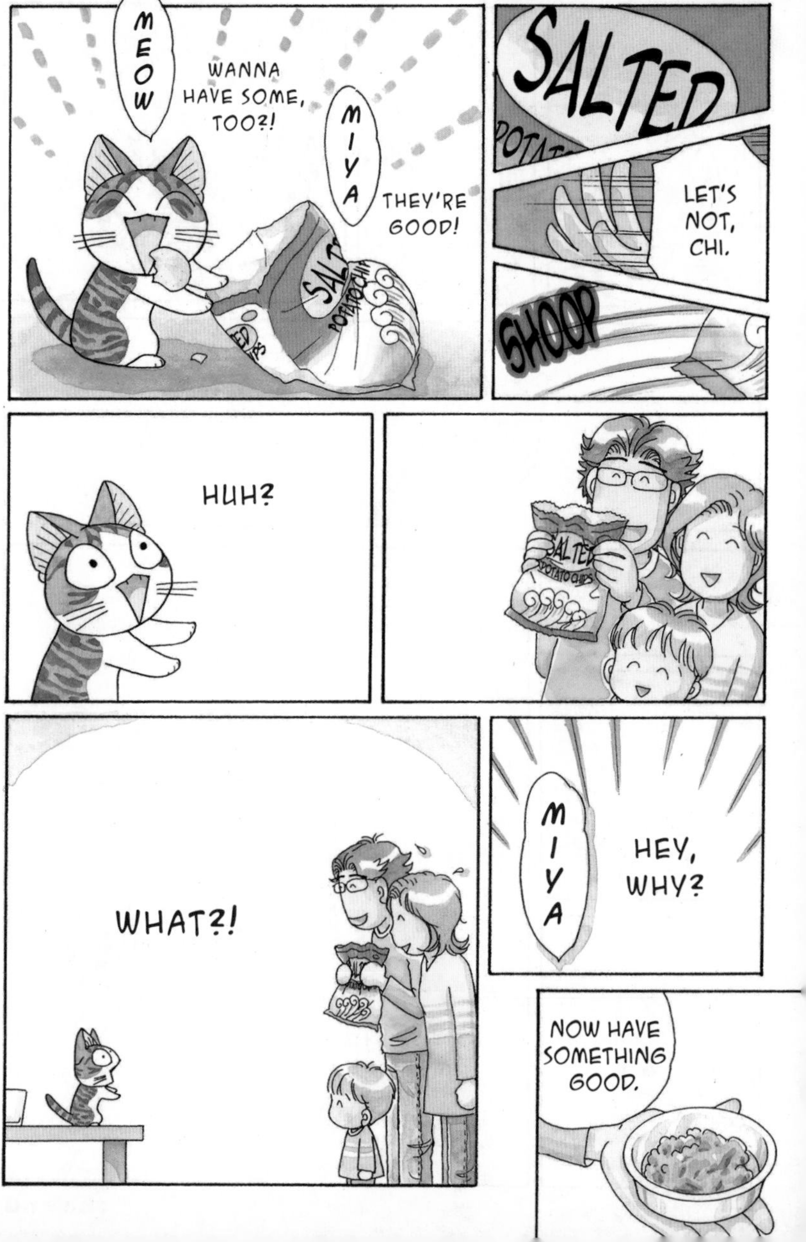
MEOW
WANNA HAVE SOME, TOO?!
MIYA
THEY'RE GOOD!
SALTED
LET'S NOT, CHI.
SHOOP
HUH?
SALTED POTATO CHIPS
WHAT?!
MIYA
HEY, WHY?
NOW HAVE SOMETHING GOOD.

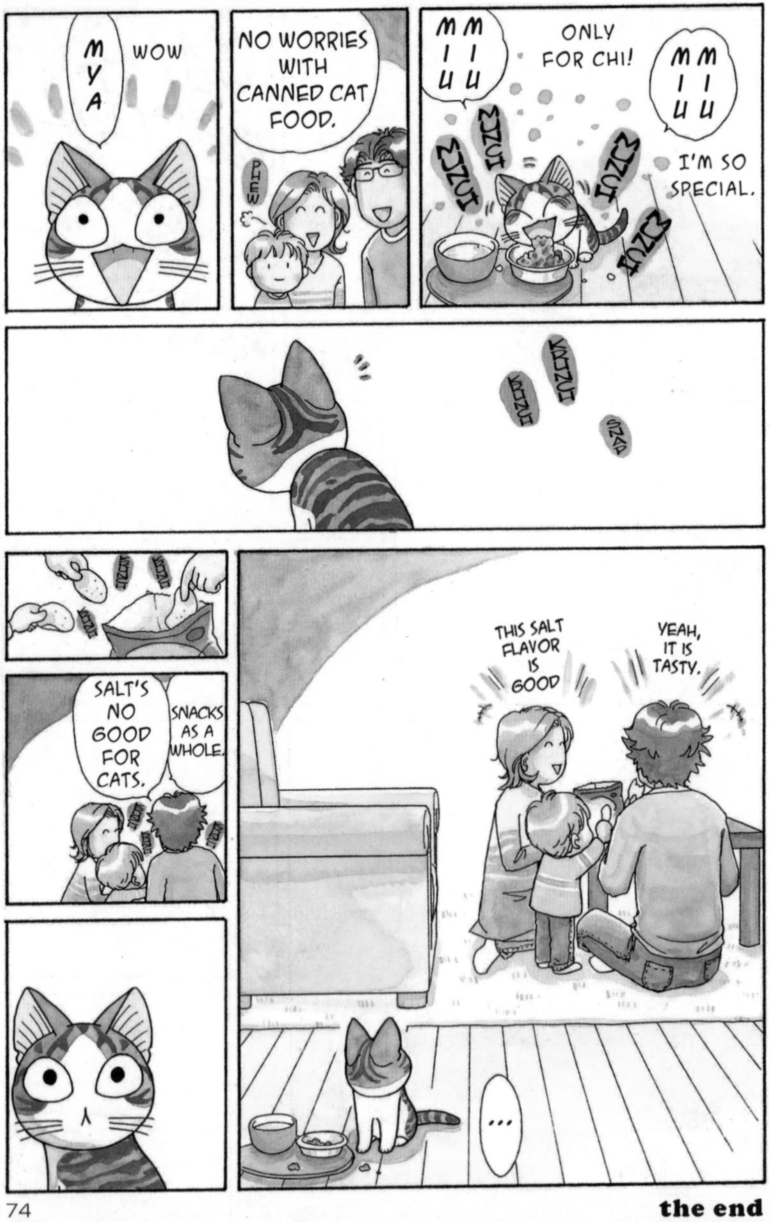
MYA
WOW
NO WORRIES WITH CANNED CAT FOOD.
PHEW
MIU MIU
ONLY FOR CHI!
MIU MIU
MUNCH
MUNCH
MUNCH
MUNCH
I'M SO SPECIAL.
KRUNCH
KRUNCH
SNAP
SALT'S NO GOOD FOR CATS.
SNACKS AS A WHOLE.
THIS SALT FLAVOR IS GOOD
YEAH, IT IS TASTY.
...

the end

homemade 138: a cat relaxes

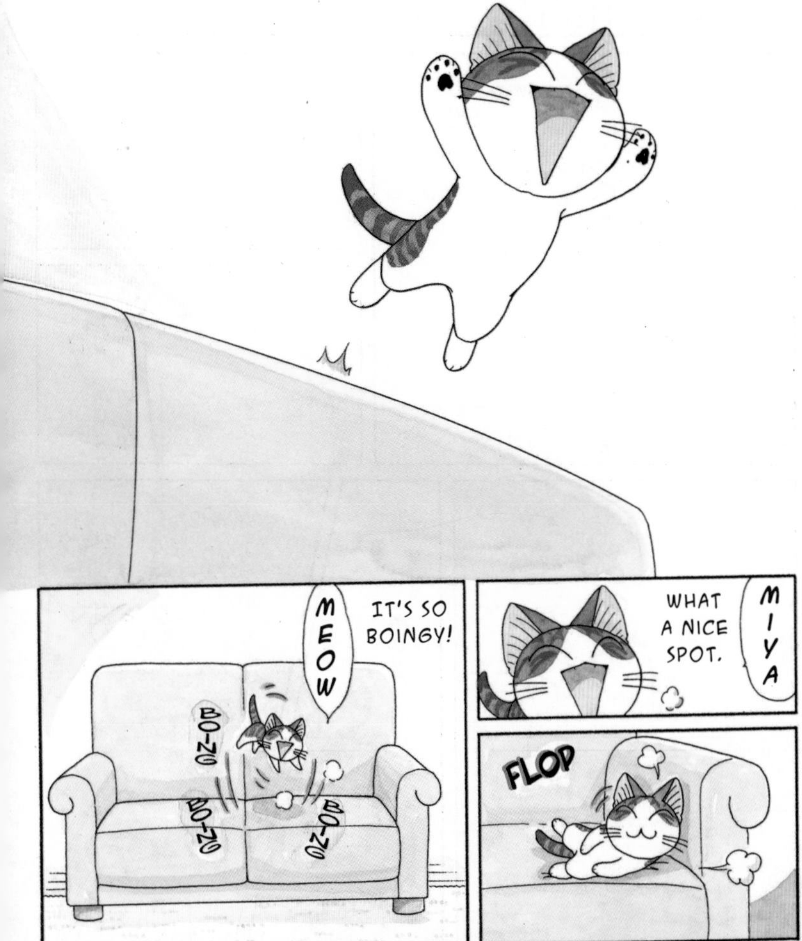
MEOW
IT'S SO BOINGY!
BOING
BOING
BOING
WHAT A NICE SPOT.
MIYA
FLOP

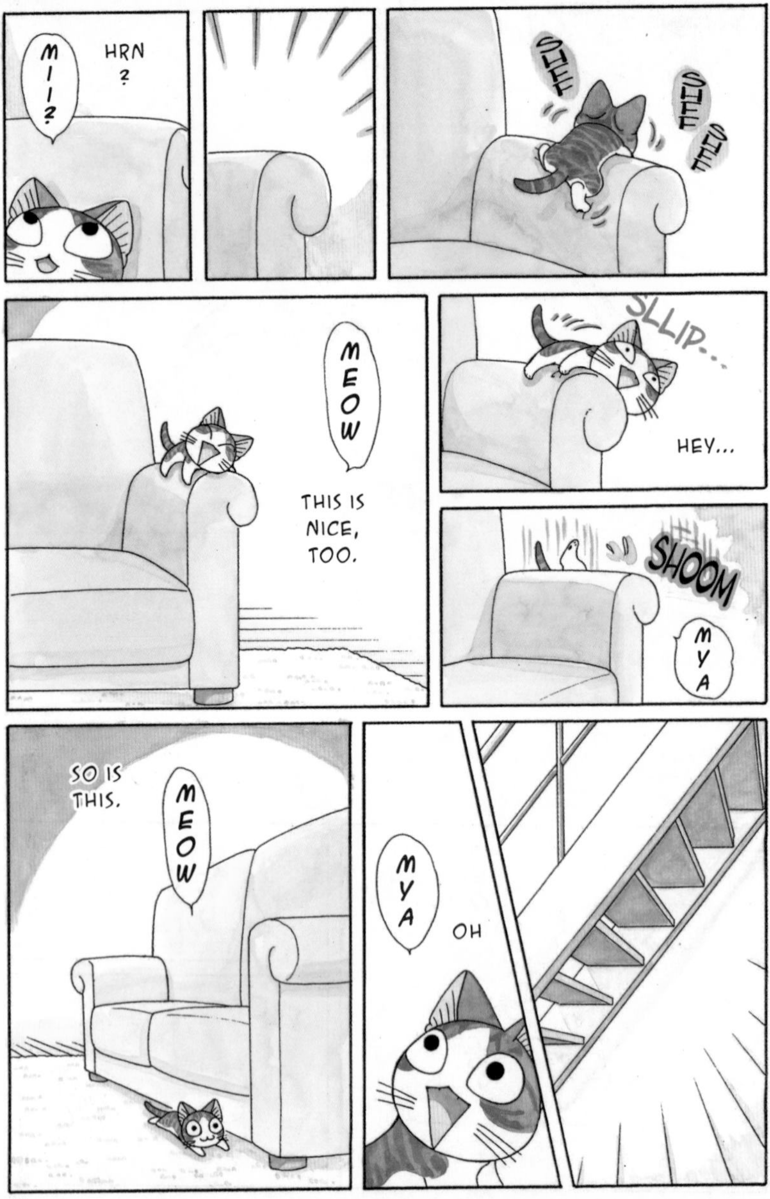
MII?
HRN?
SHFF
SHFF
SHFF
MEOW
THIS IS NICE, TOO.
SLLIP...
HEY...
SHOOM
MYA
SO IS THIS.
MEOW
MYA
OH

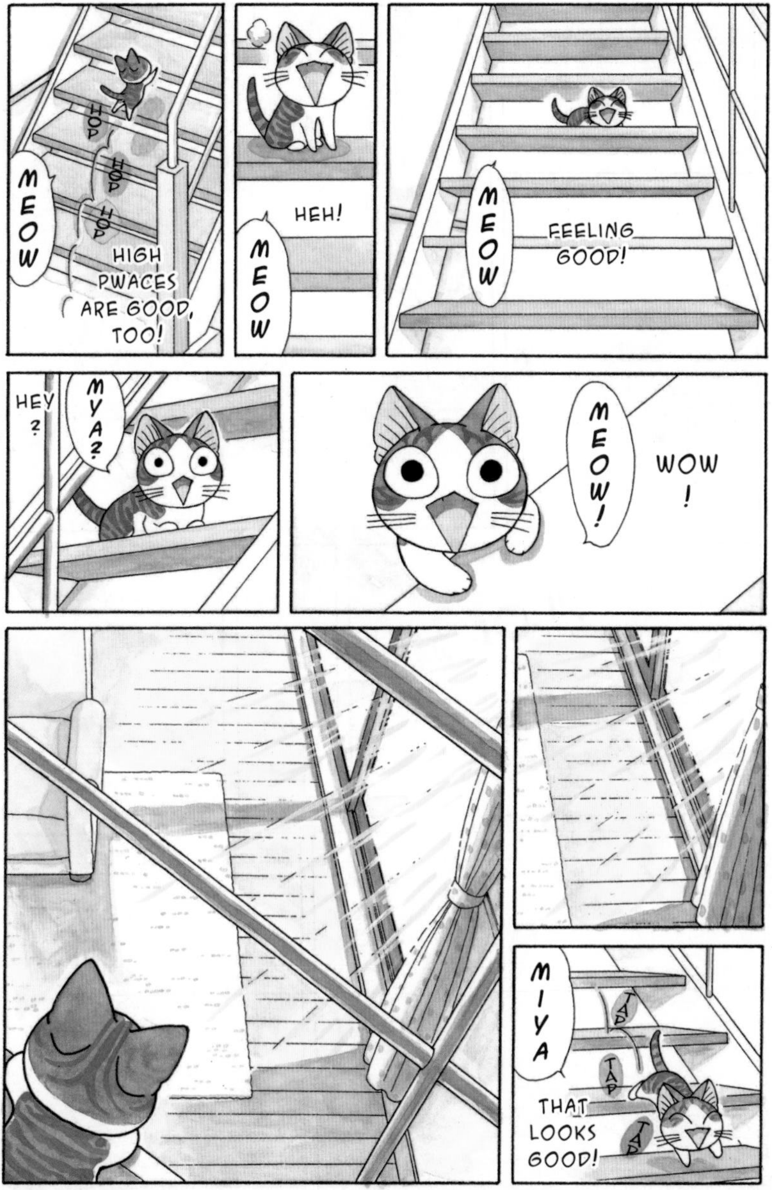
HOP
HOP
HOP
MEOW
HIGH PWACES ARE GOOD, TOO!
HEH!
MEOW
MEOW
FEELING GOOD!
HEY?
MYA?
MEOW!
WOW!
MIYA
TAP
TAP
TAP
THAT LOOKS GOOD!

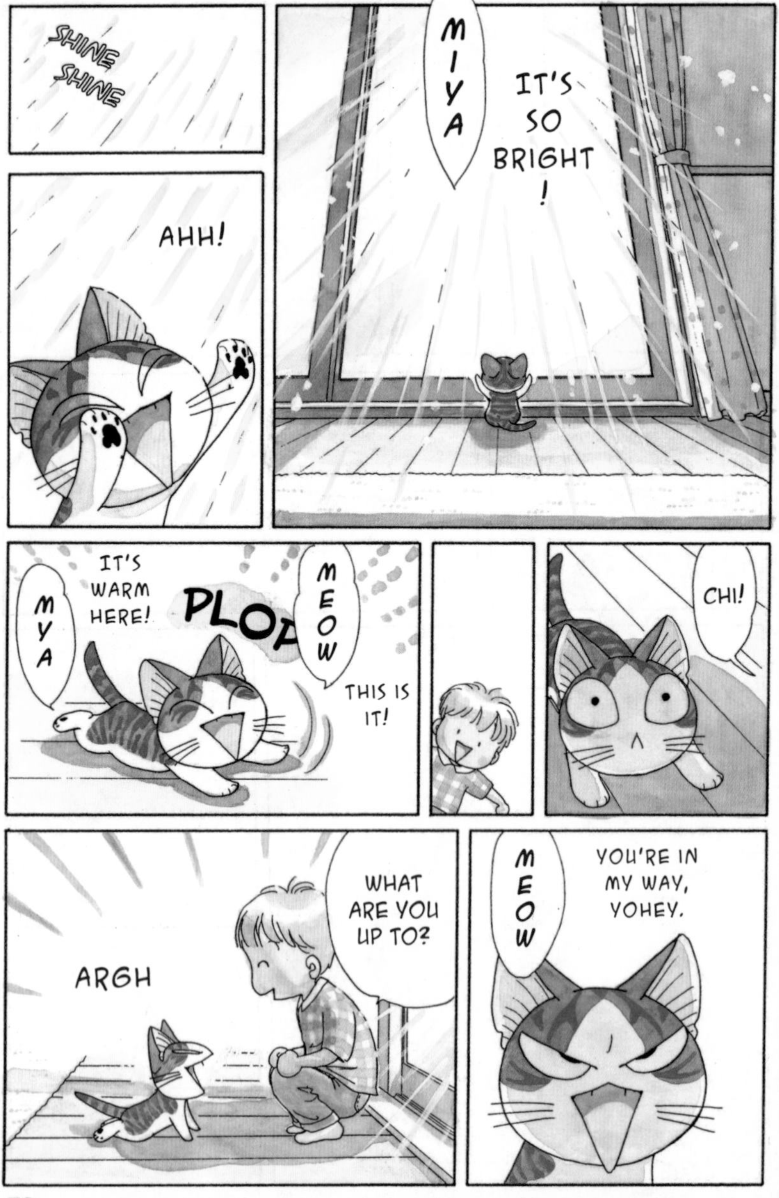
SHINE SHINE
AHH!
MIYA
IT'S SO BRIGHT!
MIYA
IT'S WARM HERE!
PLOP
MEOW
THIS IS IT!
CHI!
ARGH
WHAT ARE YOU UP TO?
MEOW
YOU'RE IN MY WAY, YOHEY.

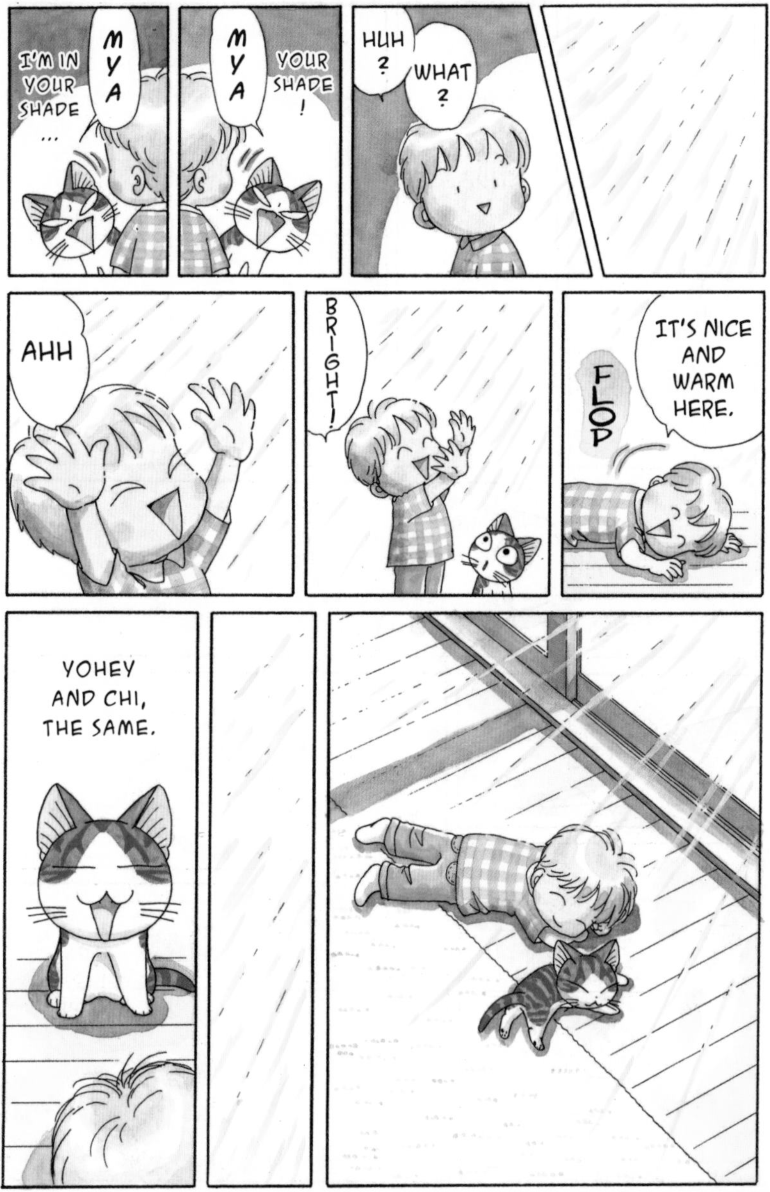
I'M IN YOUR SHADE ...
MYA
MYA
YOUR SHADE !
HUH ?
WHAT ?
AHH
BRIGHT!
FLOP
IT'S NICE AND WARM HERE.
YOHEY AND CHI, THE SAME.

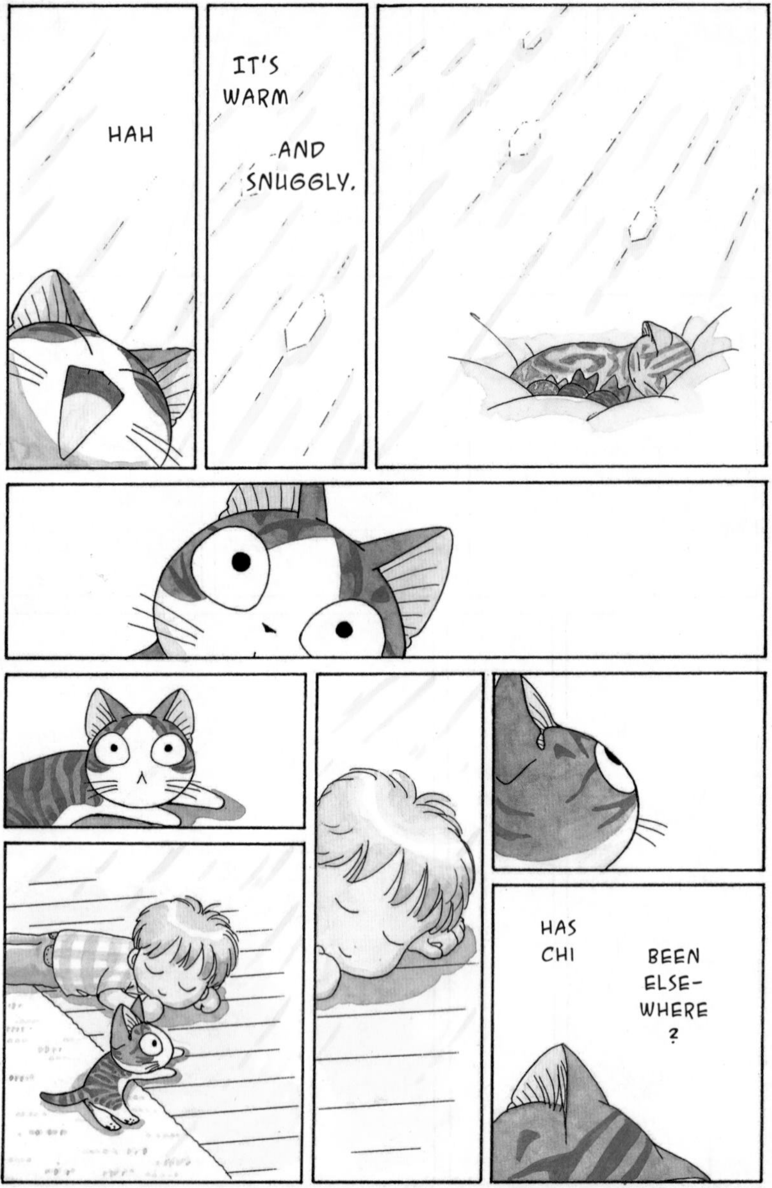
HAH
IT'S WARM
AND SNUGGLY.
HAS CHI
BEEN ELSE-WHERE?

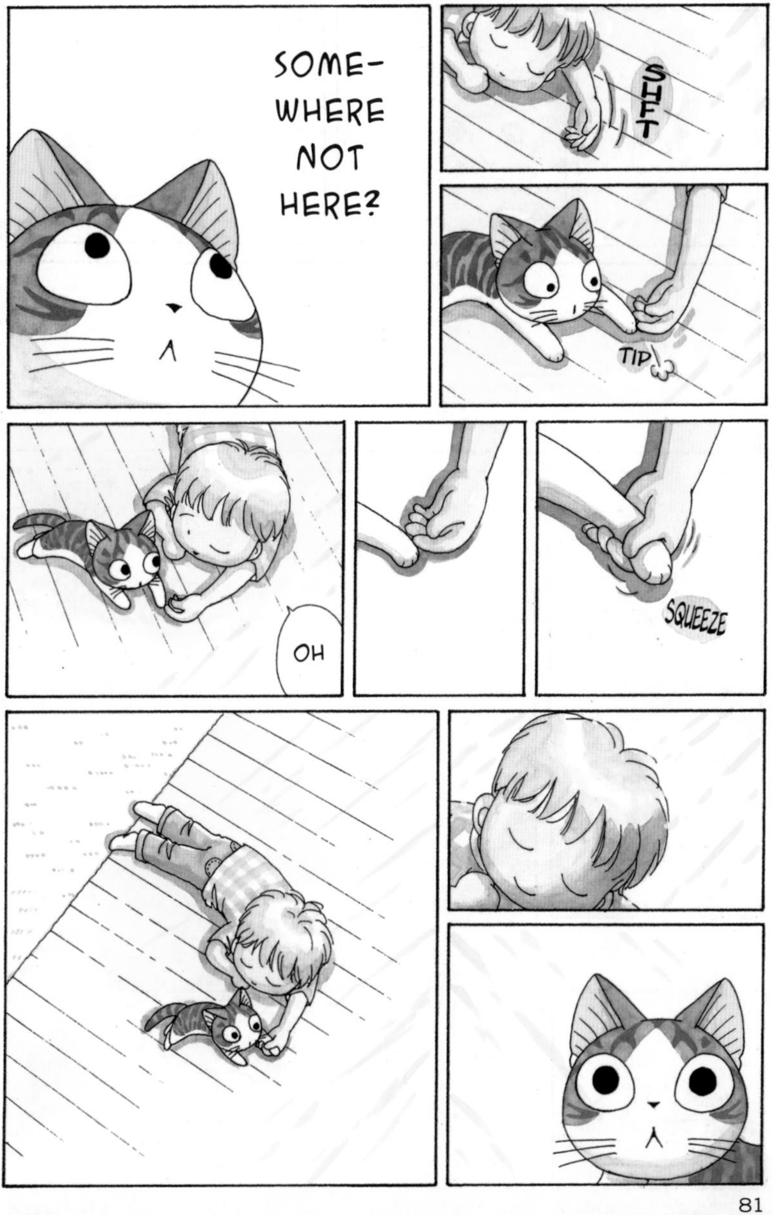
SOME-WHERE NOT HERE?
SHFT
TIP
OH
SQUEEZE

IT SURE IS WARM HERE.

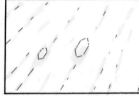

MIU

PURR PURR PURR

WHERE WAS THAT?

BUT

the end

homemade 139: a cat monitors

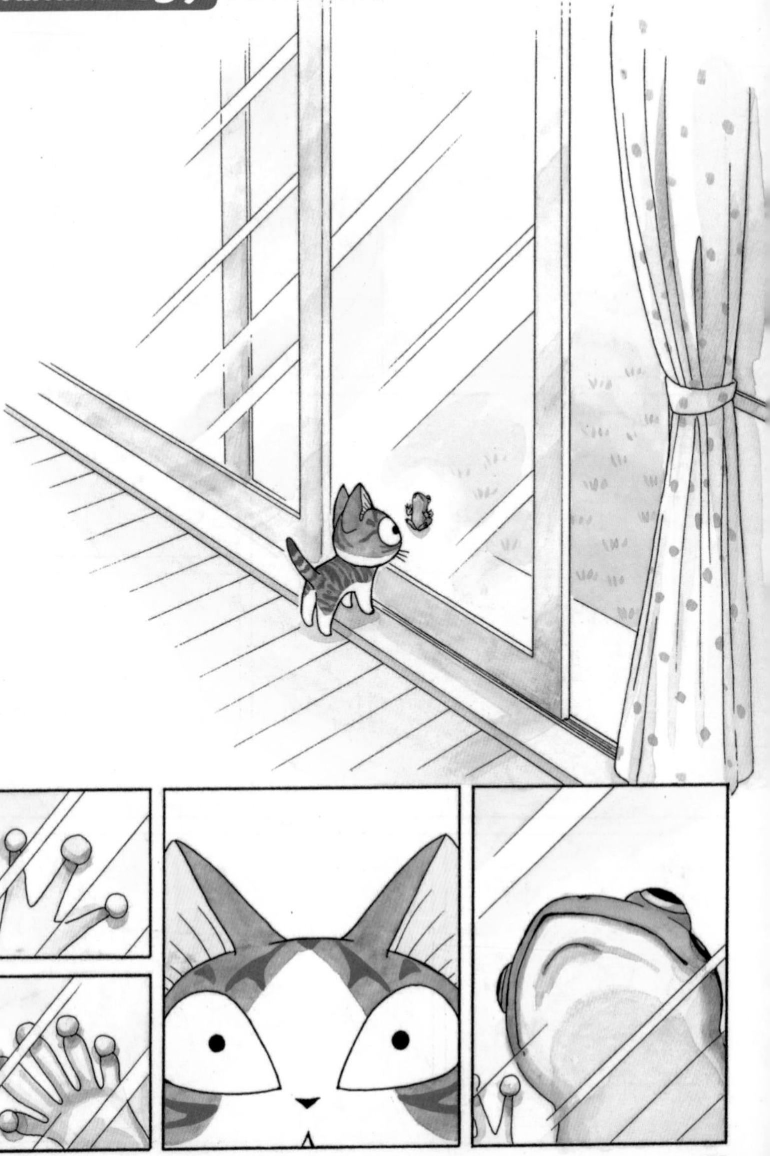

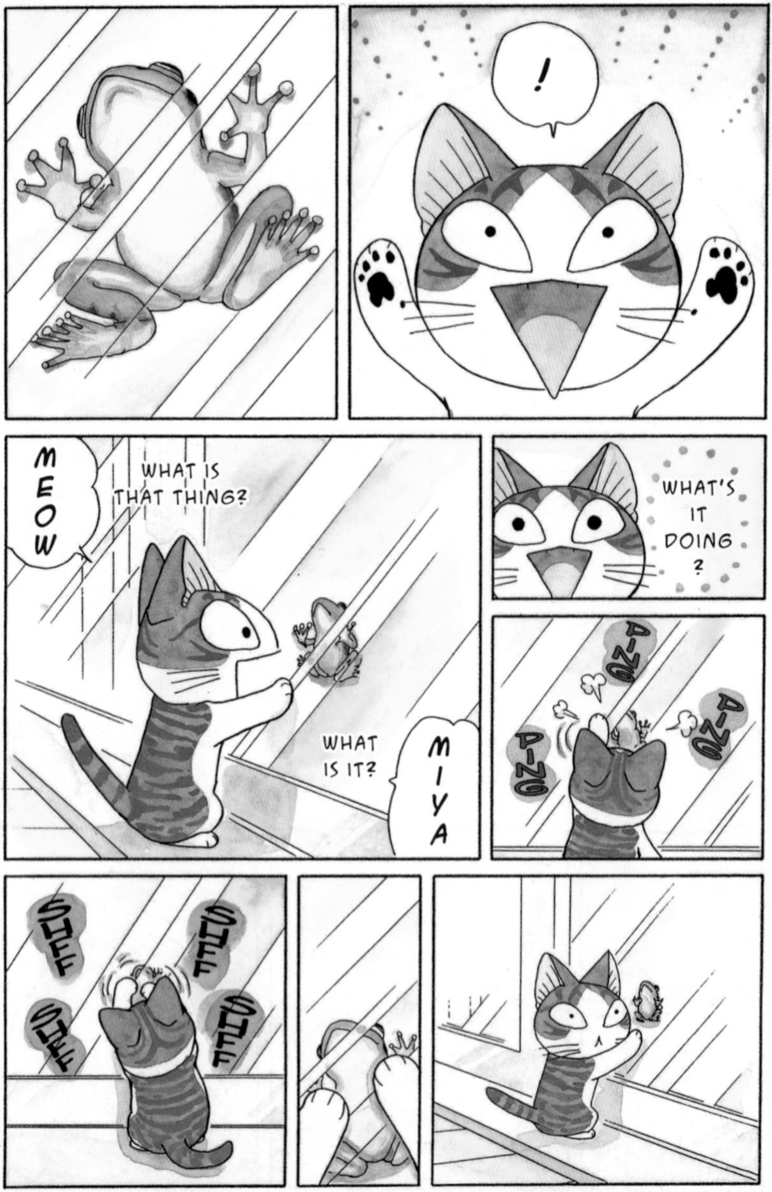
!
MEOW
WHAT IS THAT THING?
WHAT IS IT?
MIYA
WHAT'S IT DOING?
PING
PING
PING
SHFF
SHFF
SHFF
SHFF

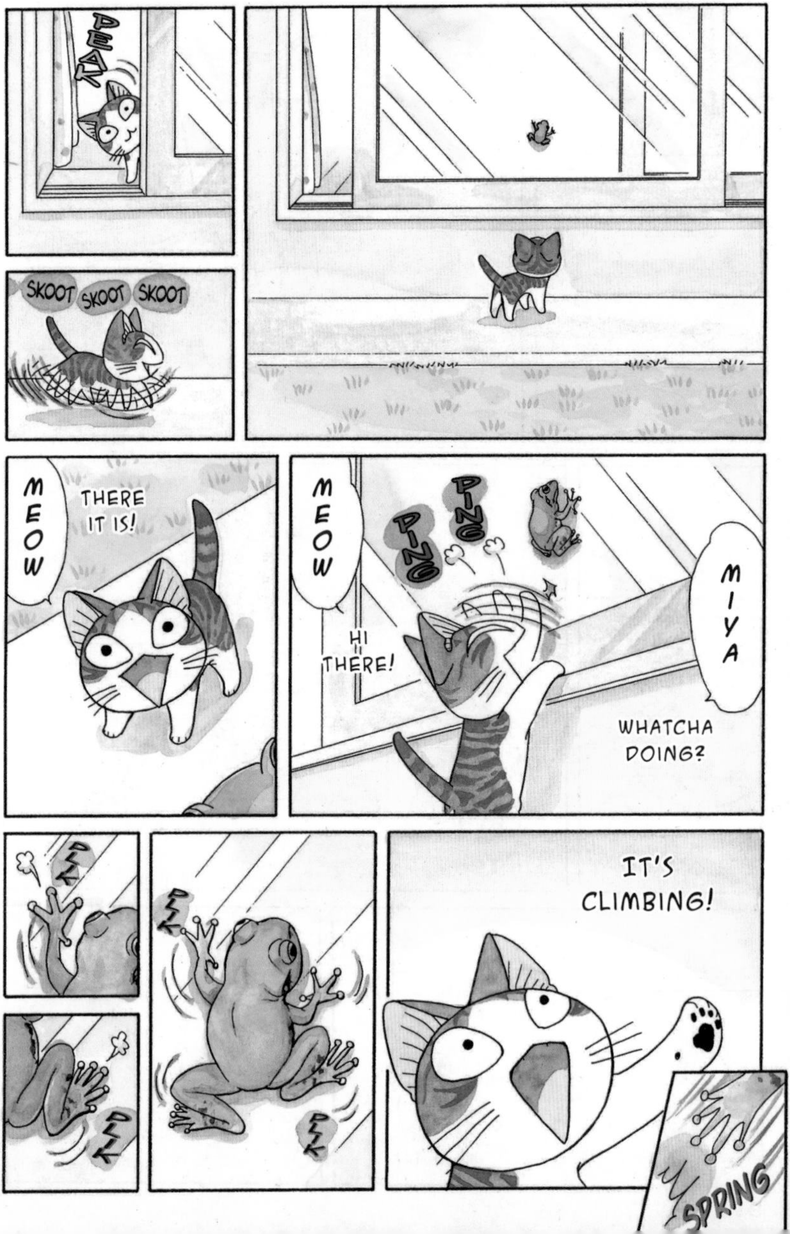
PEAK
SKOOT SKOOT SKOOT
MEOW
THERE IT IS!
MEOW
PING PING
HI THERE!
MIYA
WHATCHA DOING?
PLIK
PLIK
PLIK
PLIK
IT'S CLIMBING!
SPRING

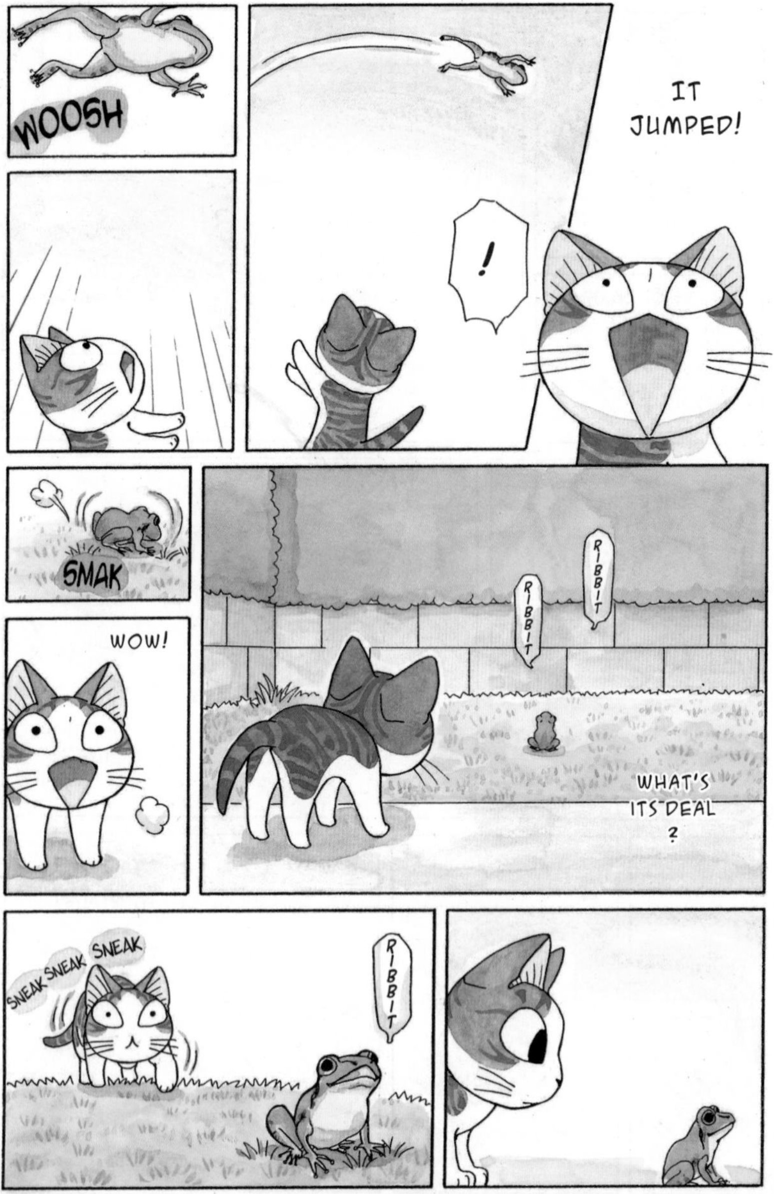
WOOSH
!
IT JUMPED!
SMAK
WOW!
RIBBIT
RIBBIT
WHAT'S ITS DEAL ?
SNEAK SNEAK SNEAK
RIBBIT

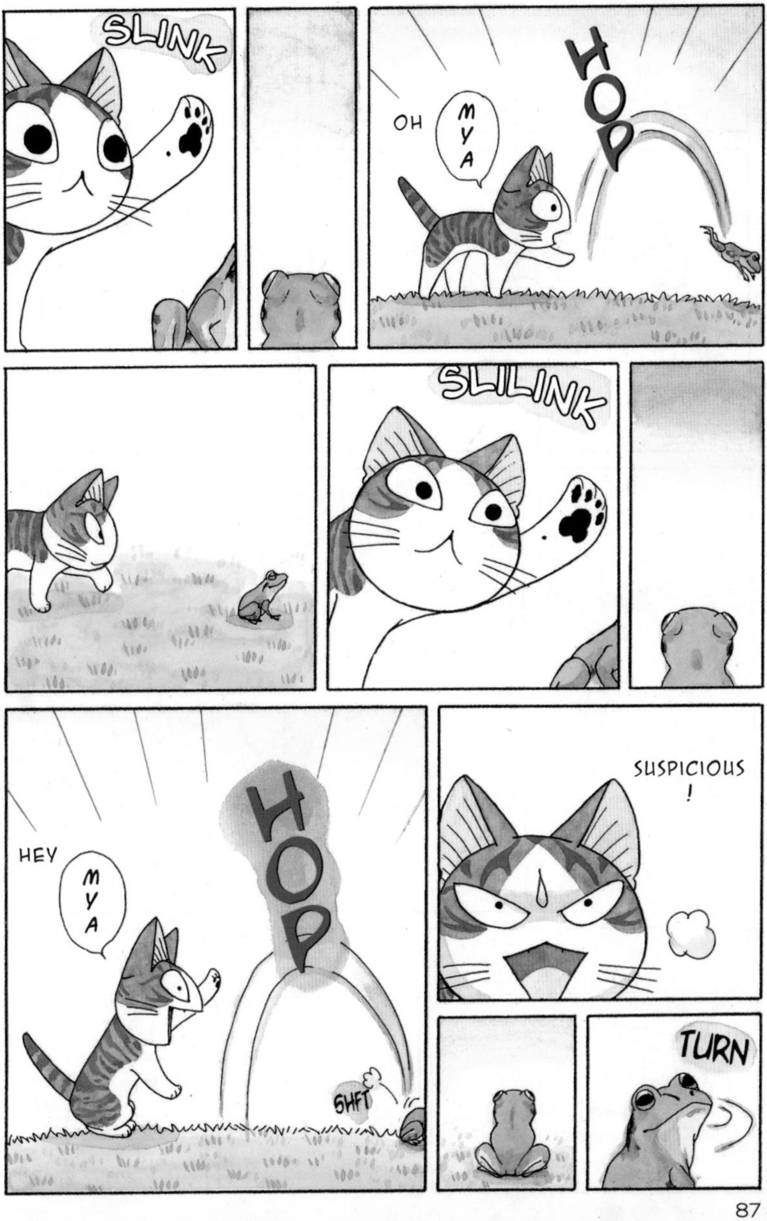
SLINK
OH
MYA
HOP
SLILINK
HEY
MYA
HOP
SHFT
SUSPICIOUS !
TURN

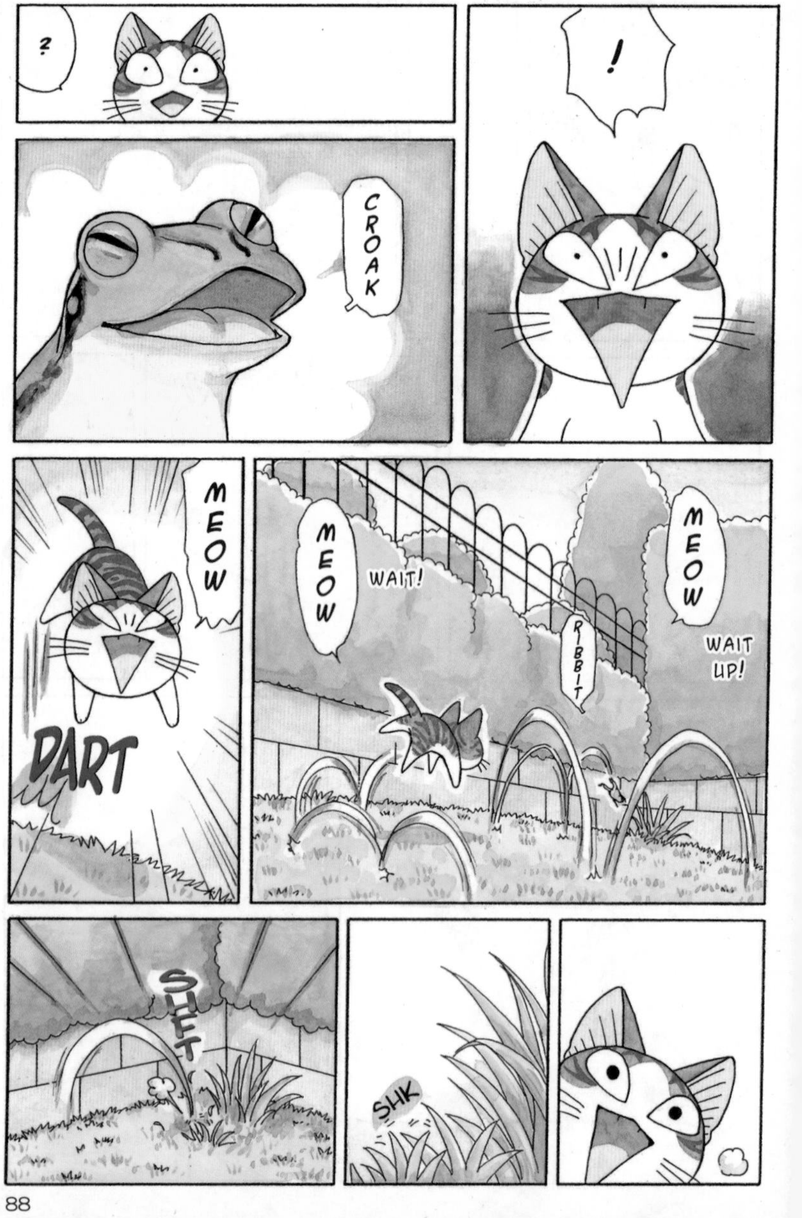
?
CROAK
!
MEOW
DART
MEOW
WAIT!
RIBBIT
MEOW
WAIT UP!
SHFT
SHK

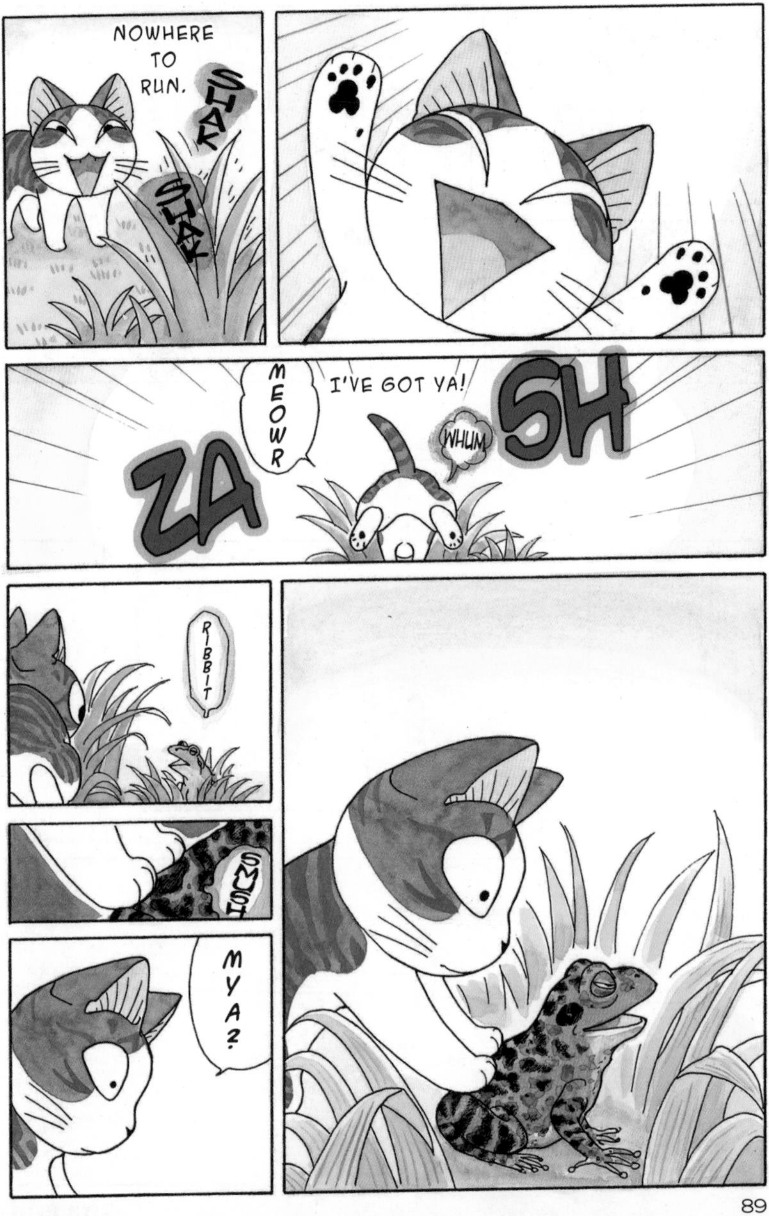
NOWHERE TO RUN.
SHAK
SHAK
MEOWR
I'VE GOT YA!
ZA
WHUM
SH
RIBBIT
SMUSH
MYA?

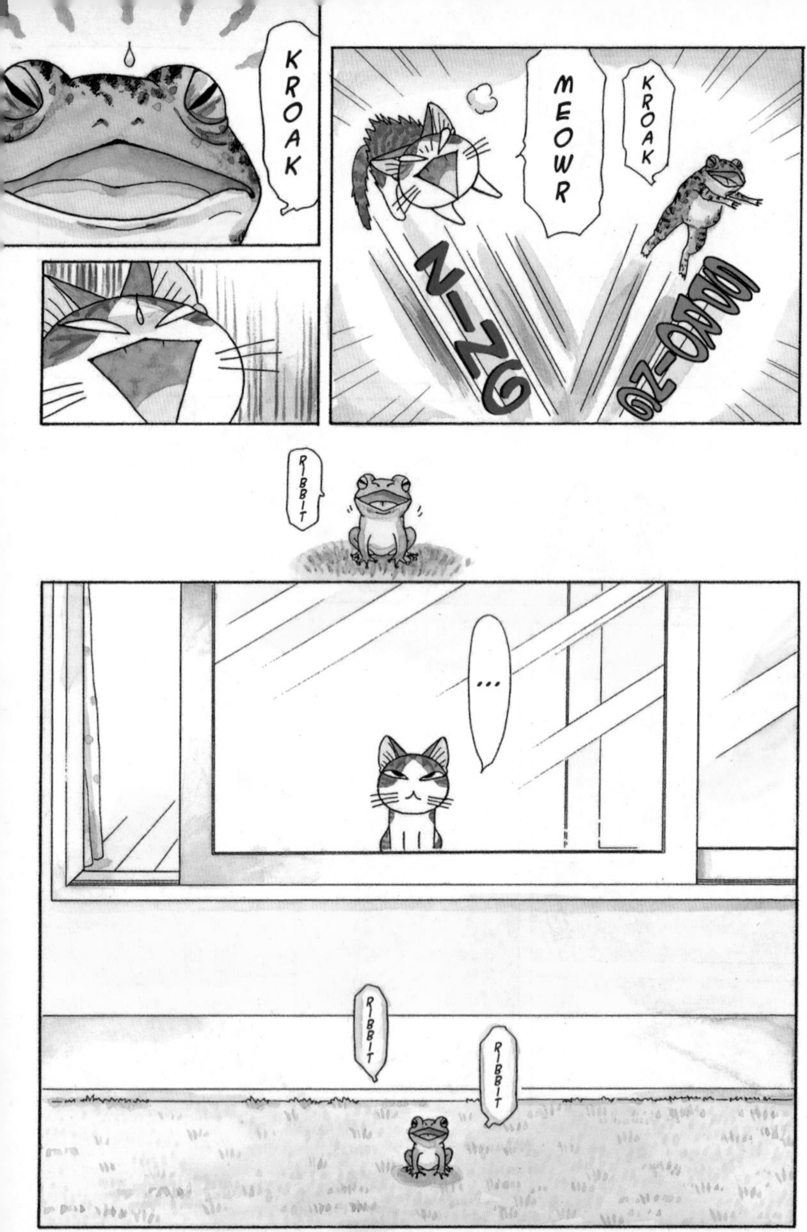
KROAK
MEOWR
KROAK
ZING
RIBBIT
...
RIBBIT
RIBBIT

the end

homemade 140: a cat steps out

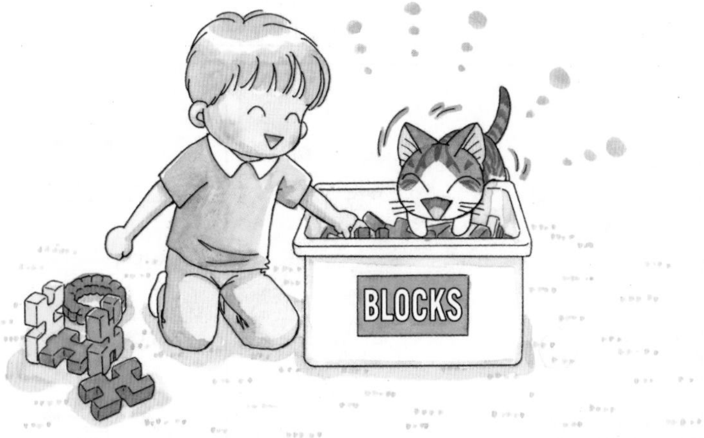

BLOCKS

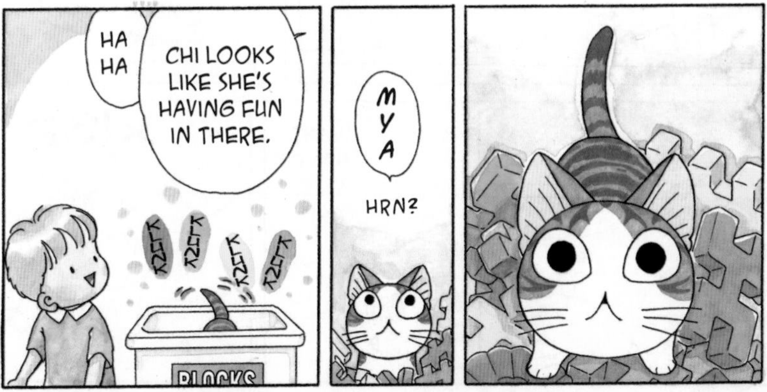

HA HA
CHI LOOKS LIKE SHE'S HAVING FUN IN THERE.
KLUNK
KLUNK
KLUNK
KLUNK
BLOCKS
MYA
HRN?

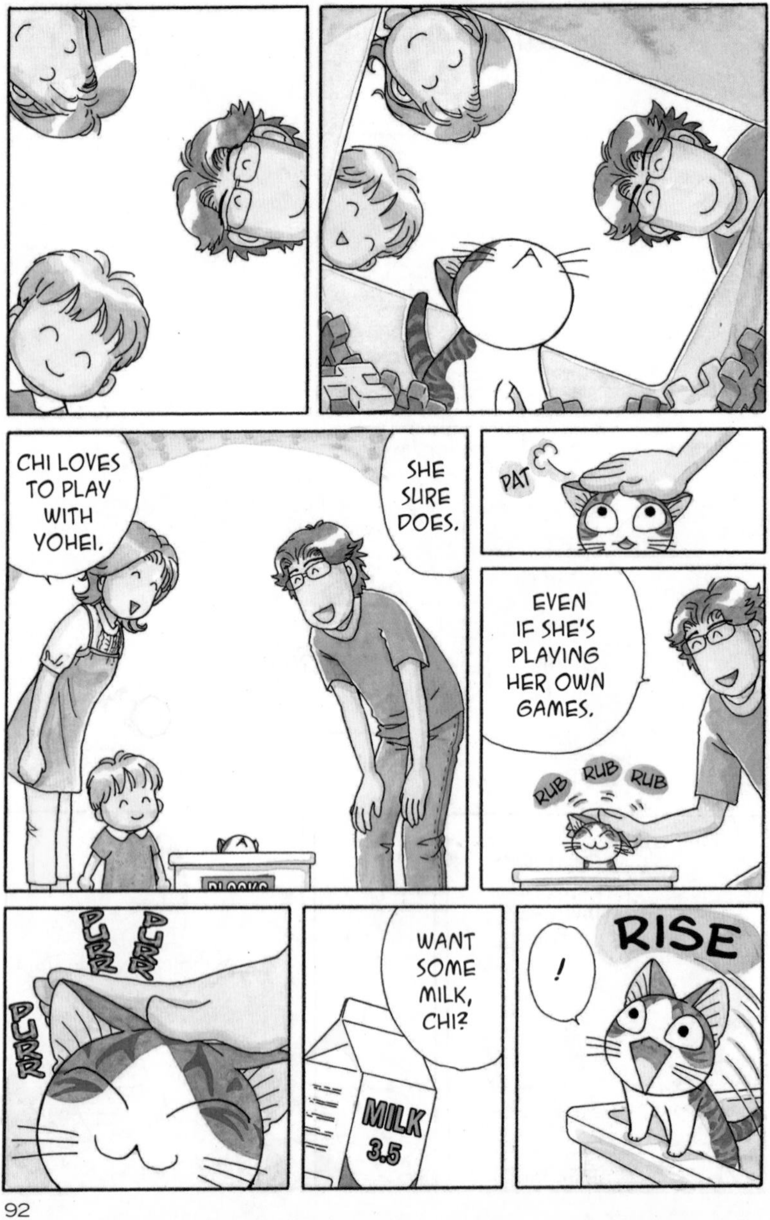
CHI LOVES TO PLAY WITH YOHEI.
SHE SURE DOES.
PAT
EVEN IF SHE'S PLAYING HER OWN GAMES.
RUB RUB RUB
PURR PURR
PURR
WANT SOME MILK, CHI?
MILK
3.5
RISE
!

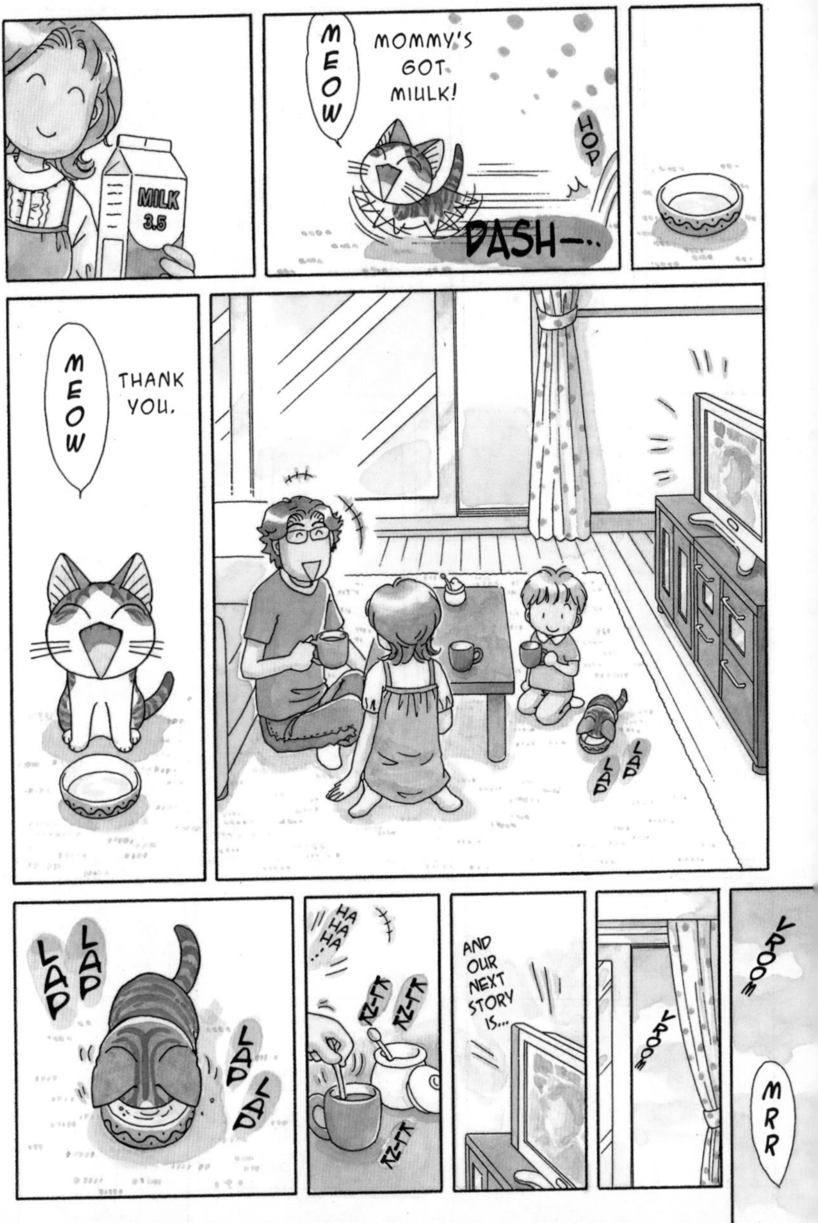
MEOW
MOMMY'S GOT MIULK!
HOP
DASH—..
MEOW
THANK YOU.
LAP
LAP
LAP LAP
LAP LAP
HA HA HA...
SWIRL
SWIRL
SWIRL
AND OUR NEXT STORY IS...
VROOM
VROOM
MRR

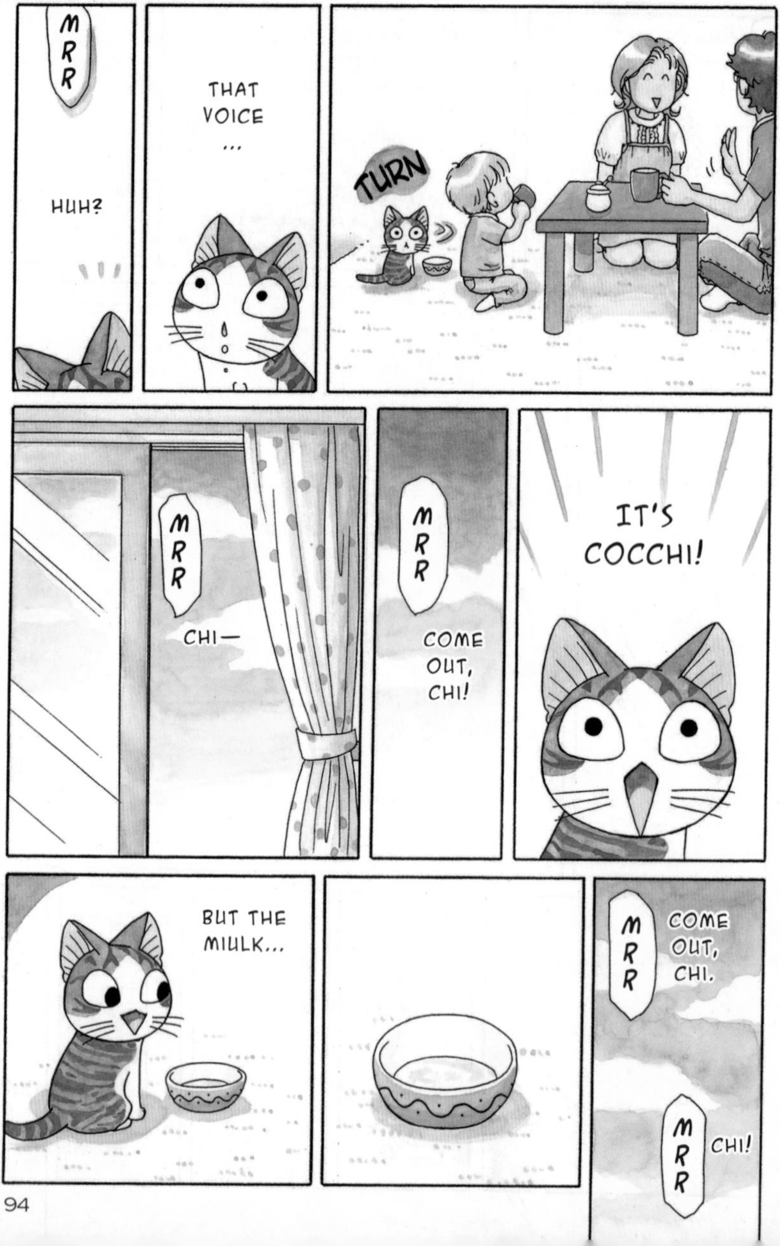
MRR
HUH?
THAT VOICE ...
TURN
MRR
CHI—
MRR
COME OUT, CHI!
IT'S COCCHI!
BUT THE MIULK...
MRR
COME OUT, CHI.
MRR
CHI!

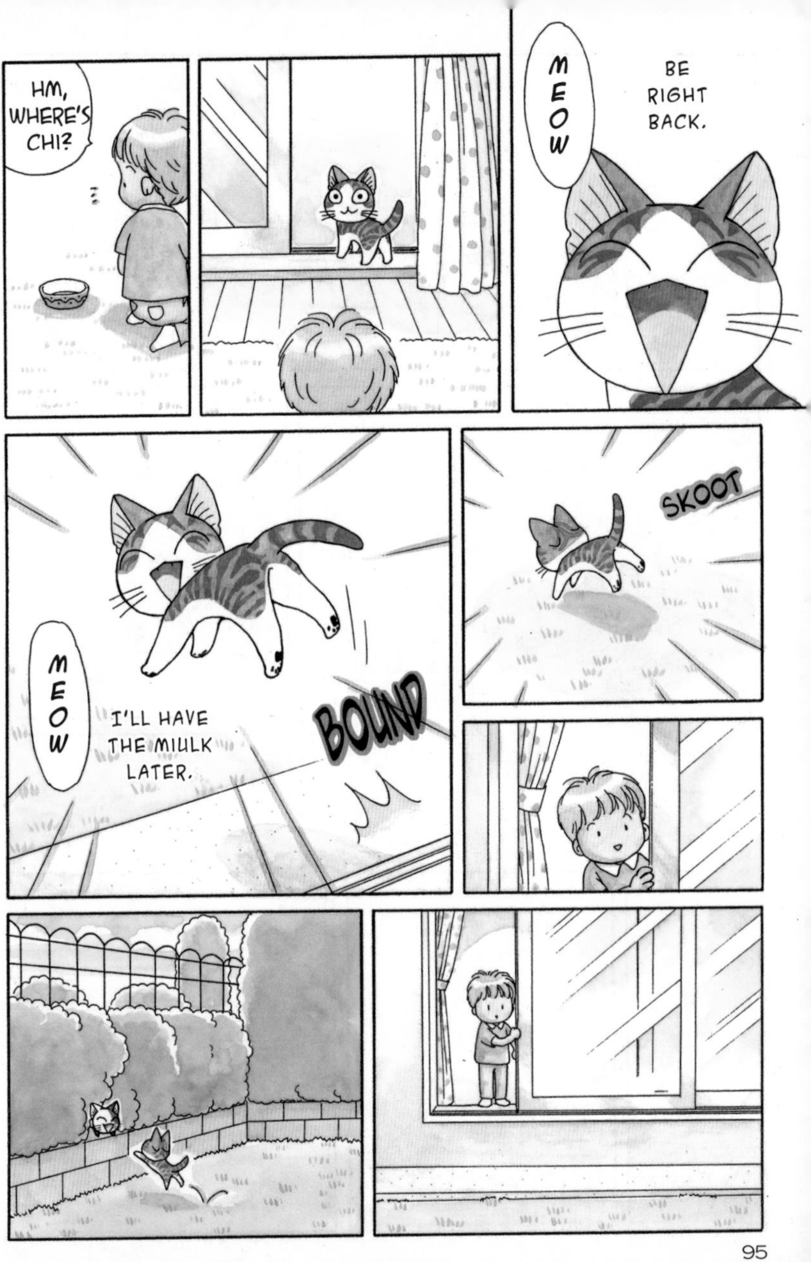
HM, WHERE'S CHI?
MEOW
BE RIGHT BACK.
MEOW
I'LL HAVE THE MIULK LATER.
BOUND
SKOOT

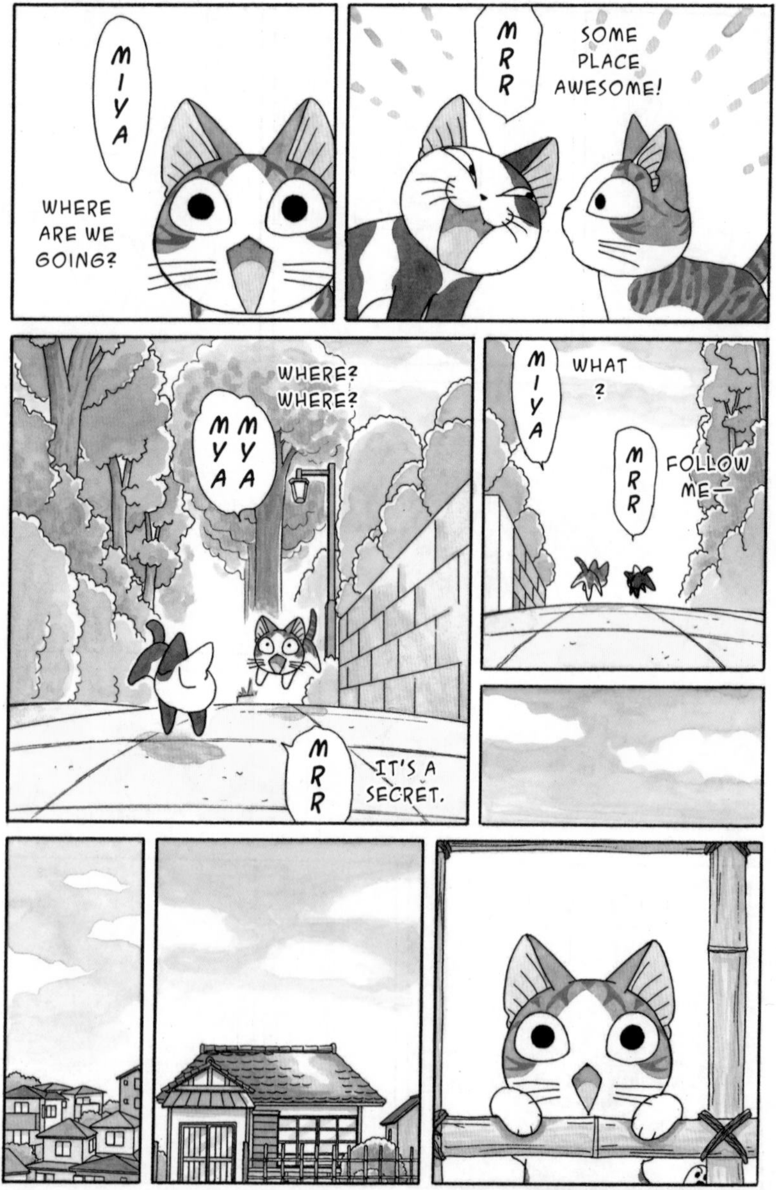
MIYA
WHERE ARE WE GOING?
MRR
SOME PLACE AWESOME!
MYA MYA
WHERE? WHERE?
MRR
IT'S A SECRET.
MIYA
WHAT?
MRR
FOLLOW ME—

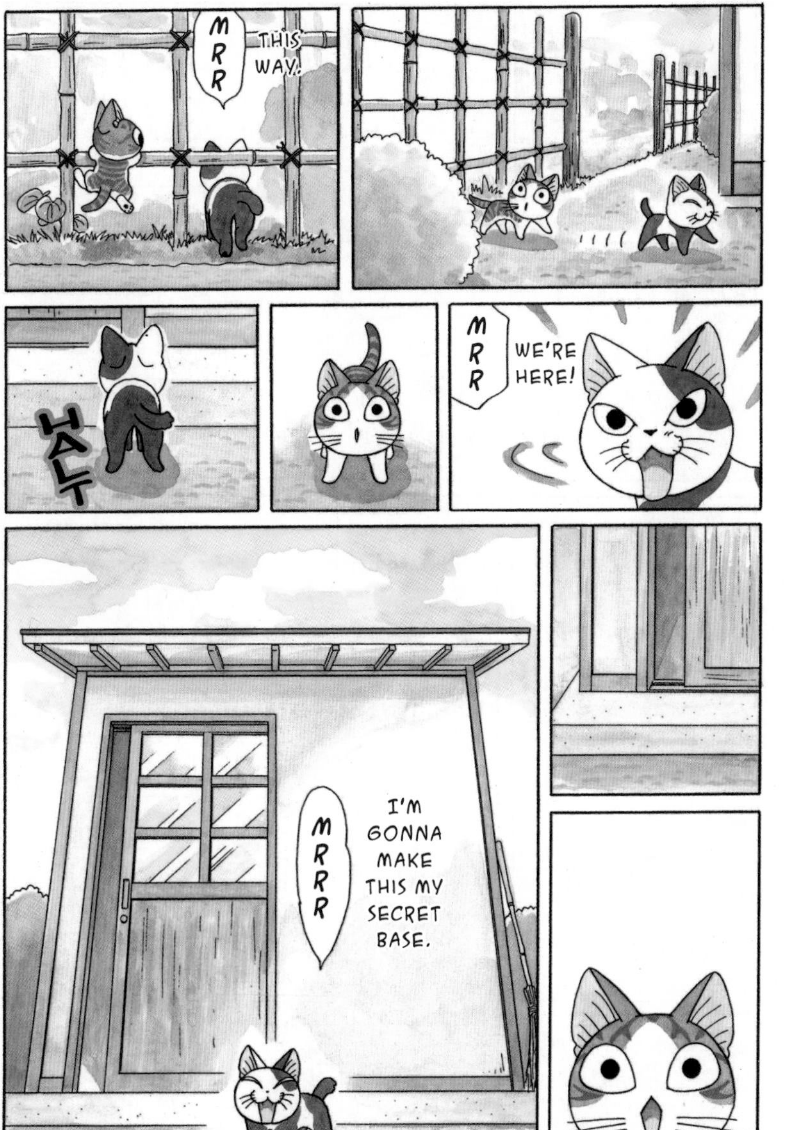
MRR
THIS WAY.
HALT
MRR
WE'RE HERE!
MRRR
I'M GONNA MAKE THIS MY SECRET BASE.

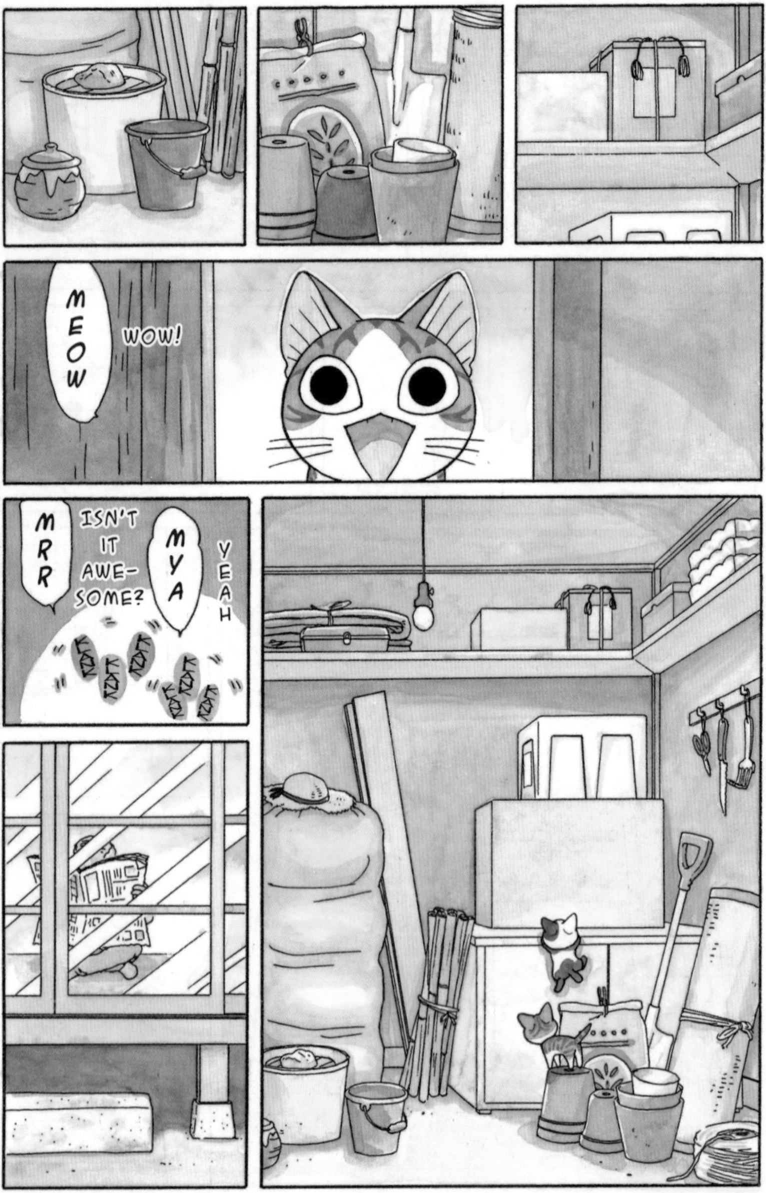
MEOW
WOW!
MRR
ISN'T IT AWESOME?
MYA
YEAH

the end

homemade 141: a cat infiltrates

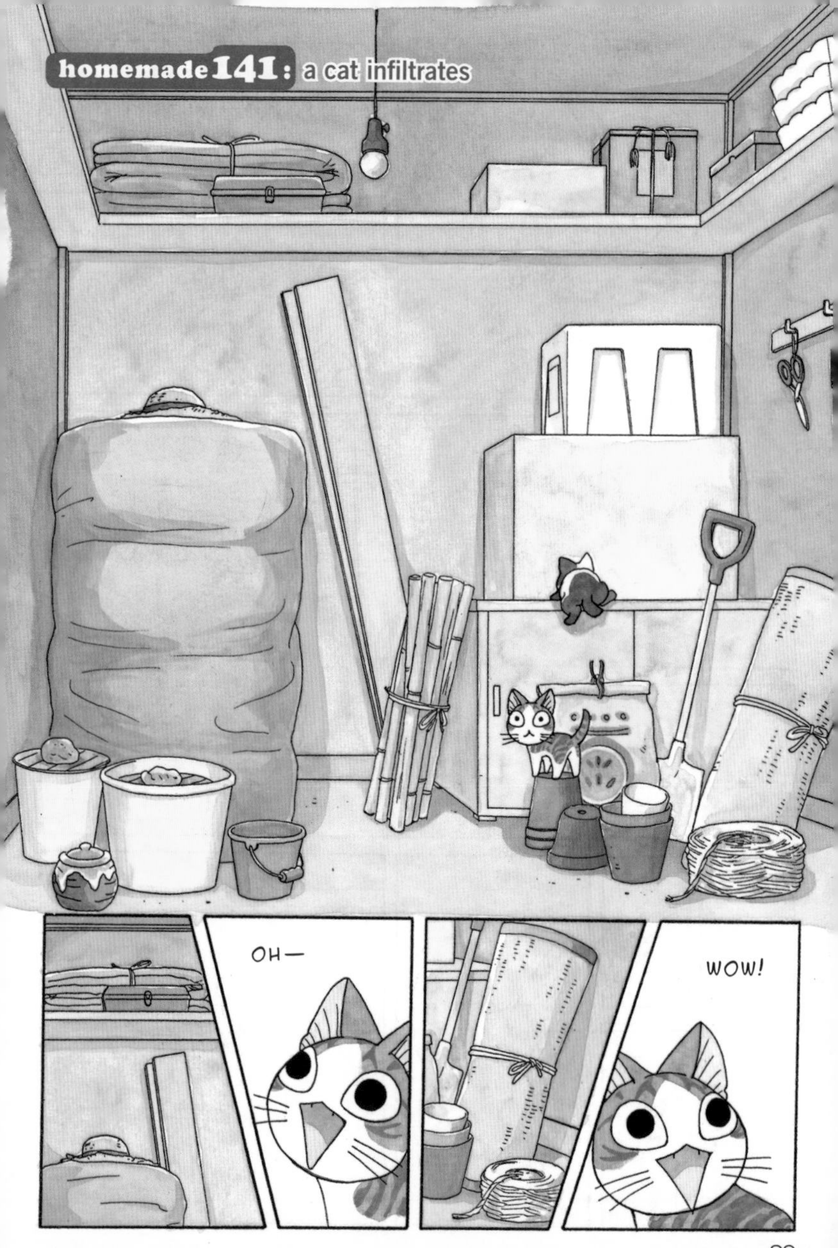
OH—
WOW!

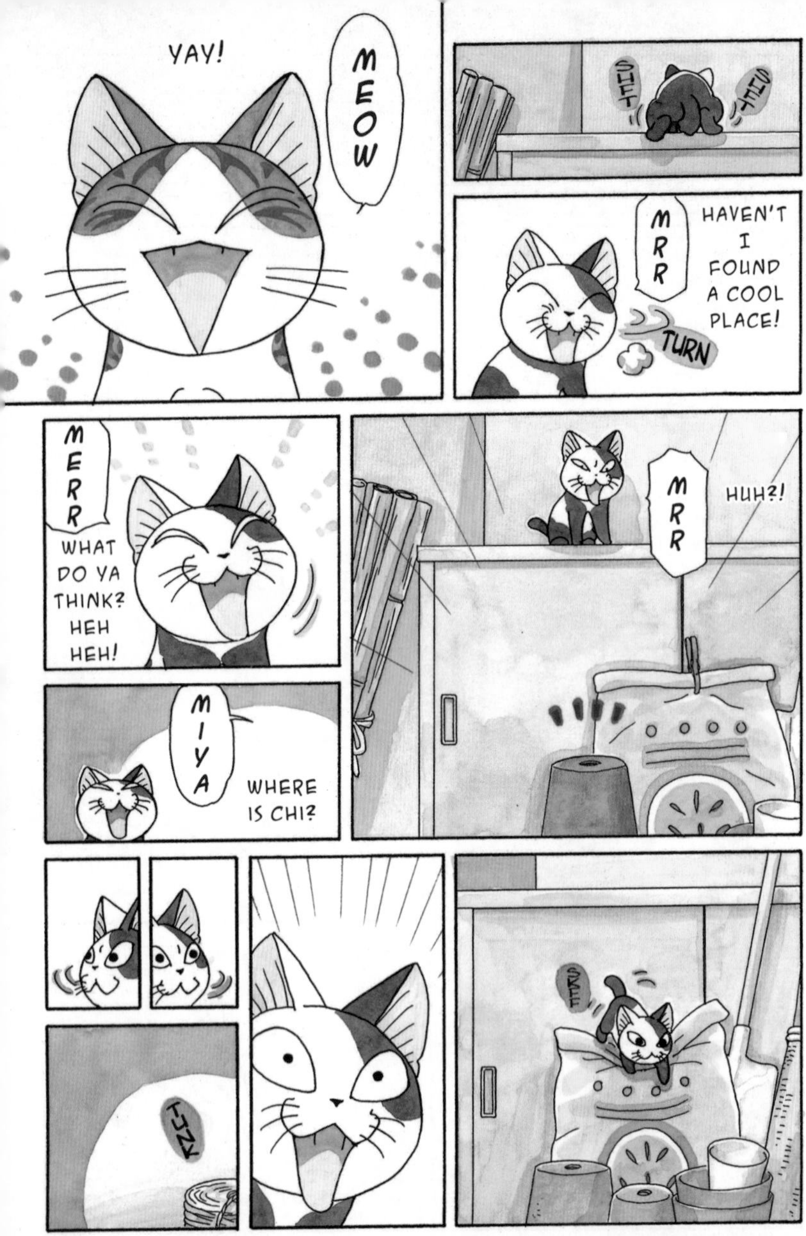
YAY!
MEOW
SHFT
SHFT
MRR
HAVEN'T I FOUND A COOL PLACE!
TURN
MERR
WHAT DO YA THINK? HEH HEH!
MIYA
WHERE IS CHI?
MRR
HUH?!
TUNK
SKFF

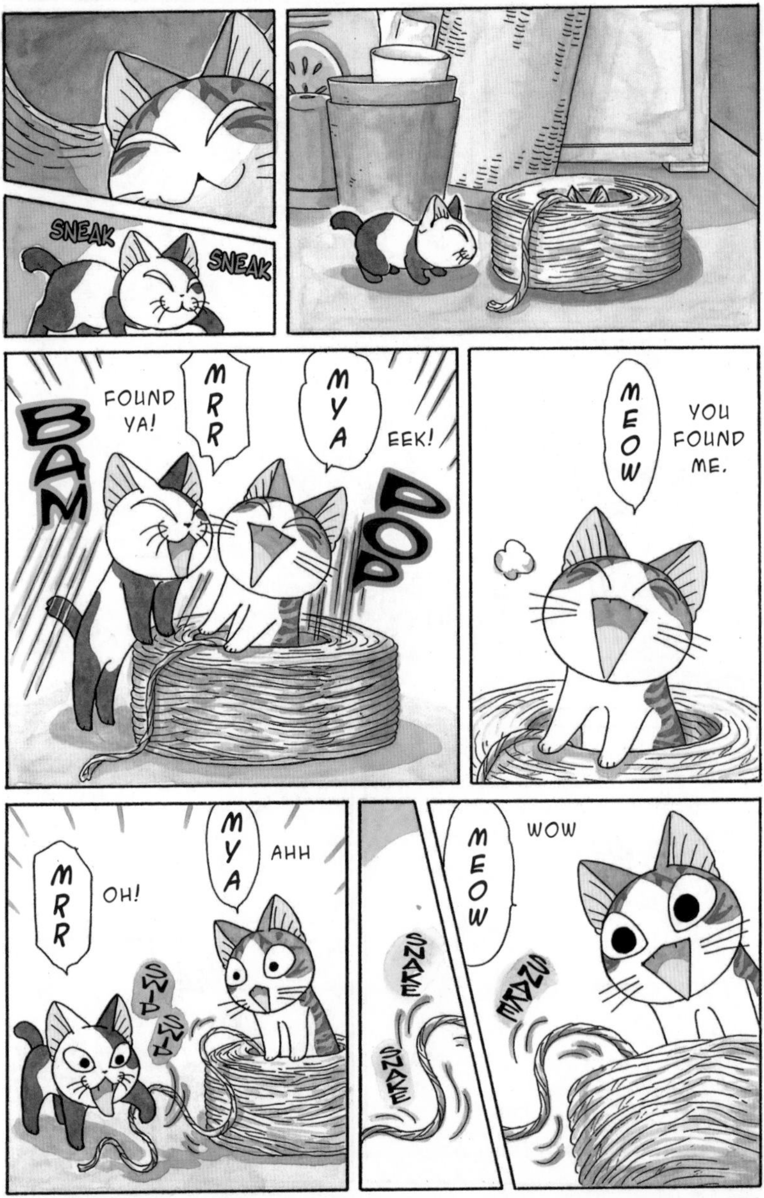
SNEAK
SNEAK
BAM
FOUND YA!
MRR
MYA
EEK!
POP
MEOW
YOU FOUND ME.
MRR
OH!
MYA
AHH
SWID
SWID
SNAKE
SNAKE
MEOW
WOW
SNAKE

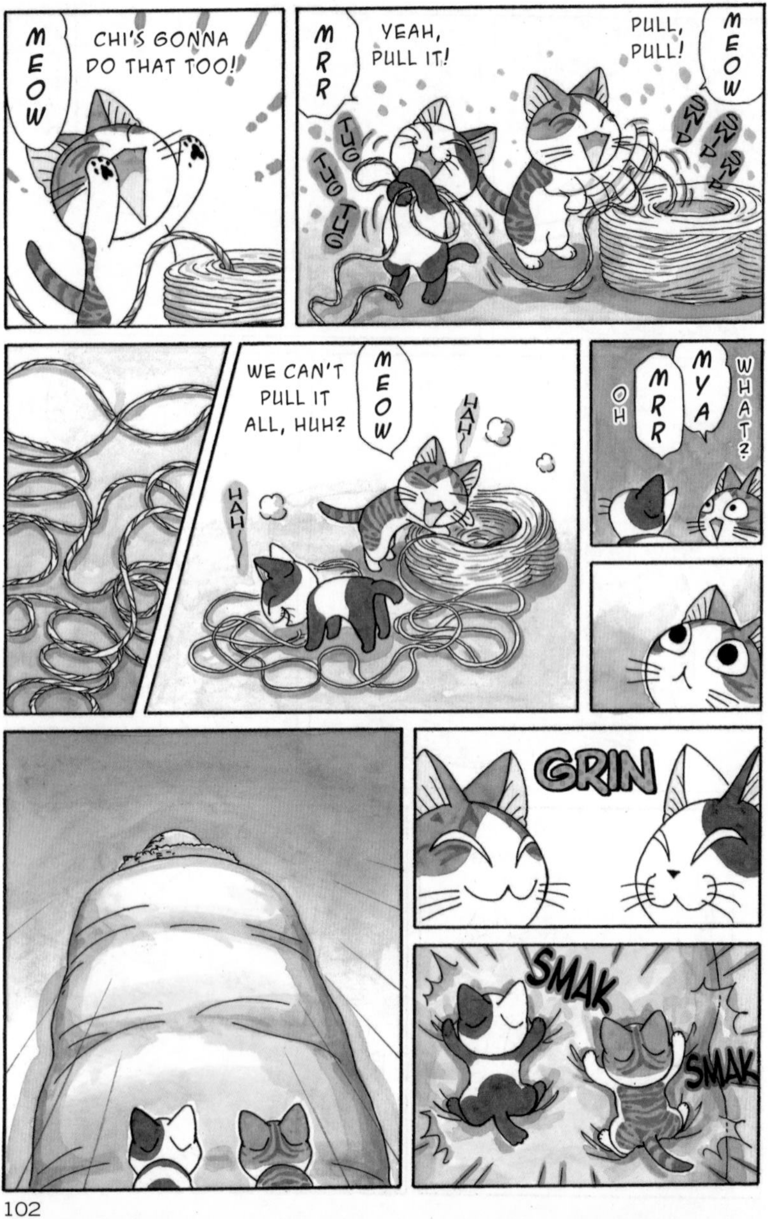
MEOW
CHI'S GONNA DO THAT TOO!
MRR
YEAH, PULL IT!
TUG TUG
TUG TUG
PULL, PULL!
MEOW
SWIP
SWIP SWIP
WE CAN'T PULL IT ALL, HUH?
MEOW
HAH~
HAH~
MYA
MRR
OH
WHAT?
GRIN
SMAK
SMAK

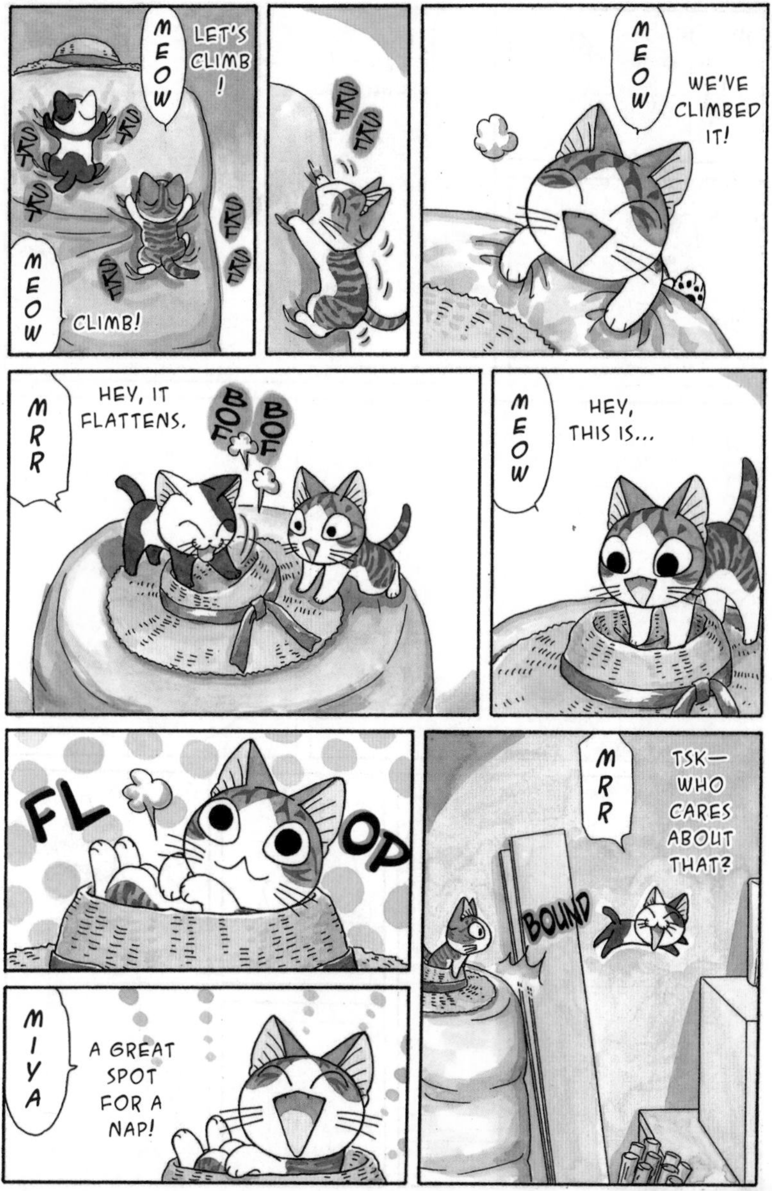
MEOW
LET'S CLIMB!
SKT SKT
SKT SKT
SKT SKT
SKT
MEOW
CLIMB!
SKT SKT
MEOW
WE'VE CLIMBED IT!
MRR
HEY, IT FLATTENS.
BOF BOF
MEOW
HEY, THIS IS...
FL OP
MIYA
A GREAT SPOT FOR A NAP!
MRR
TSK— WHO CARES ABOUT THAT?
BOUND

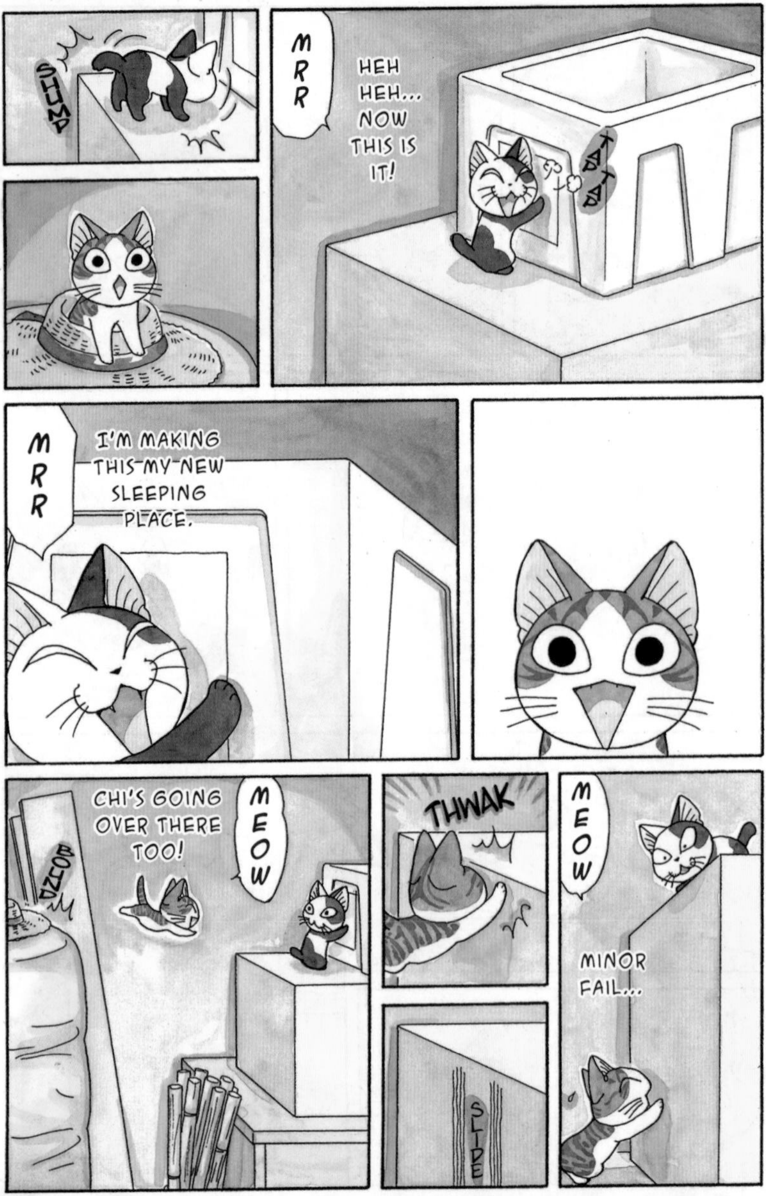
SHUMP
MRR
HEH HEH... NOW THIS IS IT!
TAP TAP
MRR
I'M MAKING THIS MY NEW SLEEPING PLACE.
BOING
CHI'S GOING OVER THERE TOO!
MEOW
THWAK
SLIDE
MEOW
MINOR FAIL...

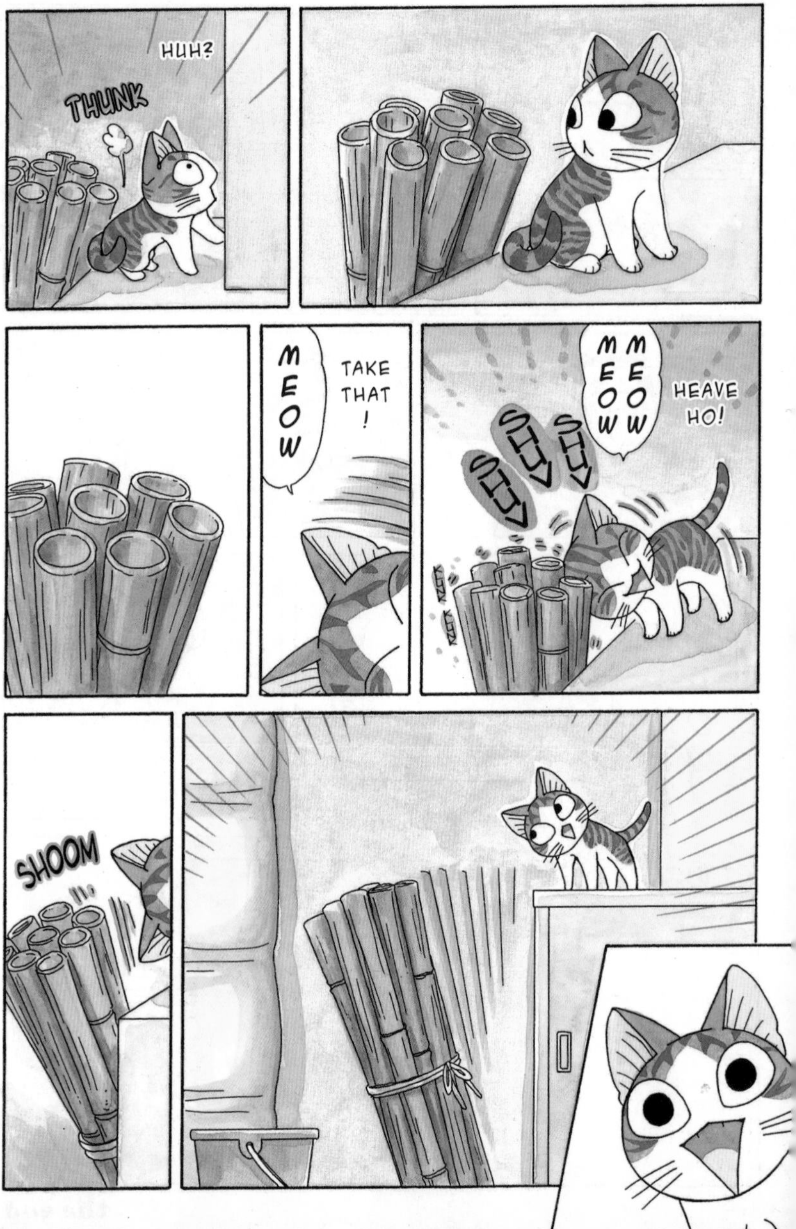
HUH?
THUNK
MEOW
TAKE THAT!
MEOW
MEOW
HEAVE HO!
SHU
SHU
SHU
SHOOM

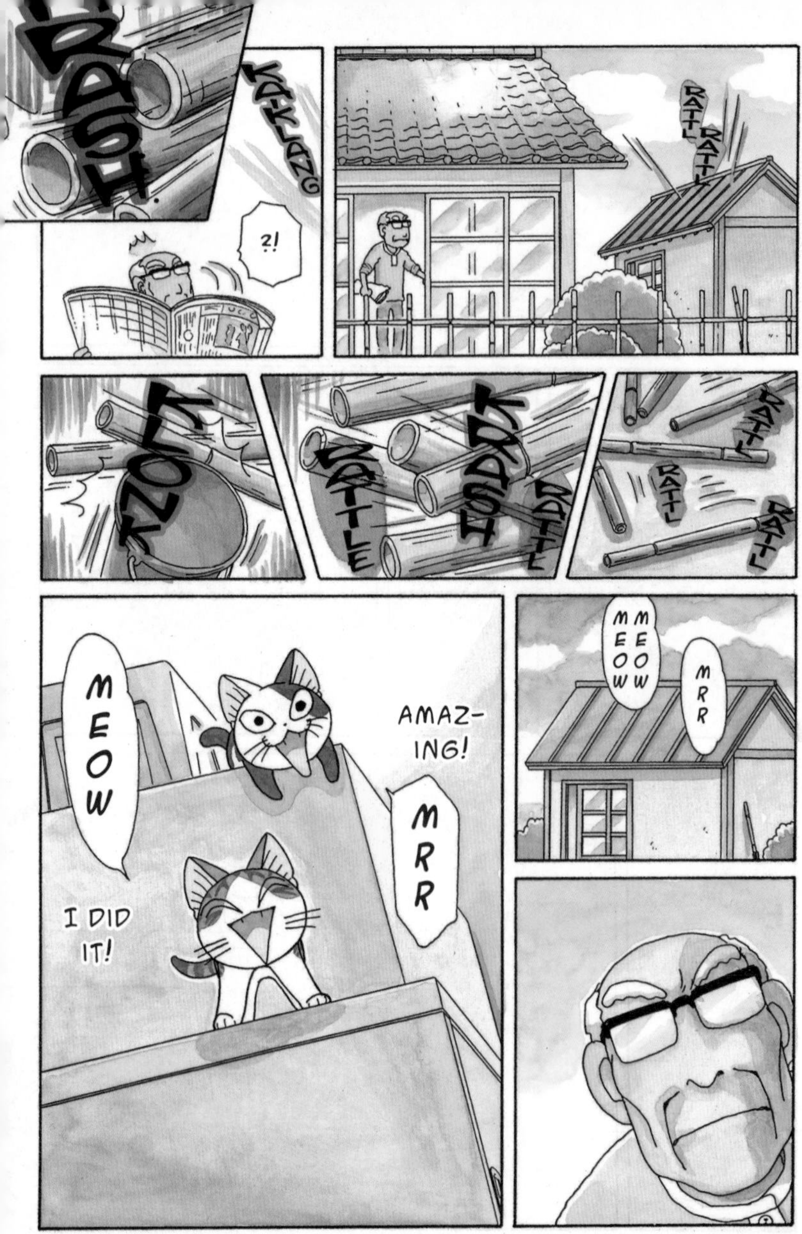
RASH
KA-KLANG
?!
RATTL
RATTL
KLONK
RATTLE
KRASH
RATTL
RATTL
RATTL
RATTL
MEOW
AMAZ-ING!
MRR
I DID IT!
MEOW MEOW
MRR

the end

homemade 142: a cat judges

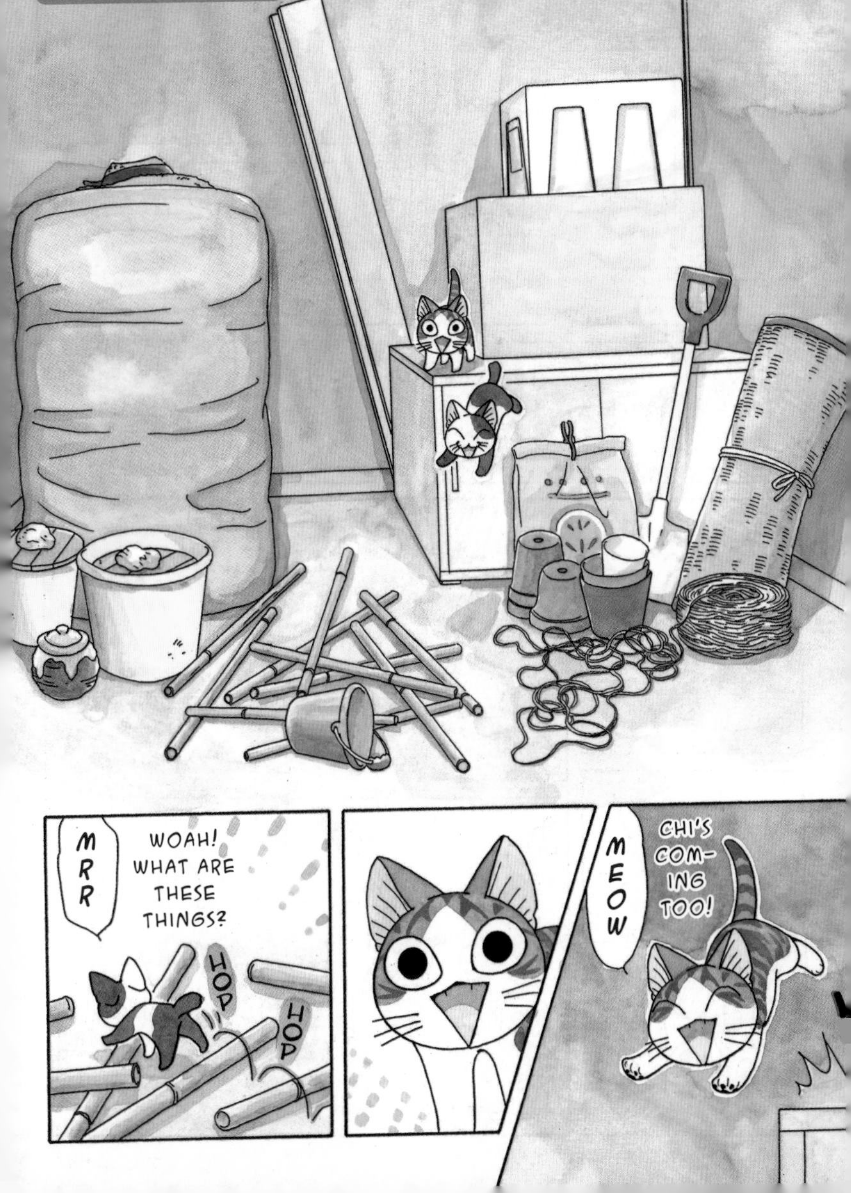
MRR
WOAH! WHAT ARE THESE THINGS?
HOP
HOP
MEOW
CHI'S COMING TOO!

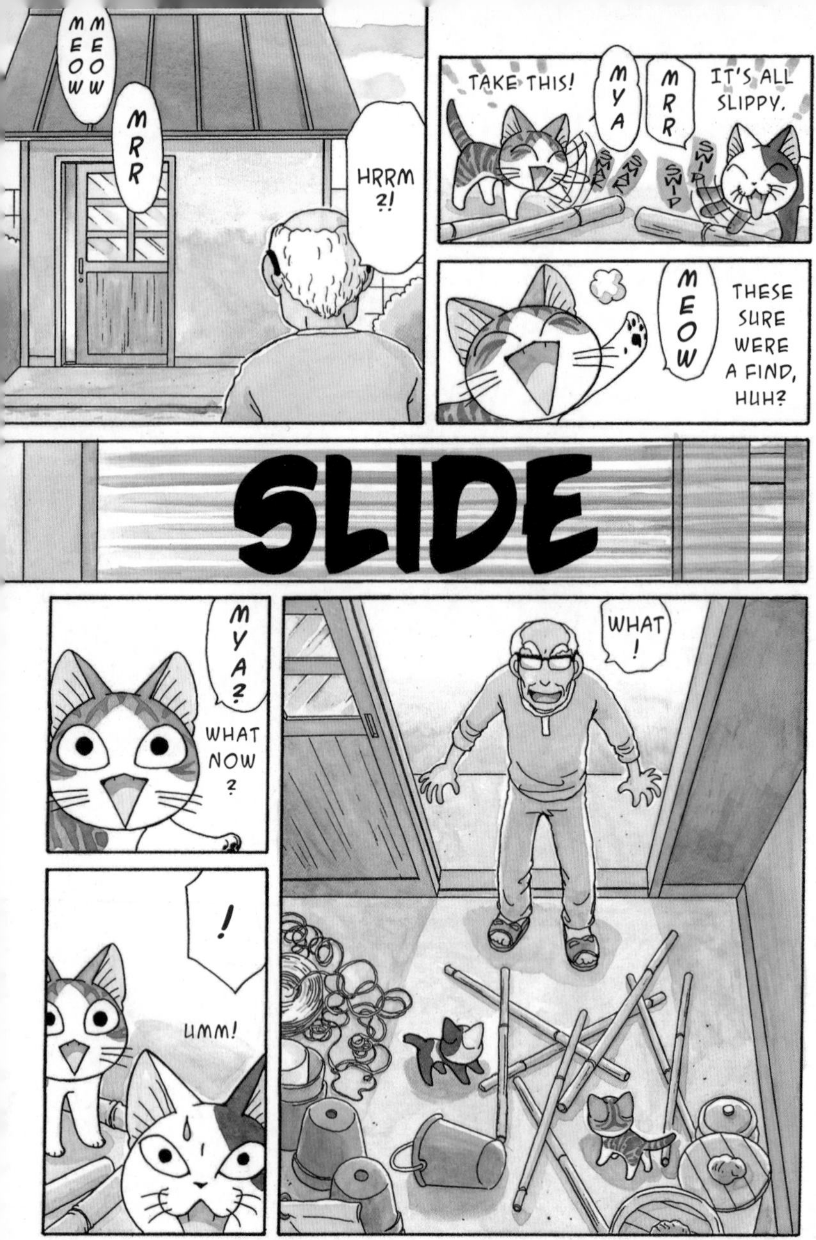
MEOW MEOW
MRR
HRRM ?!
TAKE THIS!
MYA
SMAK SMAK
MRR
SWIP SWIP
IT'S ALL SLIPPY.
MEOW
THESE SURE WERE A FIND, HUH?
SLIDE
MYA?
WHAT NOW ?
!
UMM!
WHAT !

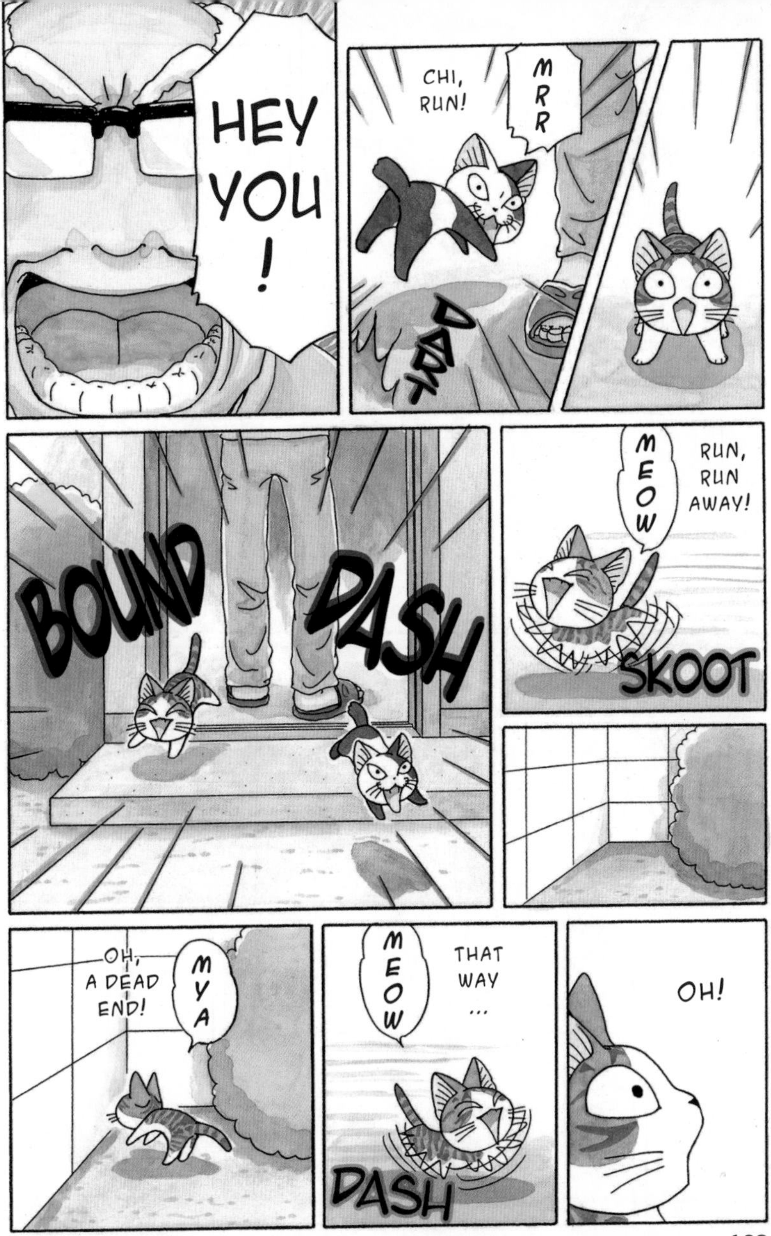
HEY YOU!
CHI, RUN!
MRR
DART
BOUND
DASH
MEOW
RUN, RUN AWAY!
SKOOT
OH, A DEAD END!
MYA
MEOW
THAT WAY ...
DASH
OH!

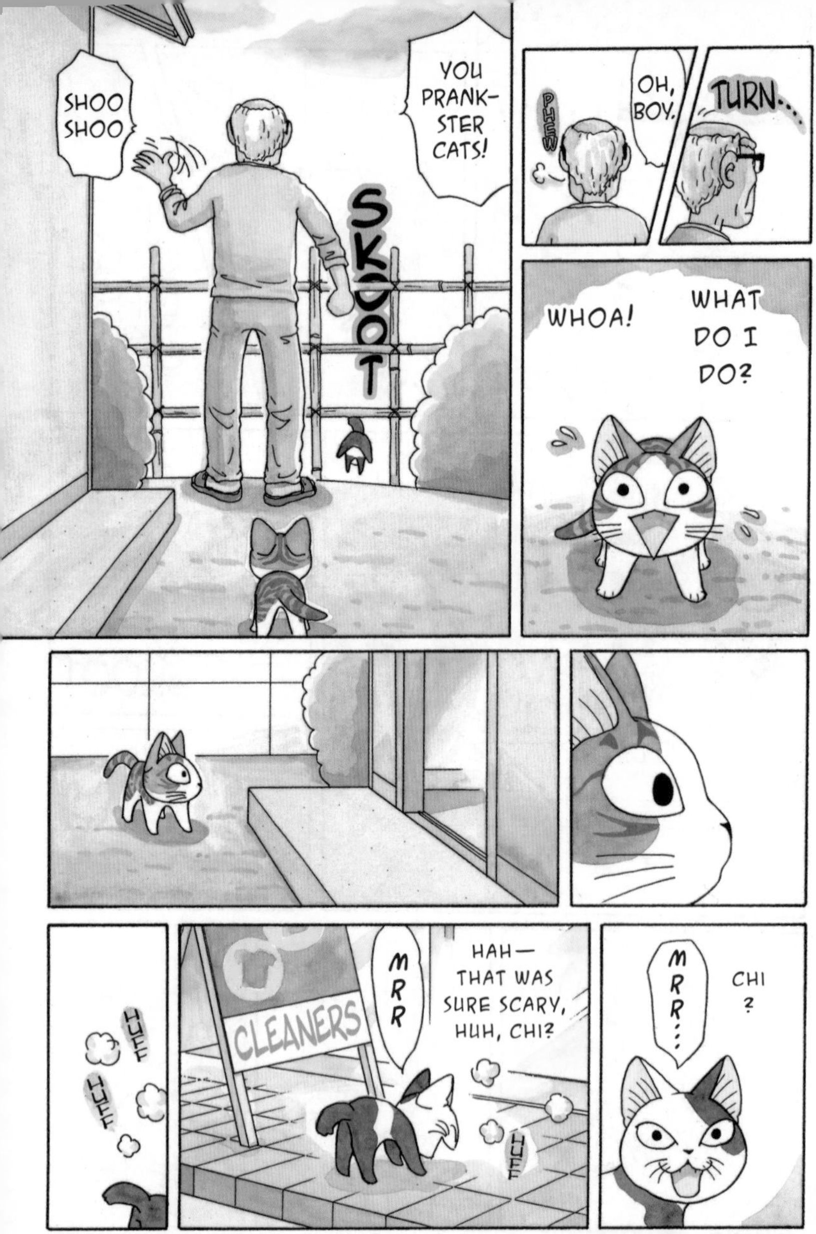
SHOO SHOO
YOU PRANK-STER CATS!
SKOOT
PHEW
OH, BOY.
TURN...
WHOA!
WHAT DO I DO?
HUFF
HUFF
MRR
HAH— THAT WAS SURE SCARY, HUH, CHI?
HUFF
CLEANERS
MRR...
CHI?

HUH?

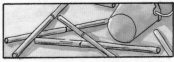

GR IN

PACE PACE PACE PACE PACE

I'LL HIDE IN HERE FOR A BIT.

MEOW

THMP THMP

THMP THMP THMP

COMING THIS WAY...

THMP THMP

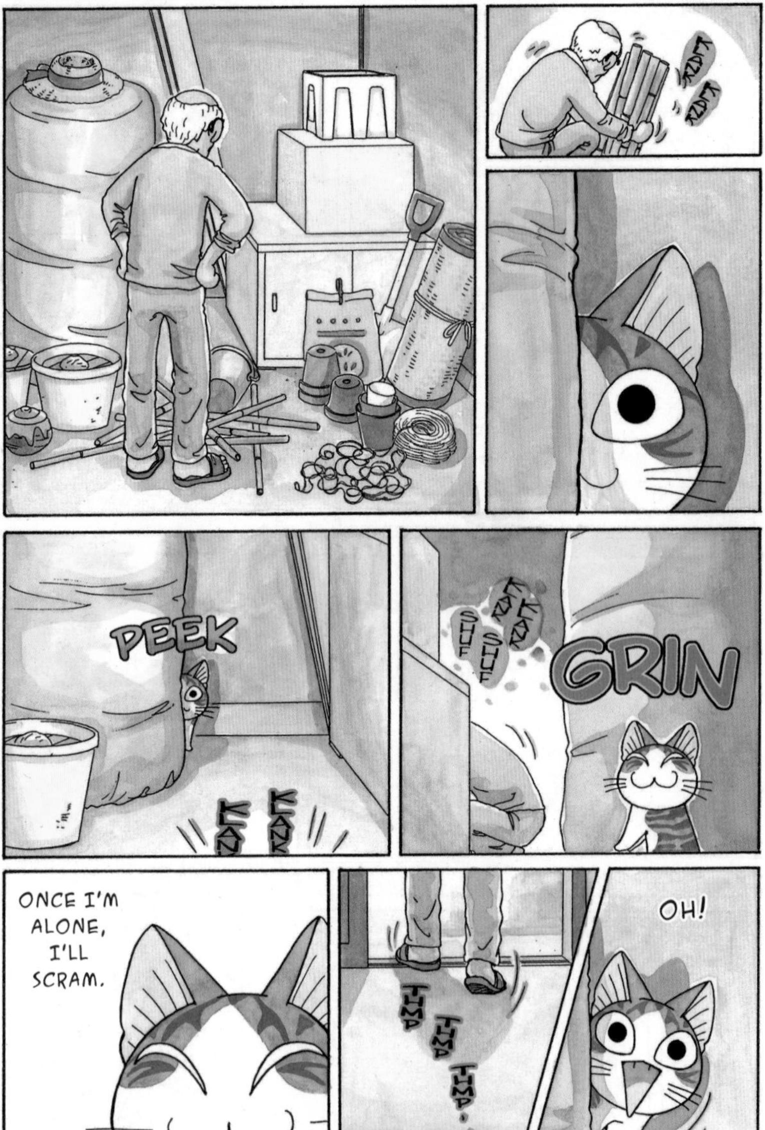
KLDK
KLDK
PEEK
KLANK
KLANK
KLANK
KLANK
SHUF
SHUF
GRIN
ONCE I'M ALONE, I'LL SCRAM.
THMP
THMP
THMP...
OH!

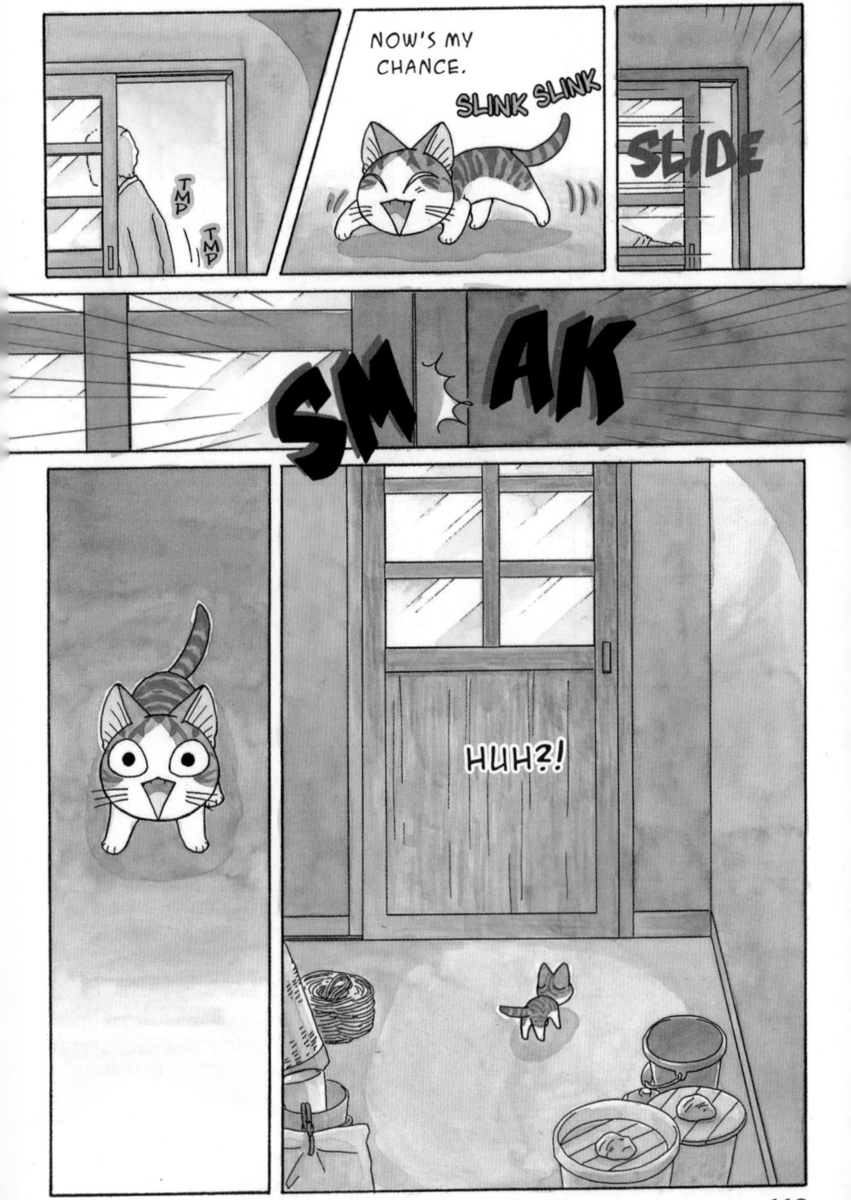
TMP
TMP
NOW'S MY CHANCE.
SLINK SLINK
SLIDE
SMAK
HUH?!

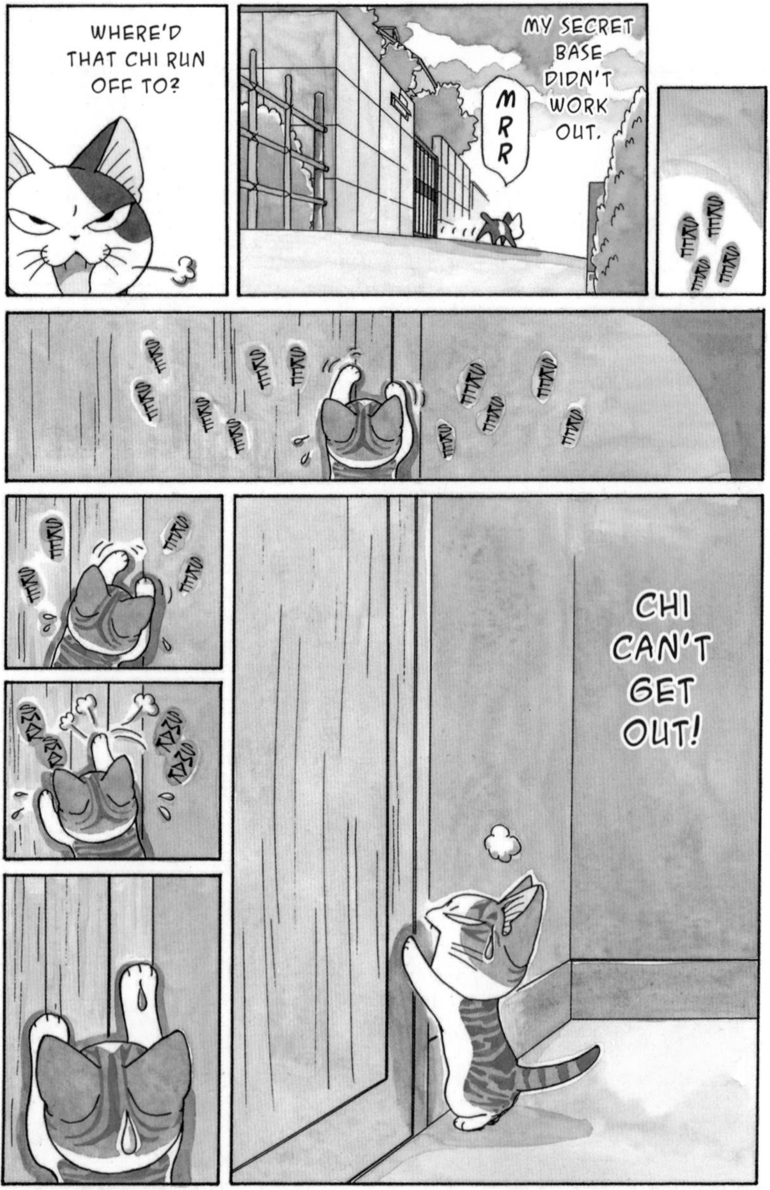
WHERE'D THAT CHI RUN OFF TO?
MY SECRET BASE DIDN'T WORK OUT.
MRR
CHI CAN'T GET OUT!

the end

homemade 143: a cat attempts

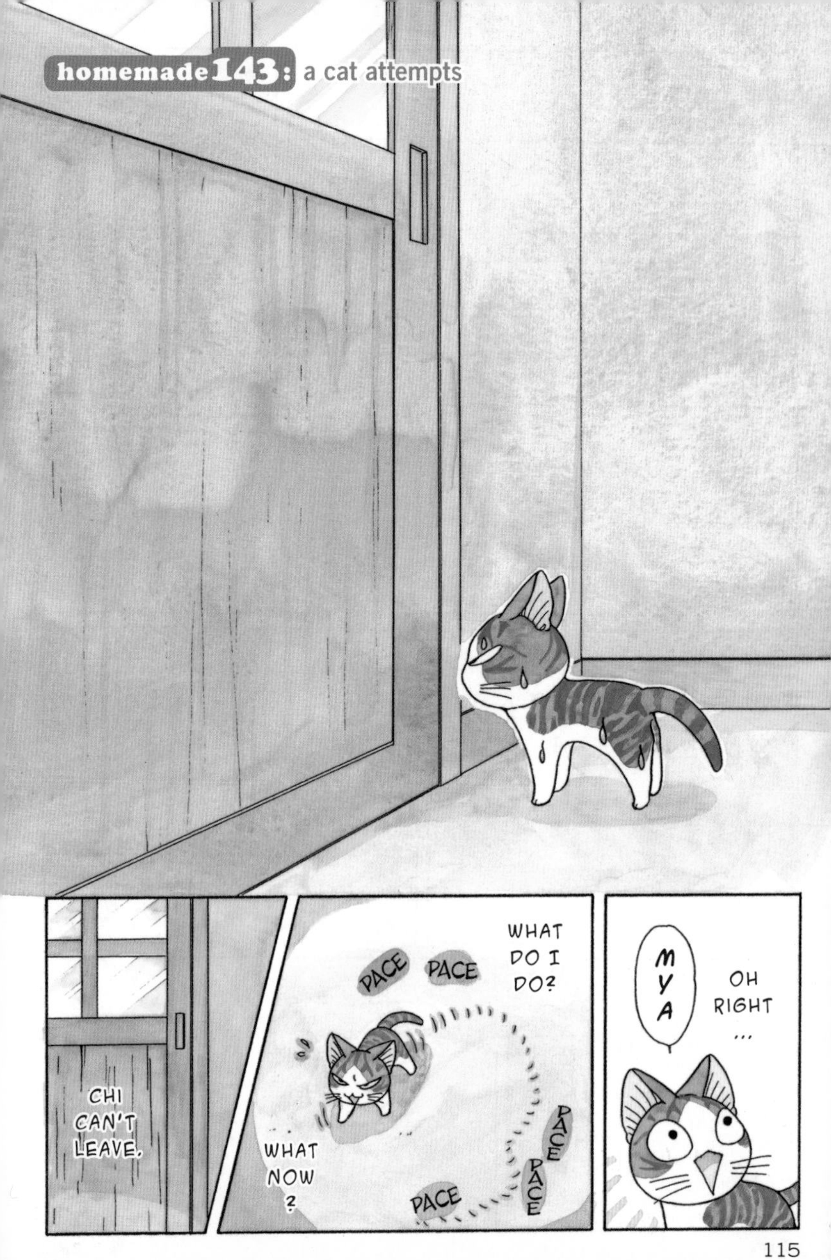
CHI CAN'T LEAVE.
PACE
PACE
WHAT DO I DO?
WHAT NOW ?
PACE
PACE
PACE
MYA
OH RIGHT ...

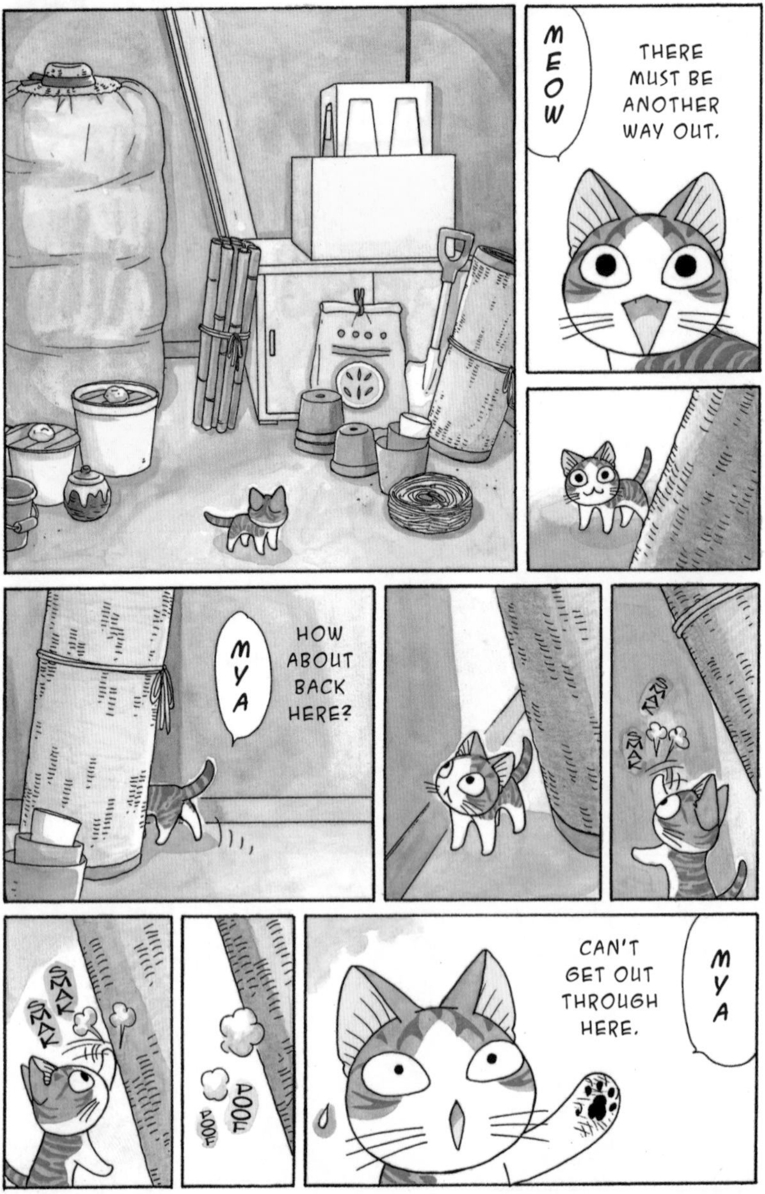
MEOW
THERE MUST BE ANOTHER WAY OUT.
MYA
HOW ABOUT BACK HERE?
SMAK
SMAK
SMAK
SMAK
POOF
POOF
CAN'T GET OUT THROUGH HERE.
MYA

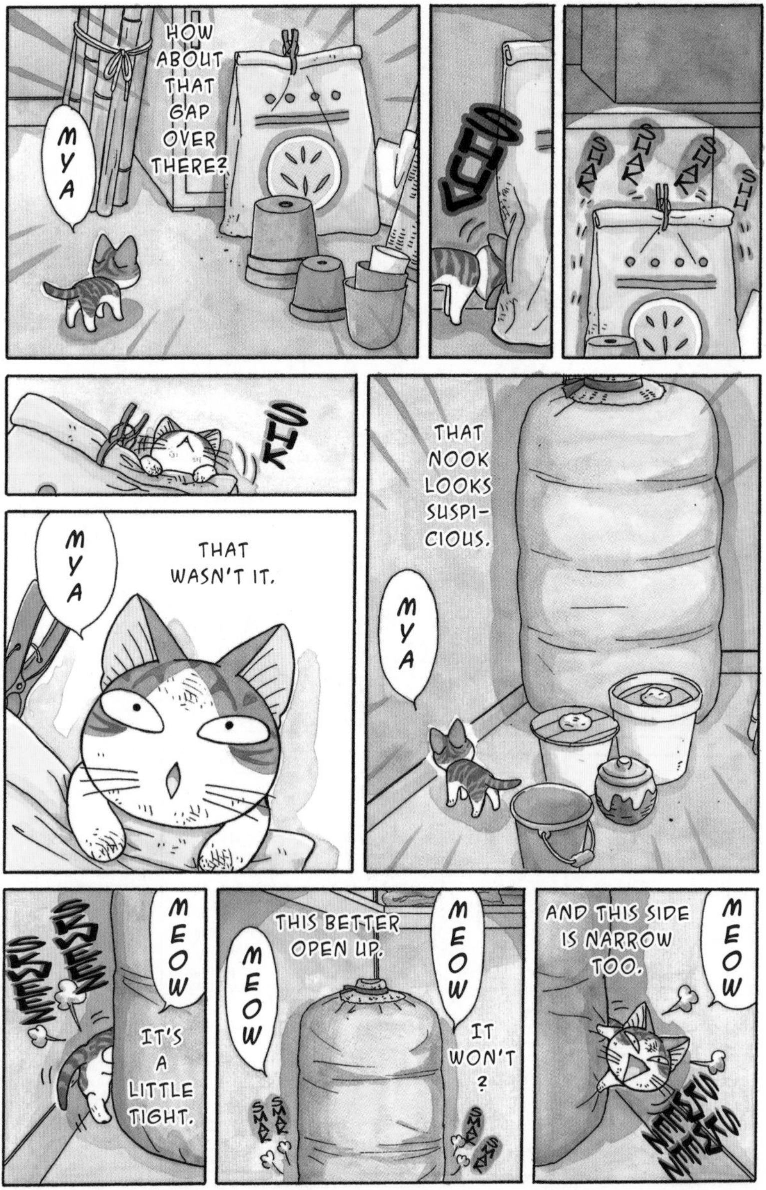
HOW ABOUT THAT GAP OVER THERE?
MYA
SHAK
SHAK
SHAK
SHU
SHK
MYA
THAT WASN'T IT.
THAT NOOK LOOKS SUSPI-CIOUS.
MYA
MEOW
IT'S A LITTLE TIGHT.
THIS BETTER OPEN UP.
MEOW
MEOW
IT WON'T ?
AND THIS SIDE IS NARROW TOO.
MEOW

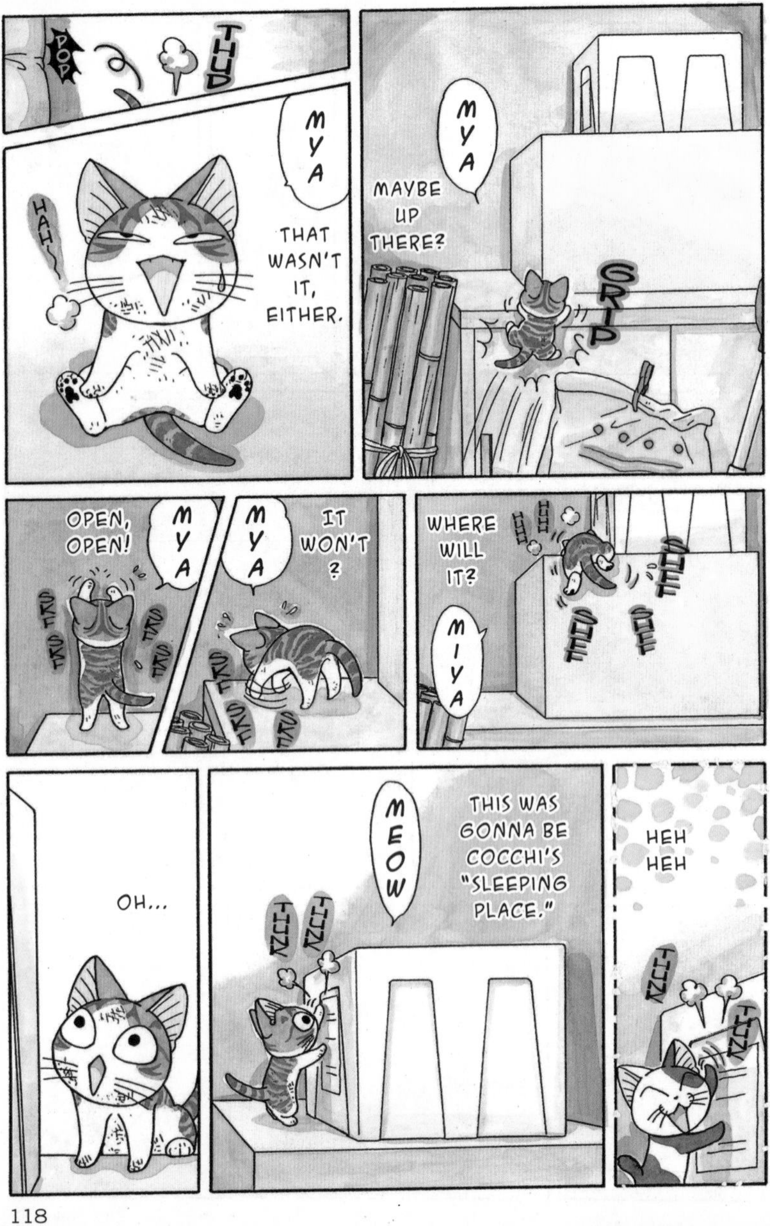
POP
THUD
HAH~
MYA
THAT WASN'T IT, EITHER.
MYA
MAYBE UP THERE?
GRIP
OPEN, OPEN!
MYA
SKF SKF
SKF SKF
MYA
IT WON'T ?
SKF SKF SKF
WHERE WILL IT?
HUH HUH
MIYA
SHFF
SHFF
SHFF
OH...
MEOW
THIS WAS GONNA BE COCCHI'S "SLEEPING PLACE."
THUNK THUNK
HEH HEH
THUNK
THUNK

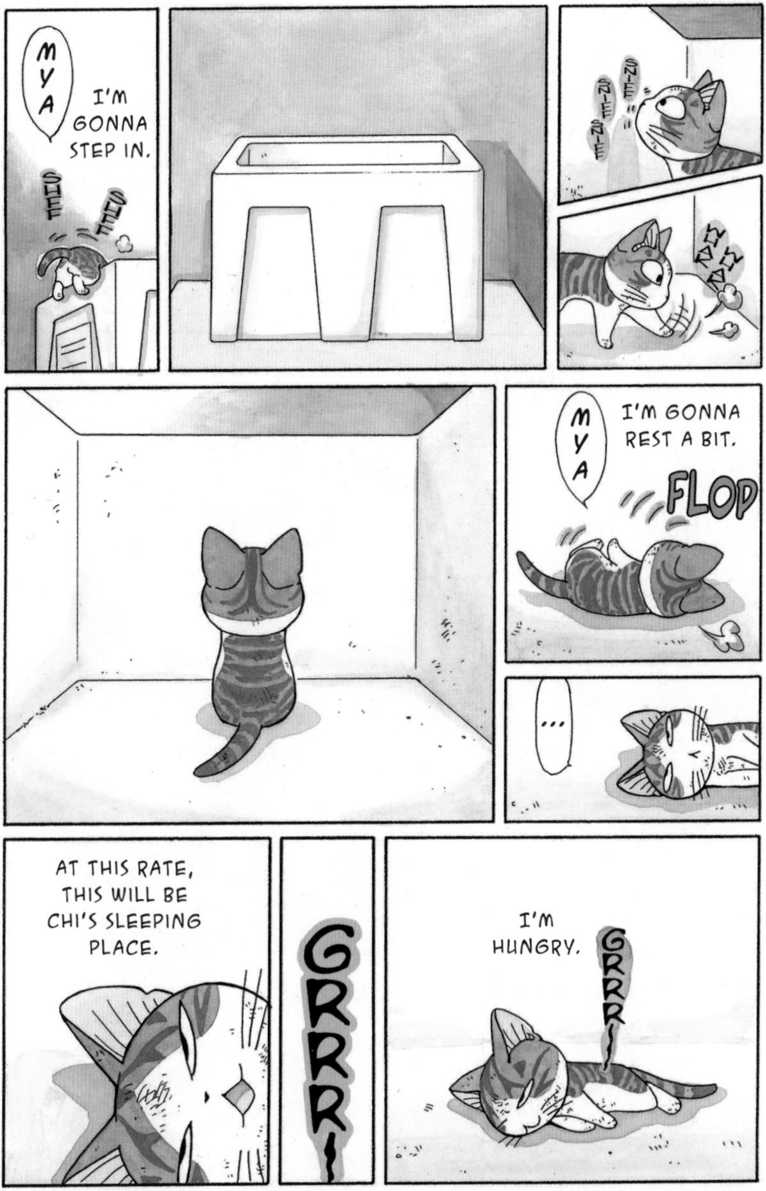
MYA
I'M GONNA STEP IN.
SHFF
SHFF
SNIFF
SNIFF
SNIFF
SWIP
SWIP
MYA
I'M GONNA REST A BIT.
FLOP
...
AT THIS RATE, THIS WILL BE CHI'S SLEEPING PLACE.
GRRRI
I'M HUNGRY.
GRRRI

MIULK

I SHOULD HAVE DRANK IT ALL.

GRRRR

BLOCKS

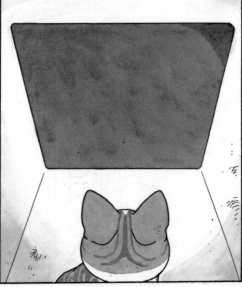

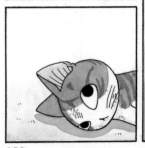

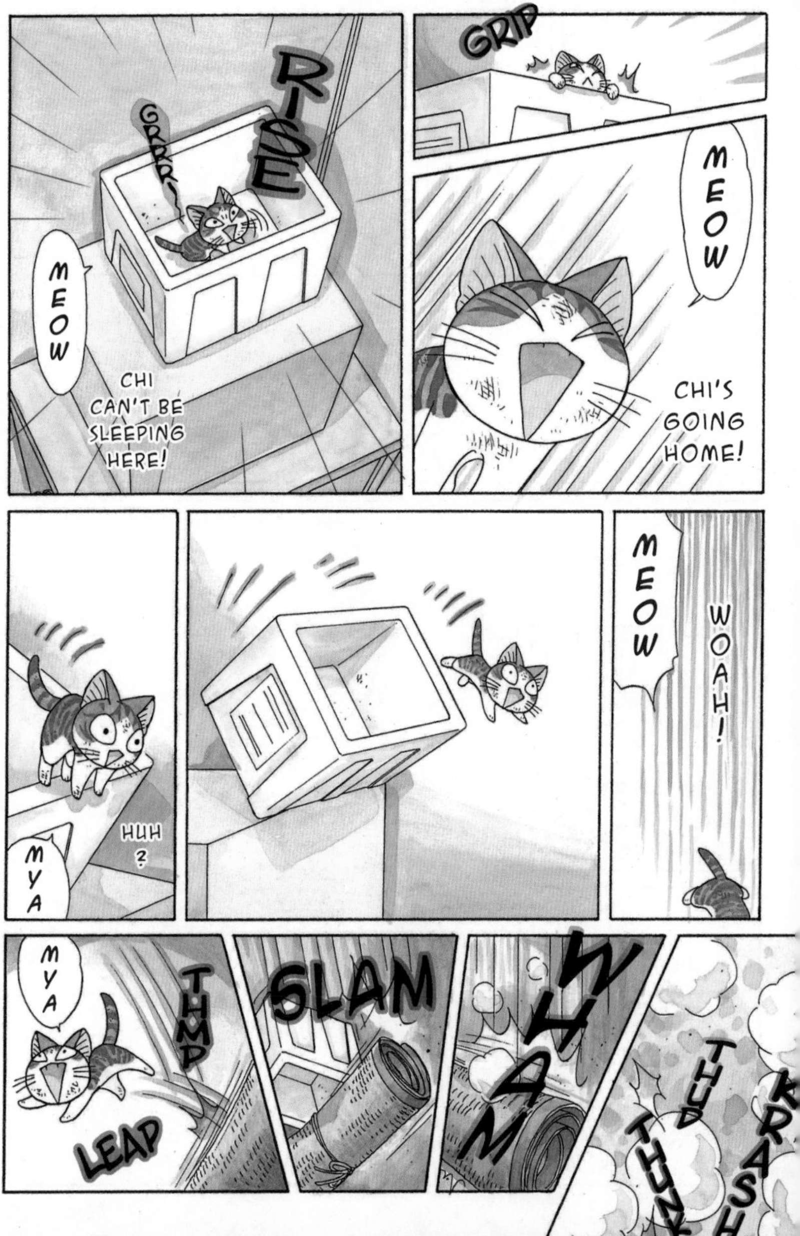
RISE
GRRRR~
MEOW
CHI CAN'T BE SLEEPING HERE!
GRIP
MEOW
CHI'S GOING HOME!
MYA
HUH?
MEOW
WOAH!
MYA
LEAP
THUMP
SLAM
WHAM
THUD
THUNK
KRASH

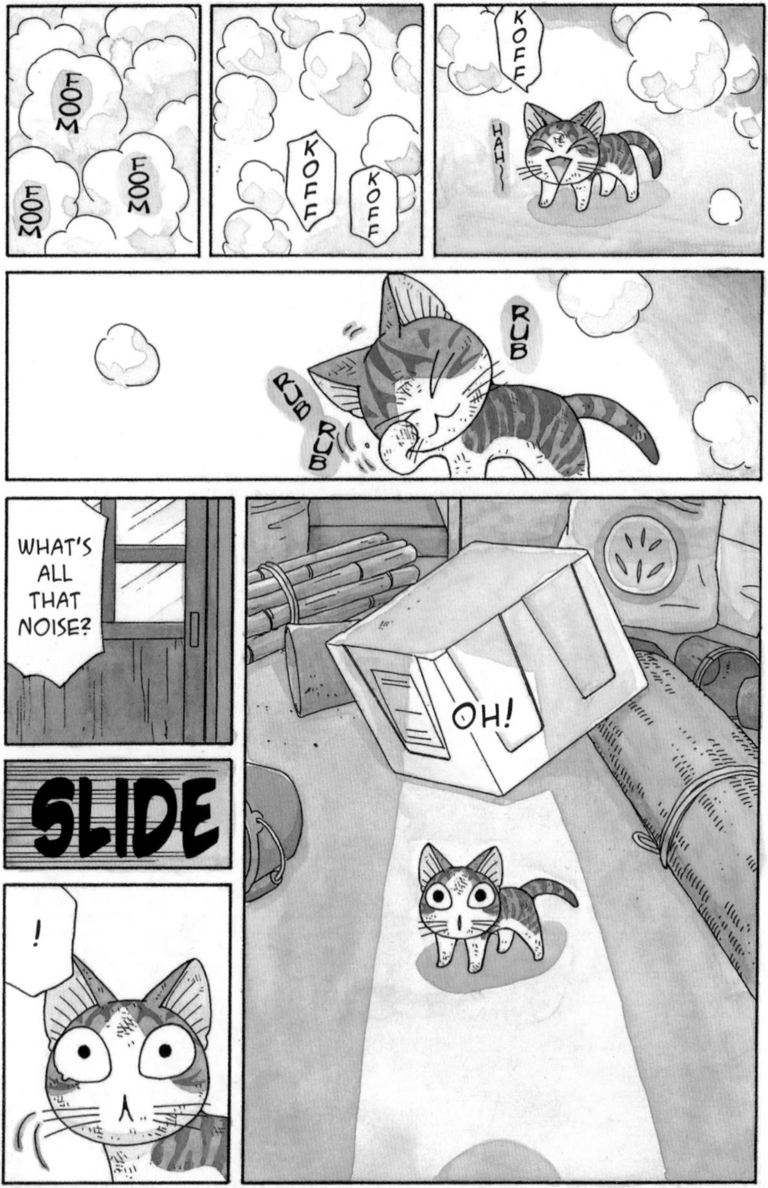
FOOM
FOOM
FOOM
KOFF
KOFF
KOFF
HAH~
RUB
RUB RUB
WHAT'S ALL THAT NOISE?
SLIDE
!
OH!

the end

homemade 144: a cat concerns

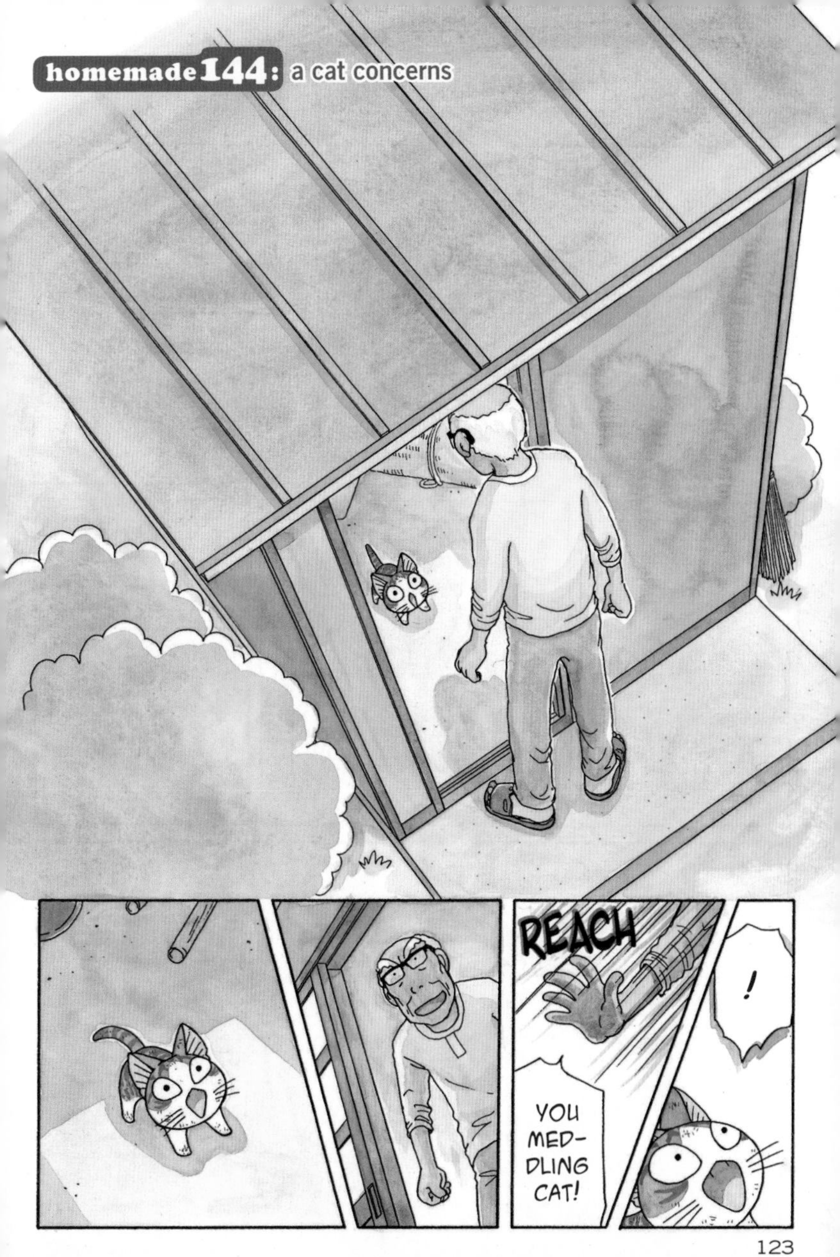
REACH
!
YOU MED-DLING CAT!

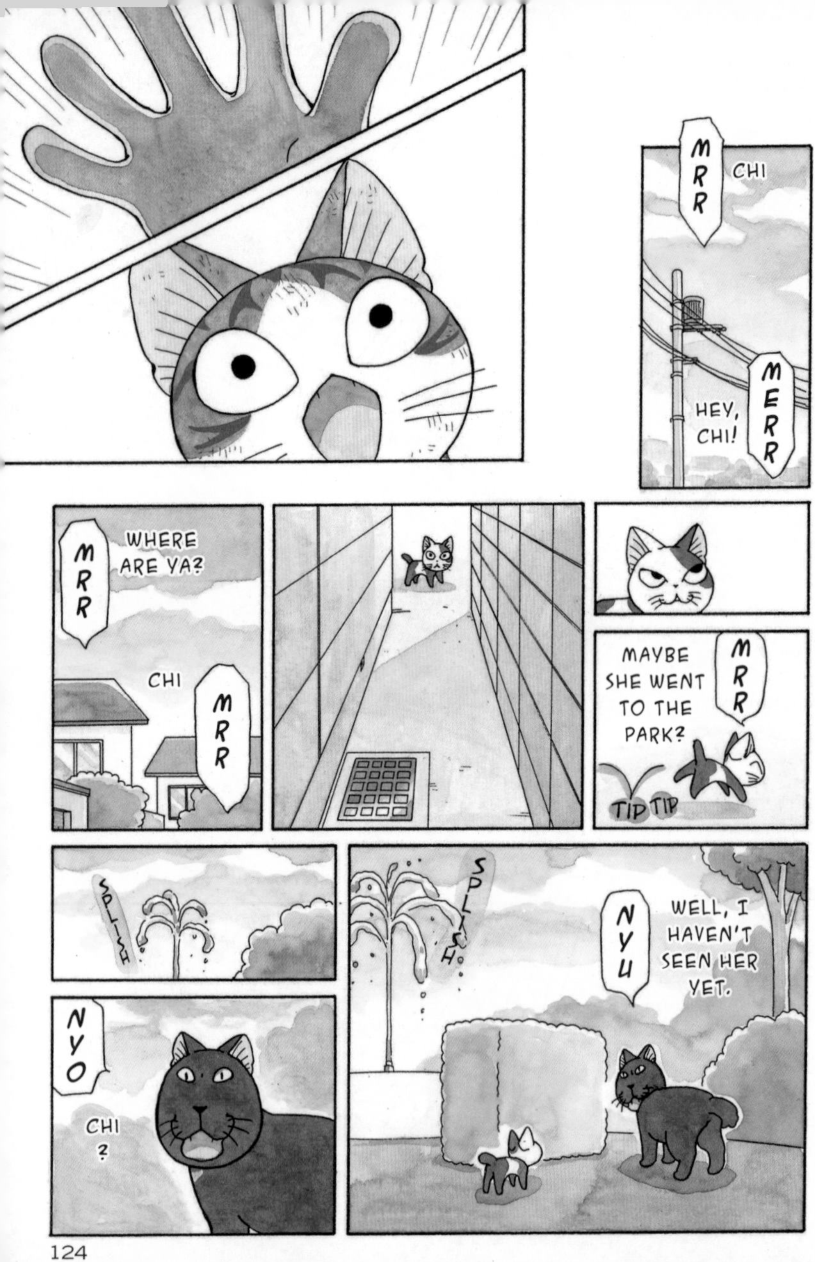
MRR
CHI
MERR
HEY, CHI!
MRR
WHERE ARE YA?
CHI
MRR
MAYBE SHE WENT TO THE PARK?
MRR
TIP TIP
SPLISH
NYO
CHI?
SPLISH
NYU
WELL, I HAVEN'T SEEN HER YET.

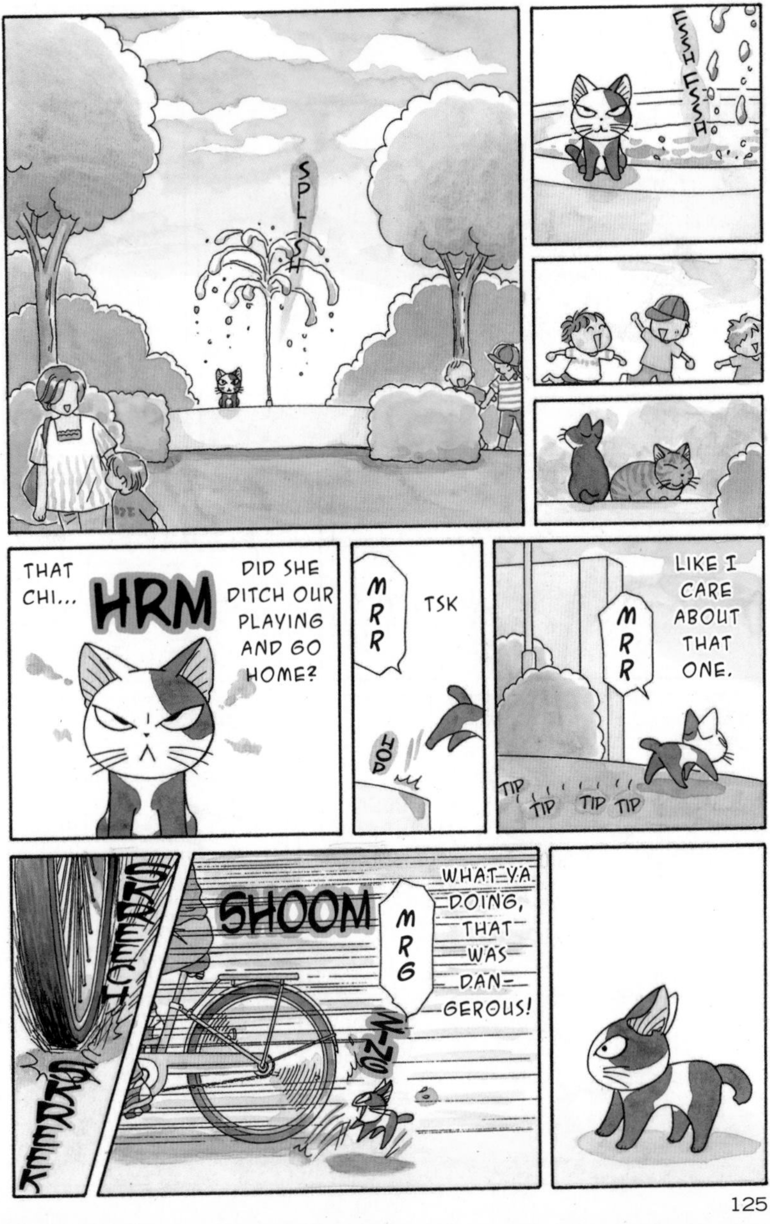
SPLISH
FSSH FSSH
THAT CHI...
HRM
DID SHE DITCH OUR PLAYING AND GO HOME?
MRR
TSK
HOP
MRR
LIKE I CARE ABOUT THAT ONE.
TIP TIP TIP TIP
SKREECH
SKREEEEK
SHOOM
MRG
WHAT YA DOING, THAT WAS DAN-GEROUS!
ZING

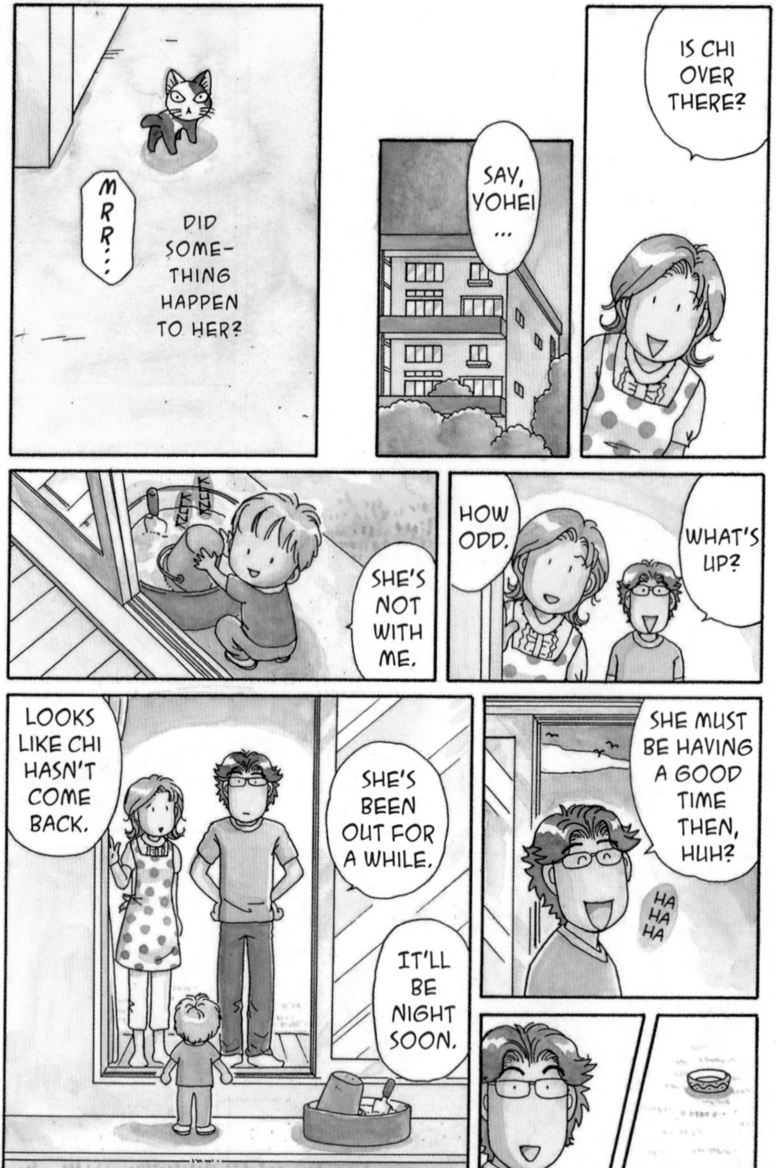
MRR...
DID SOMETHING HAPPEN TO HER?
SAY, YOHEI ...
IS CHI OVER THERE?
SHE'S NOT WITH ME.
HOW ODD.
WHAT'S UP?
LOOKS LIKE CHI HASN'T COME BACK.
SHE'S BEEN OUT FOR A WHILE.
IT'LL BE NIGHT SOON.
SHE MUST BE HAVING A GOOD TIME THEN, HUH?
HA HA HA

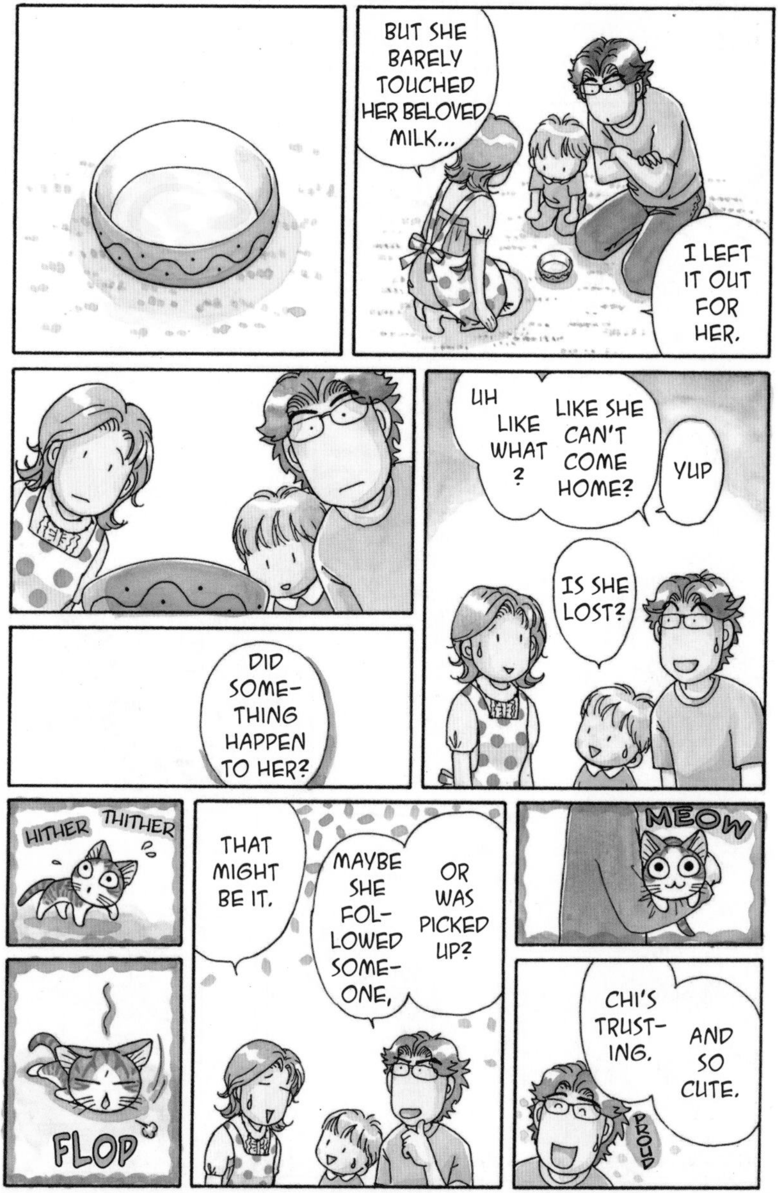
BUT SHE BARELY TOUCHED HER BELOVED MILK...
I LEFT IT OUT FOR HER.
DID SOME-THING HAPPEN TO HER?
UH LIKE WHAT?
LIKE SHE CAN'T COME HOME?
YUP
IS SHE LOST?
HITHER THITHER
FLOP
THAT MIGHT BE IT.
MAYBE SHE FOL-LOWED SOME-ONE,
OR WAS PICKED UP?
MEOW
CHI'S TRUST-ING.
AND SO CUTE.
PROUD

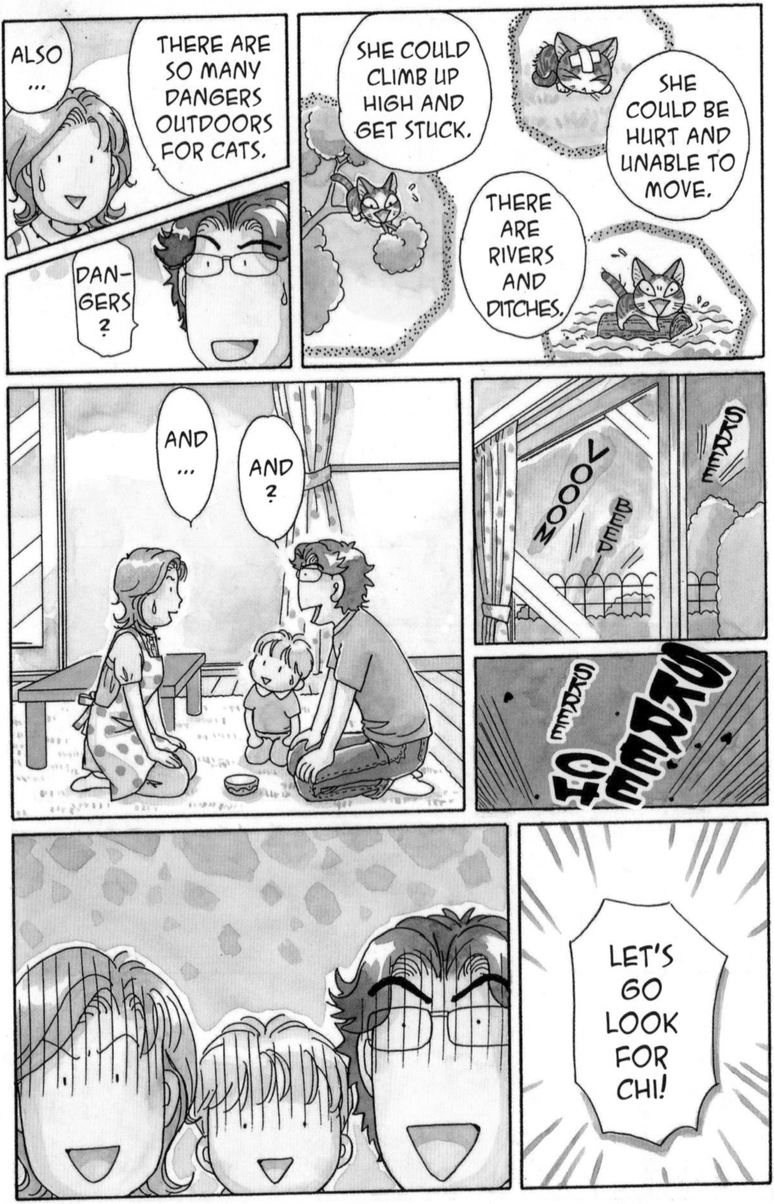
ALSO ...
THERE ARE SO MANY DANGERS OUTDOORS FOR CATS.
DANGERS?
SHE COULD CLIMB UP HIGH AND GET STUCK.
SHE COULD BE HURT AND UNABLE TO MOVE.
THERE ARE RIVERS AND DITCHES.
AND ...
AND?
VOOOM
BEEP
SKREE
SKREE
SKREECH
LET'S GO LOOK FOR CHI!

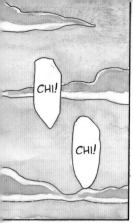

CHI!

CHI!

GLARE

GRIT

MEOWR

SHLOOM

WHUP

DASH

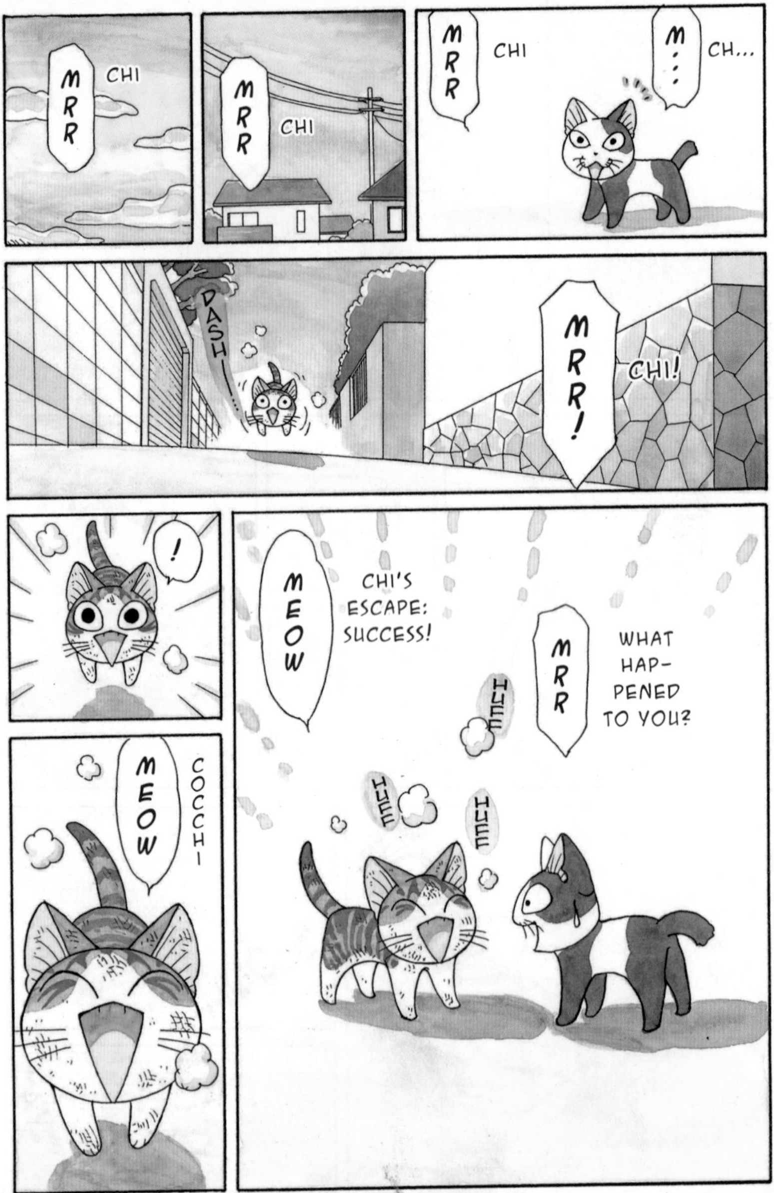
MRR
CHI
MRR
CHI
MRR
CHI
M...
CH...
DASH
MRR!
CHI!
!
MEOW
COCCHI
MEOW
CHI'S ESCAPE: SUCCESS!
HUFF
MRR
WHAT HAP-PENED TO YOU?
HUFF
HUFF

the end

homemade 145: a cat reconnects

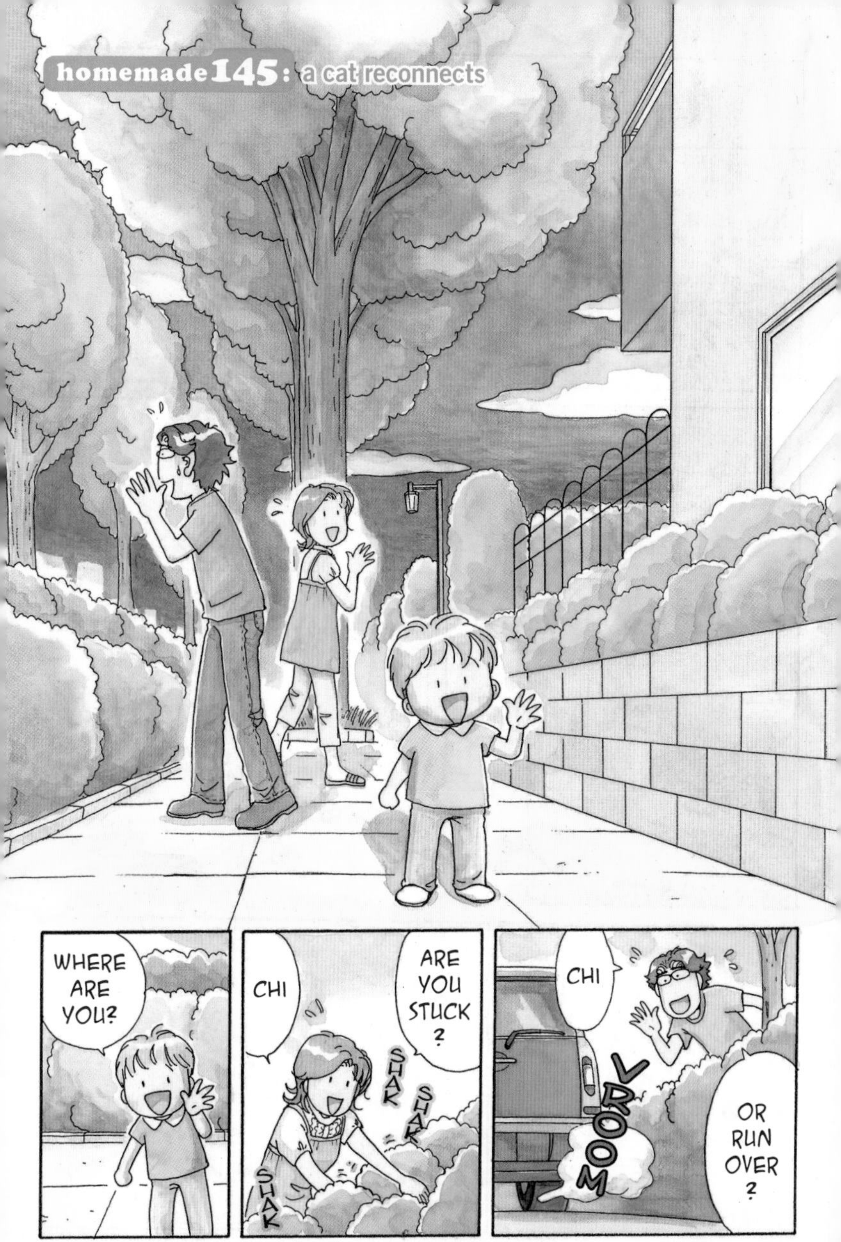
WHERE ARE YOU?
CHI
ARE YOU STUCK?
SHAK SHAK
SHAK
CHI
VROOM
OR RUN OVER?

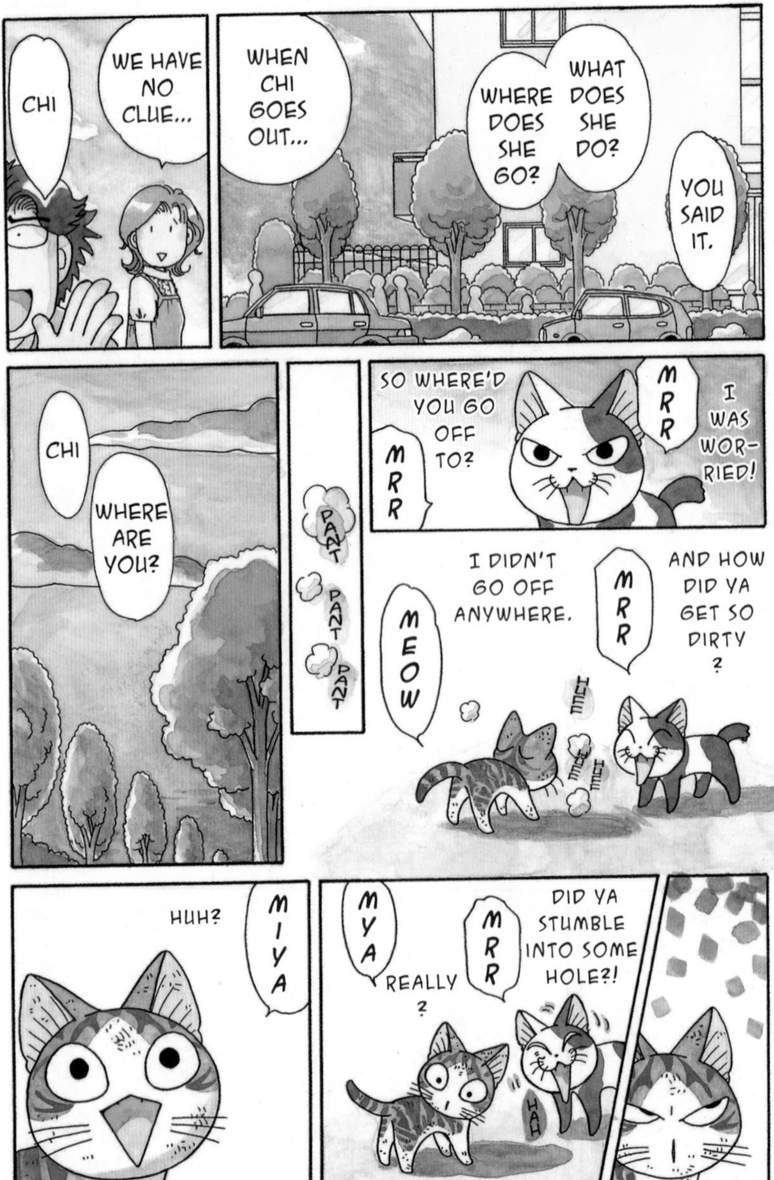
CHI
WE HAVE NO CLUE...
WHEN CHI GOES OUT...
WHERE DOES SHE GO?
WHAT DOES SHE DO?
YOU SAID IT.
CHI
WHERE ARE YOU?
PANT
PANT
PANT
SO WHERE'D YOU GO OFF TO?
MRR
MRR
I WAS WOR-RIED!
MEOW
I DIDN'T GO OFF ANYWHERE.
MRR
AND HOW DID YA GET SO DIRTY?
HUH?
MIYA
MYA
REALLY?
MRR
DID YA STUMBLE INTO SOME HOLE?!
HAH

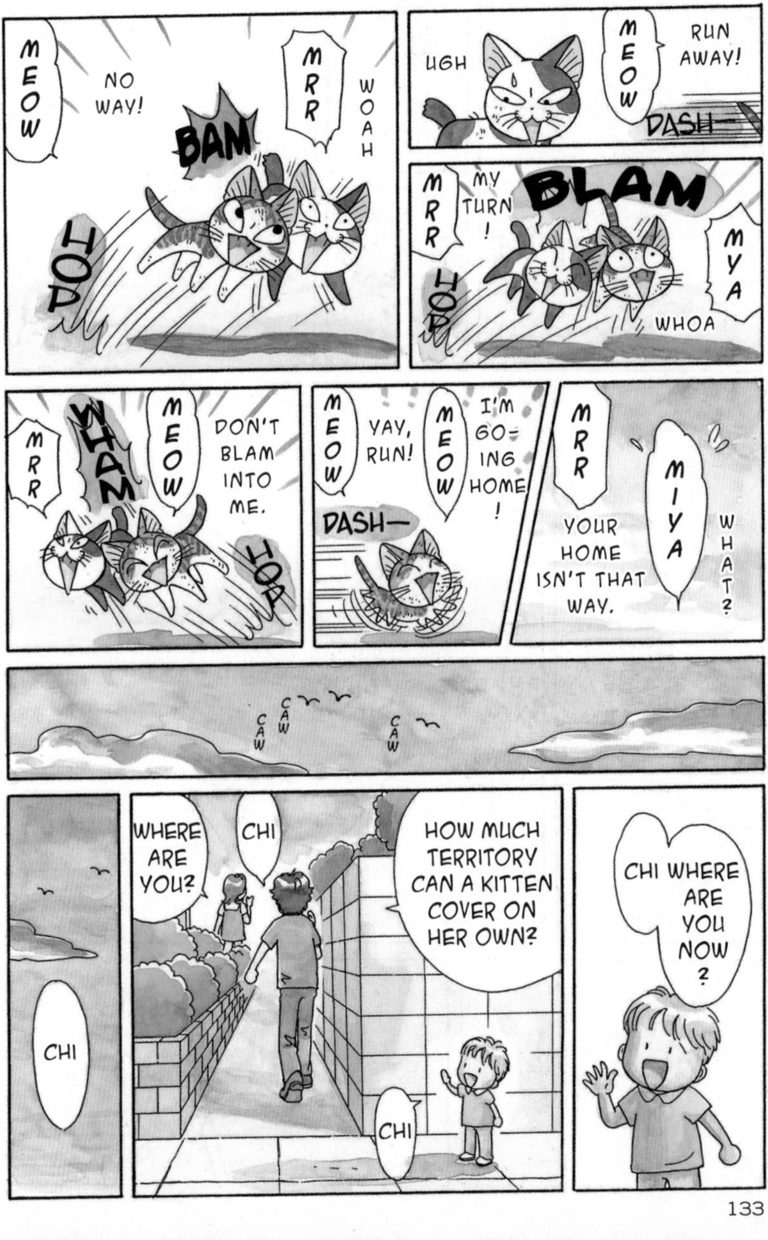
MEOW
NO WAY!
MRR
BAM
WOAH
HOP
UGH
MEOW
RUN AWAY!
DASH—
MRR
MY TURN!
BLAM
MYA
HOP
WHOA
MRR
WHAM
MEOW
DON'T BLAM INTO ME.
HOP
MEOW
YAY, RUN!
MEOW
I'M GO-ING HOME!
DASH—
MRR
MIYA
YOUR HOME ISN'T THAT WAY.
WHAT?
CAW
CAW
CAW
CAW
CHI
WHERE ARE YOU?
CHI
HOW MUCH TERRITORY CAN A KITTEN COVER ON HER OWN?
CHI
CHI WHERE ARE YOU NOW?

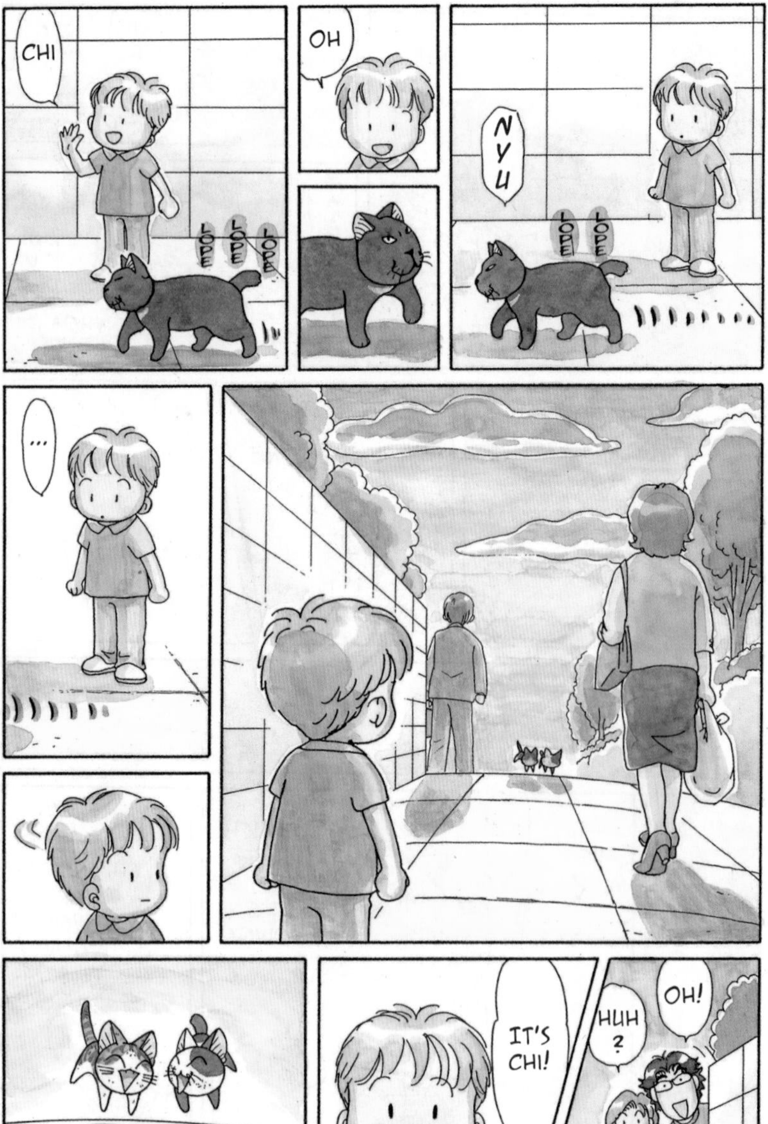
CHI
LOPE LOPE LOPE
OH
NYU
LOPE LOPE
...
IT'S CHI!
HUH?
OH!

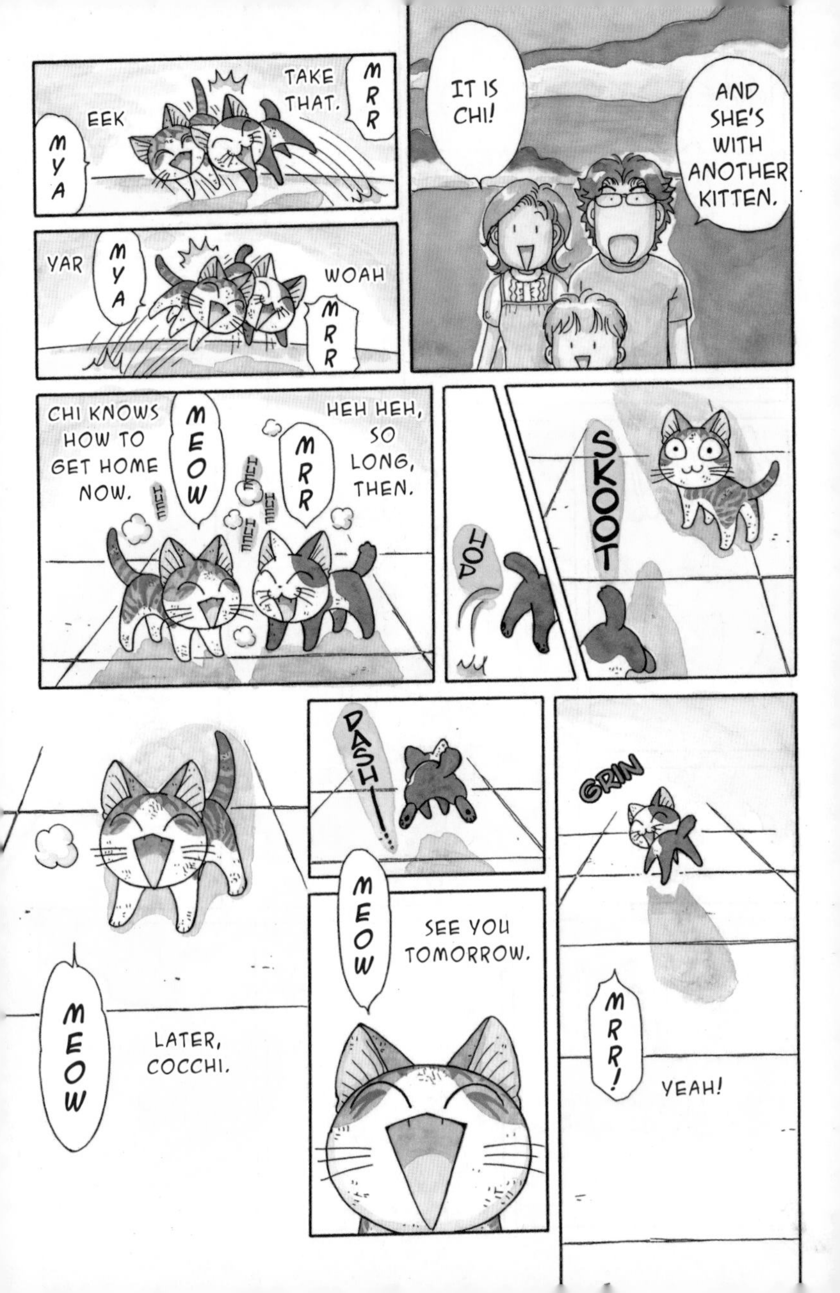
MYA
EEK
TAKE THAT.
MRR
YAR
MYA
WOAH
MRR
IT IS CHI!
AND SHE'S WITH ANOTHER KITTEN.
CHI KNOWS HOW TO GET HOME NOW.
MEOW
MRR
HEH HEH, SO LONG, THEN.
HOP
SKOOT
MEOW
LATER, COCCHI.
DASH!
MEOW
SEE YOU TOMORROW.
GRIN
MRR!
YEAH!

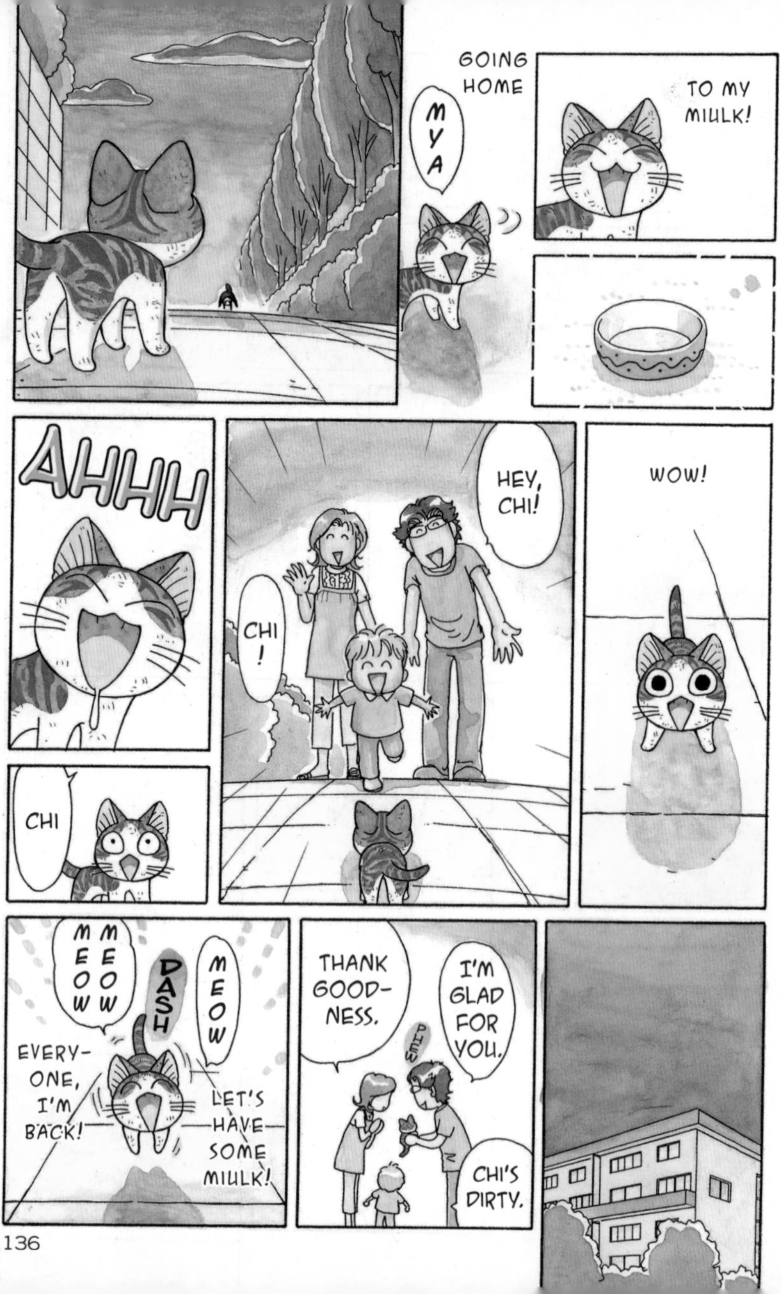
GOING HOME
MYA
TO MY MIULK!
AHHHH
CHI
CHI!
HEY, CHI!
WOW!
MEOW MEOW
DASH
MEOW
EVERYONE, I'M BACK!
LET'S HAVE SOME MIULK!
THANK GOODNESS.
I'M GLAD FOR YOU.
CHI'S DIRTY.

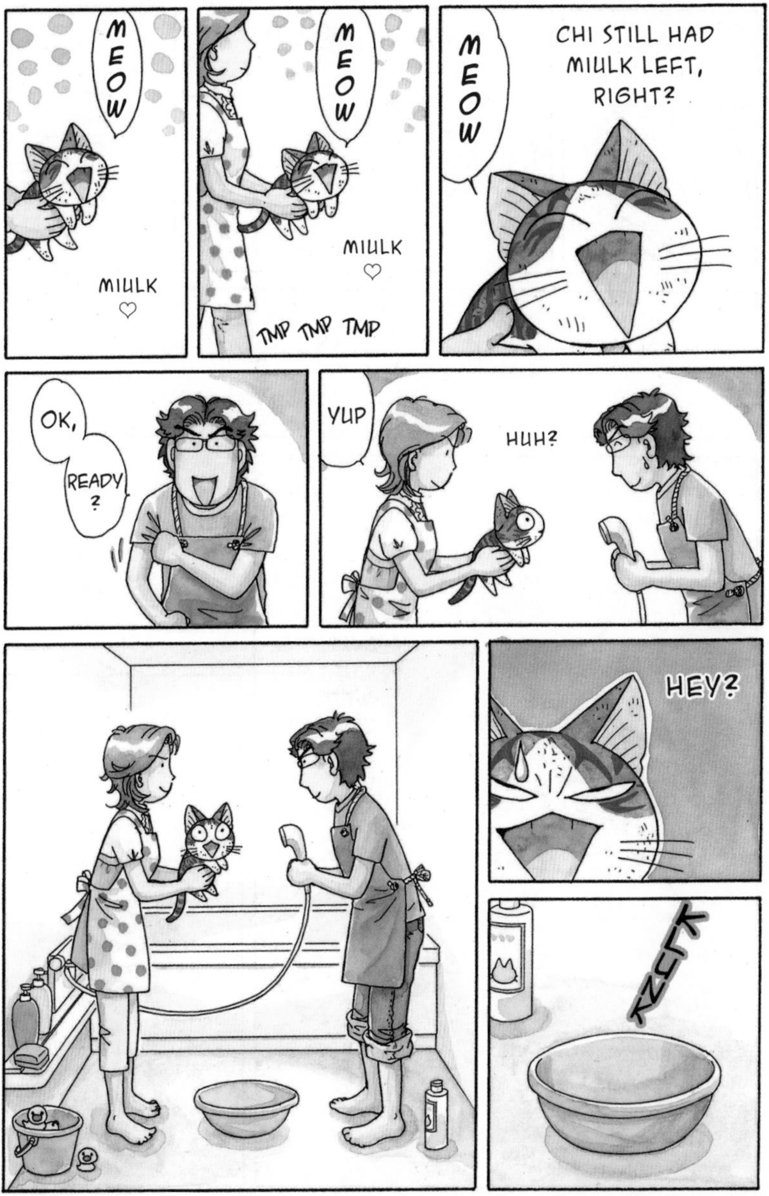
MEOW
MIULK ♡
MEOW
MIULK ♡
TMP TMP TMP
MEOW
CHI STILL HAD MIULK LEFT, RIGHT?
OK,
READY?
YUP
HUH?
HEY?

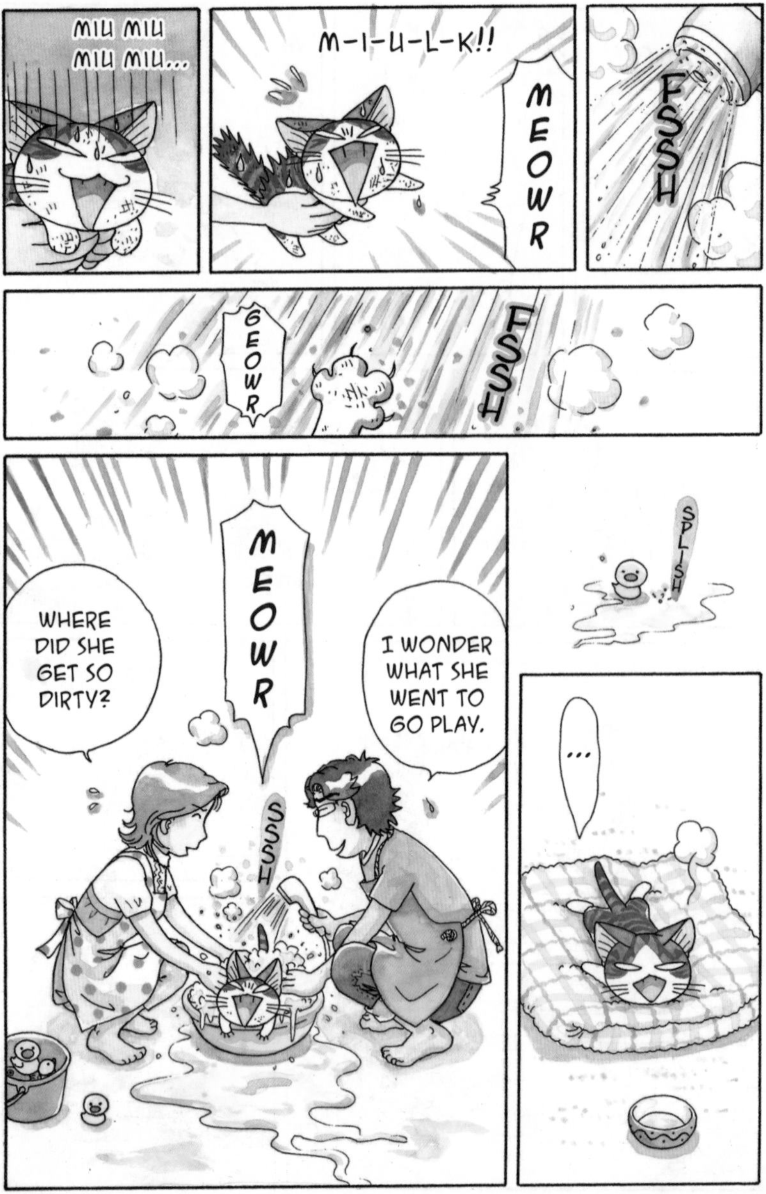
MIU MIU MIU MIU...
M-I-U-L-K!!
MEOWR
FSSH
GEOWR
FSSH
WHERE DID SHE GET SO DIRTY?
MEOWR
I WONDER WHAT SHE WENT TO GO PLAY.
SSSH
SPLISH
...

the end

homemade 146: a cat sheds tears

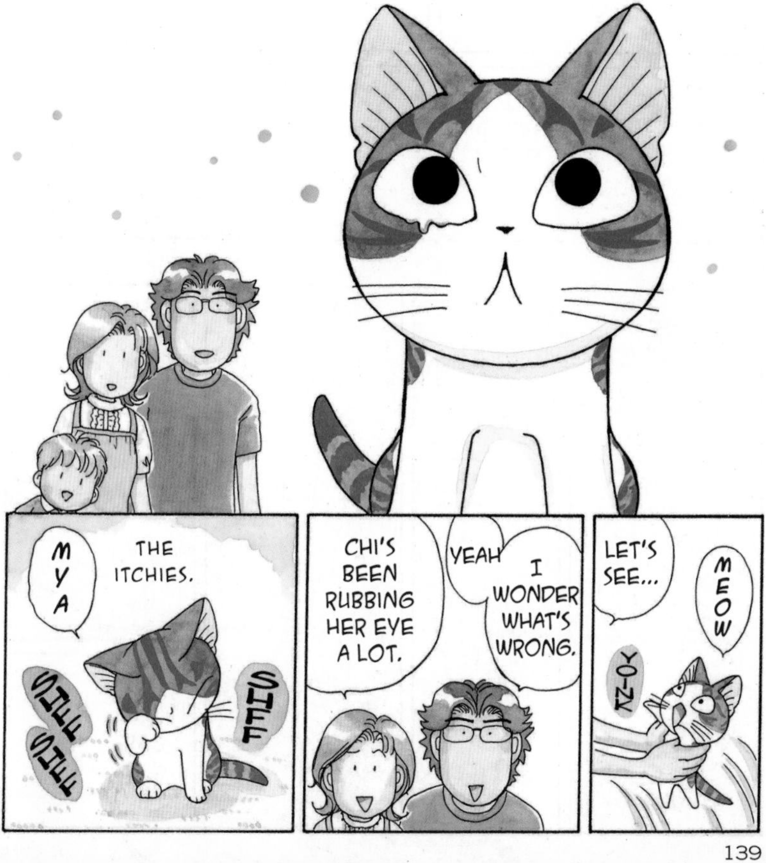
MYA
THE ITCHIES.
SHFF SHFF
SHFF
CHI'S BEEN RUBBING HER EYE A LOT.
YEAH
I WONDER WHAT'S WRONG.
LET'S SEE...
MEOW
YOINK

UH HER LEFT EYE IS ALL DROOPY WITH TEARS.

IS SHE OKAY?

DID SHE GET HURT WHILE SHE WAS OUT?

DOES YOUR EYE HURT?

DROOP

WE'LL TAKE HER TO THE VET TOMORROW!

KITA□□O VETERINARY HOSPITAL

MEOW

MEOW

MEO

MEO

LOOKS LIKE CONJUNCTIVITIS.

MEOW

CONJUNCTIVITIS?!

IS SHE OKAY?

OKAY, WE'RE DONE.

PINKEYE CAN BE CAUSED BY BACTERIA OR COLDS

BUT IN HER CASE, DUST AND GRIME SEEM TO HAVE BROUGHT IT ON.

LET'S TRY EYEDROPS FOR A FEW DAYS.

HAH

MYA

JUST IN CASE, PUT THIS ON HER, TOO.

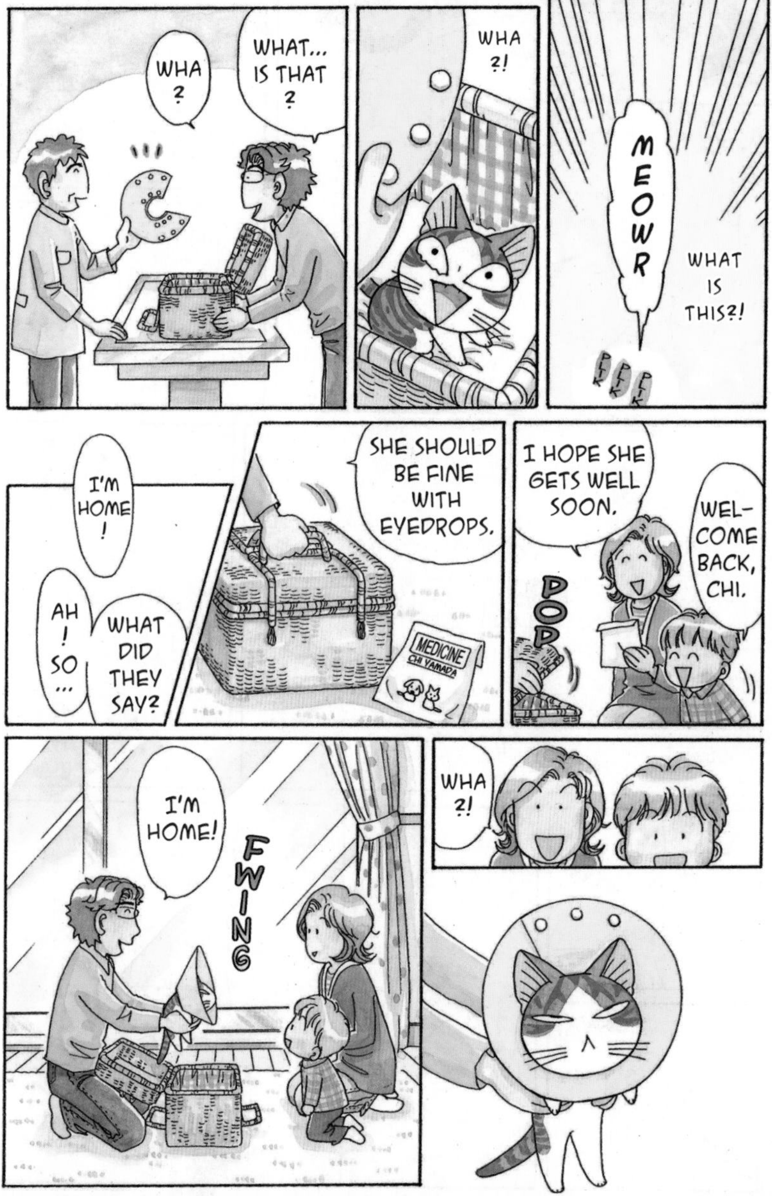
WHA?
WHAT... IS THAT?
WHA?!
MEOWR
WHAT IS THIS?!
PTIK PTIK PTIK
I'M HOME!
AH! SO...
WHAT DID THEY SAY?
SHE SHOULD BE FINE WITH EYEDROPS.
MEDICINE
CHI YAMADA
I HOPE SHE GETS WELL SOON.
POP
WEL-COME BACK, CHI.
I'M HOME!
FWING
WHA?!

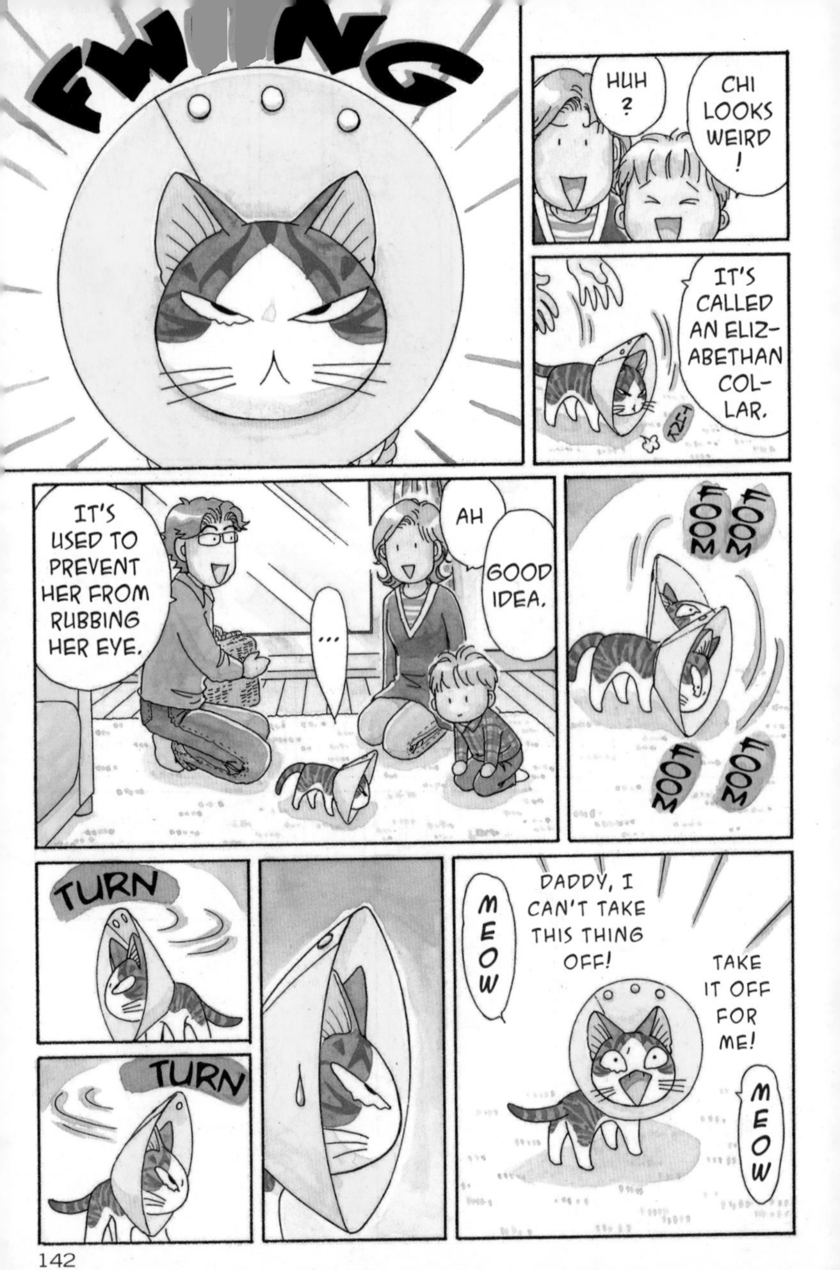
FWING
HUH?
CHI LOOKS WEIRD!
IT'S CALLED AN ELIZABETHAN COLLAR.
IT'S USED TO PREVENT HER FROM RUBBING HER EYE.
...
AH
GOOD IDEA.
FOOM FOOM
FOOM FOOM
TURN
TURN
MEOW
DADDY, I CAN'T TAKE THIS THING OFF!
TAKE IT OFF FOR ME!
MEOW

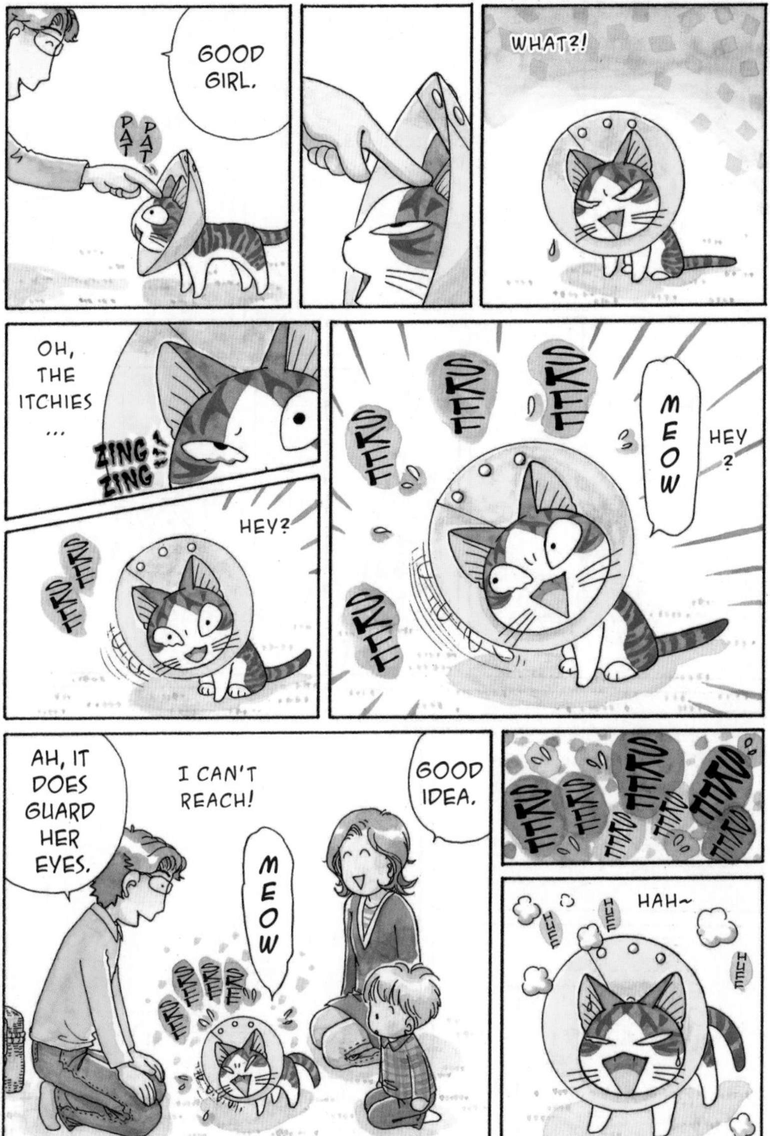
GOOD GIRL.
PAT PAT
WHAT?!
OH, THE ITCHIES ...
ZING ZING
HEY?
SKFF SKFF SKFF SKFF
MEOW
HEY?
AH, IT DOES GUARD HER EYES.
I CAN'T REACH!
GOOD IDEA.
MEOW
HAH~
HUFF HUFF HUFF

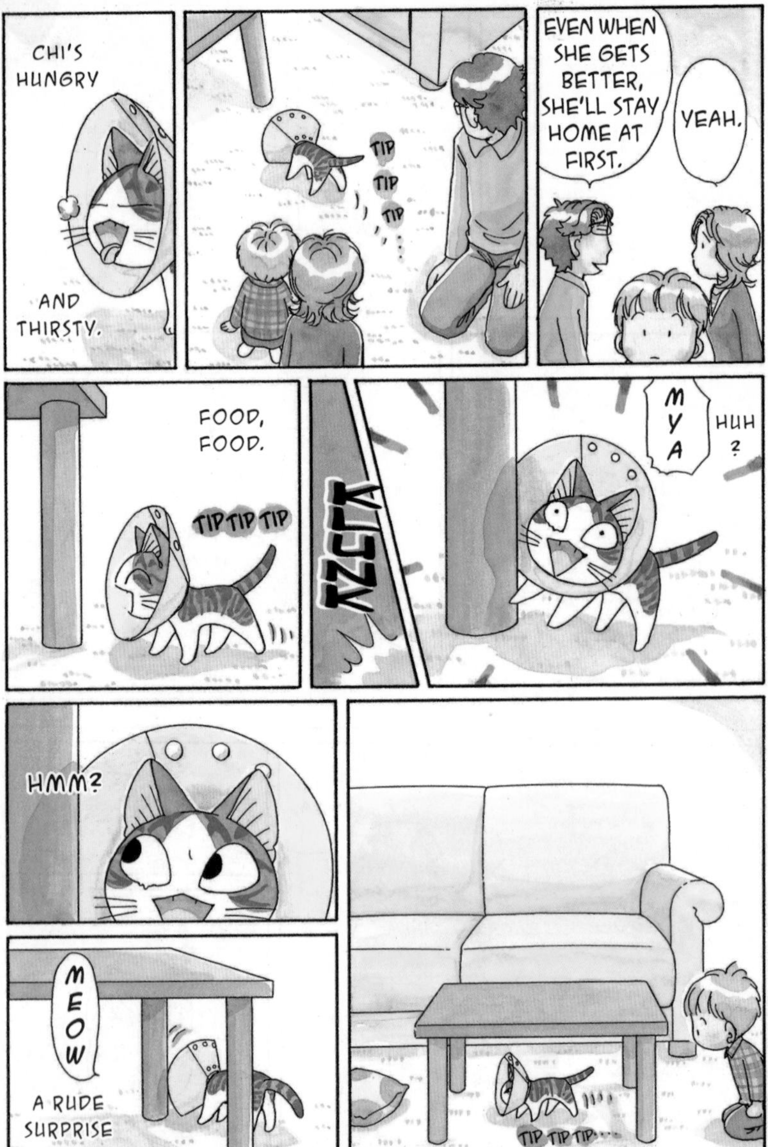
CHI'S HUNGRY
AND THIRSTY.
TIP
TIP
TIP
EVEN WHEN SHE GETS BETTER, SHE'LL STAY HOME AT FIRST.
YEAH.
FOOD, FOOD.
TIP TIP TIP
KLUNK
MYA
HUH?
HMM?
MEOW
A RUDE SURPRISE ...
TIP TIP TIP...

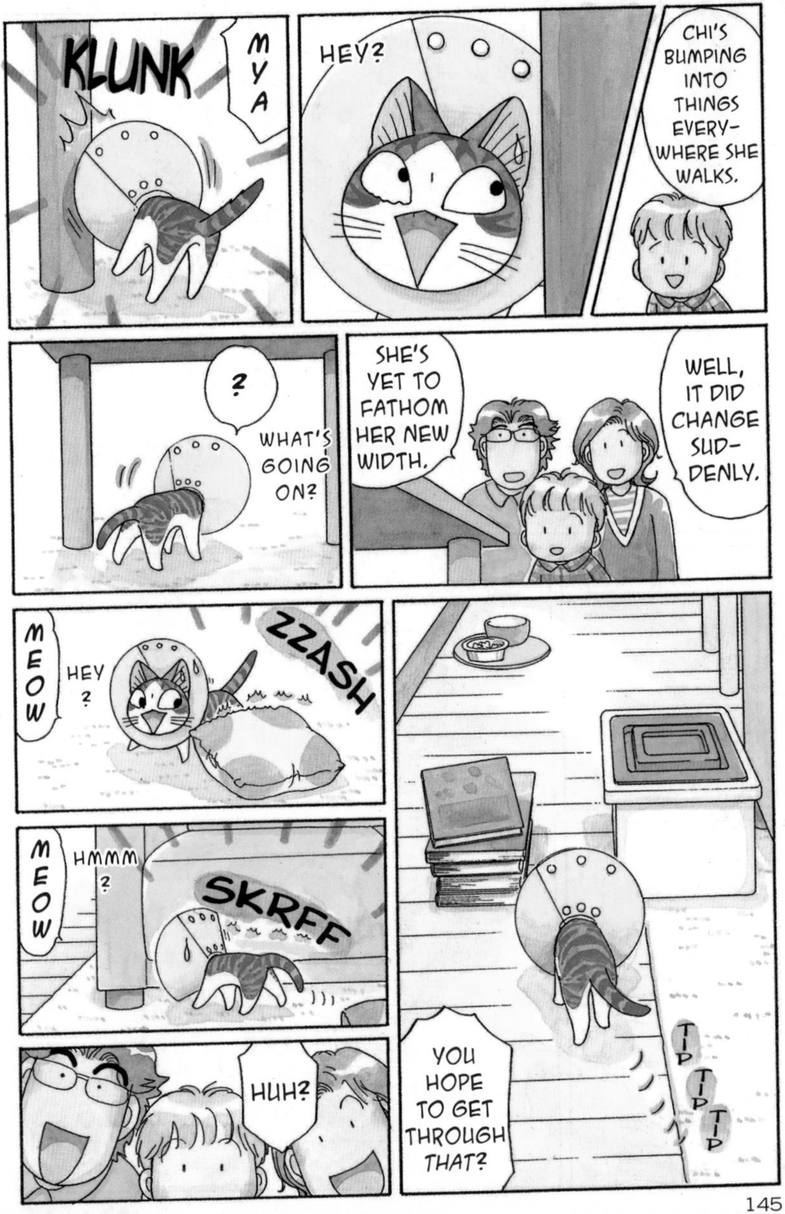
KLUNK
MYA
HEY?
CHI'S BUMPING INTO THINGS EVERY-WHERE SHE WALKS.
?
WHAT'S GOING ON?
SHE'S YET TO FATHOM HER NEW WIDTH.
WELL, IT DID CHANGE SUD-DENLY.
MEOW
HEY?
ZZASH
MEOW
HMMM?
SKRFF
HUH?
YOU HOPE TO GET THROUGH THAT?
TIP
TIP
TIP
TIP

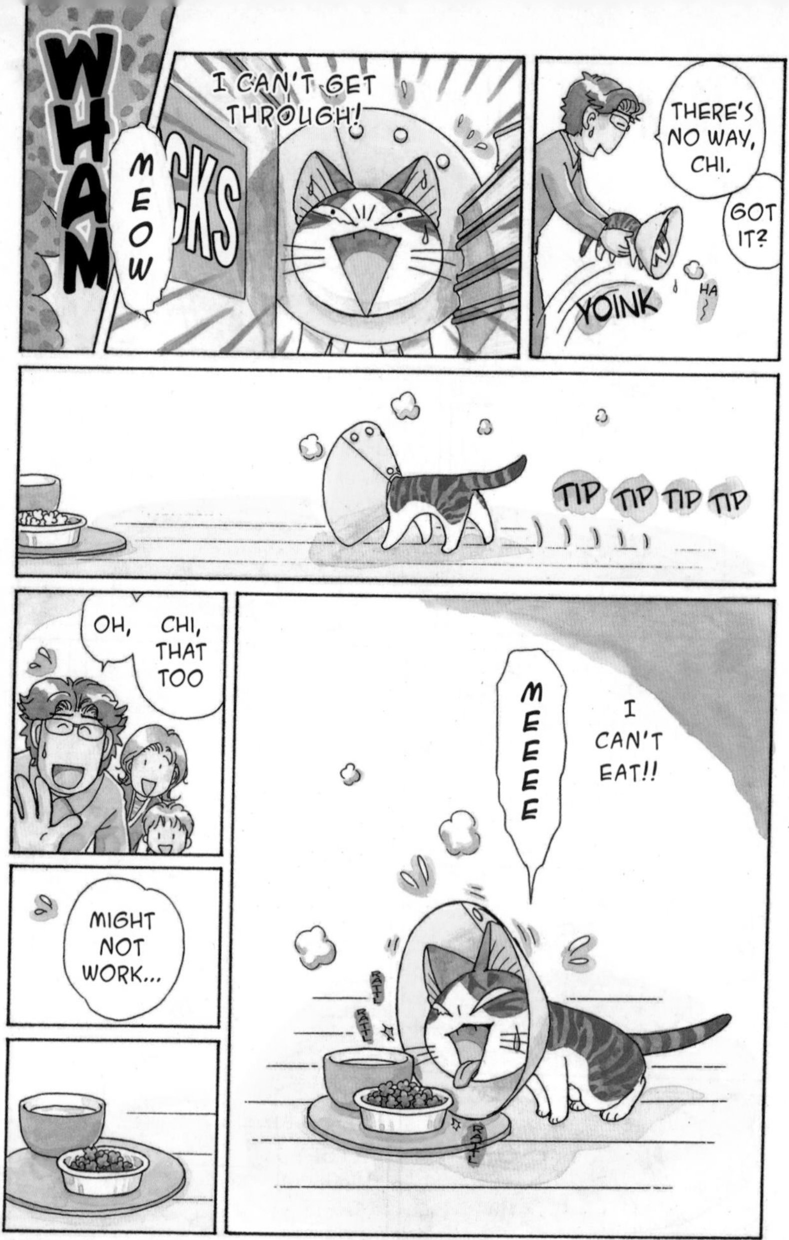
WHAM
MEOW
I CAN'T GET THROUGH!
THERE'S NO WAY, CHI.
GOT IT?
YOINK
HA
TIP TIP TIP TIP
OH, CHI, THAT TOO
MIGHT NOT WORK...
MEEEEE
I CAN'T EAT!!
RATTL
RATTL
RATTL

the end

Extra
Chi's Sweet Origami!

Let's Make a Chi Face!!

Copy or cut out the image to the right and fold using the following instructions.

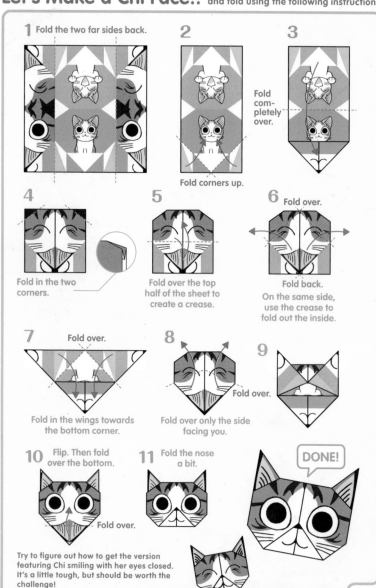

1 Fold the two far sides back.

2 Fold corners up.

3 Fold completely over.

4 Fold in the two corners.

5 Fold over the top half of the sheet to create a crease.

6 Fold over. Fold back. On the same side, use the crease to fold out the inside.

7 Fold over. Fold in the wings towards the bottom corner.

8 Fold over only the side facing you. Fold over.

9

10 Flip. Then fold over the bottom. Fold over.

11 Fold the nose a bit.

DONE!

Try to figure out how to get the version featuring Chi smiling with her eyes closed. It's a little tough, but should be worth the challenge!

Origami (instructions on facing page)

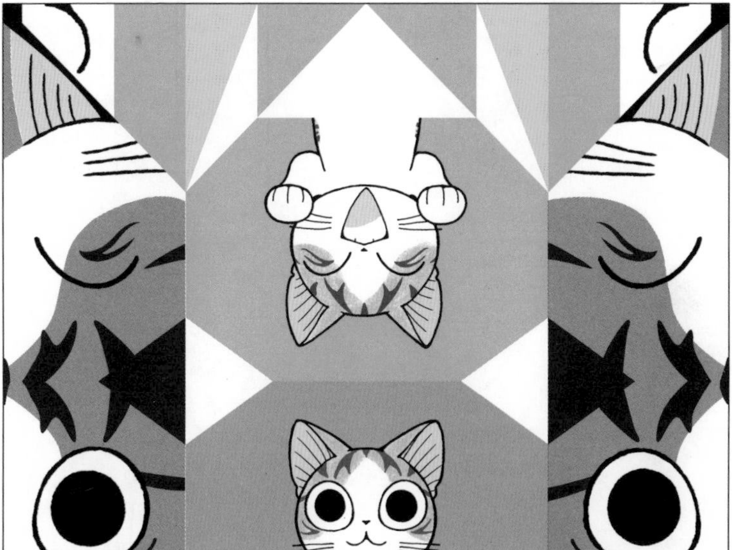

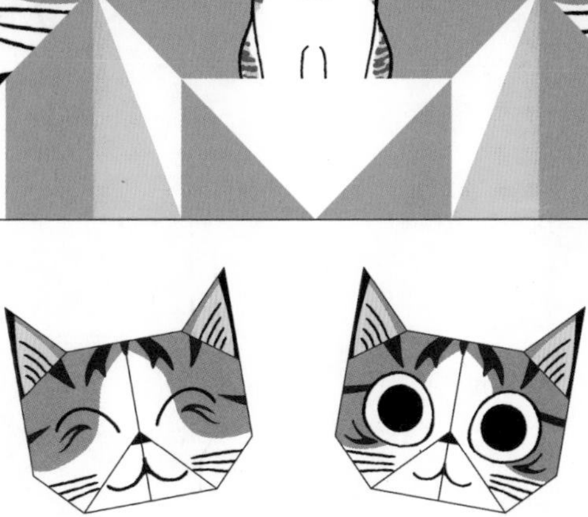

Let's try to fold our way to both
of Chi's origami faces!

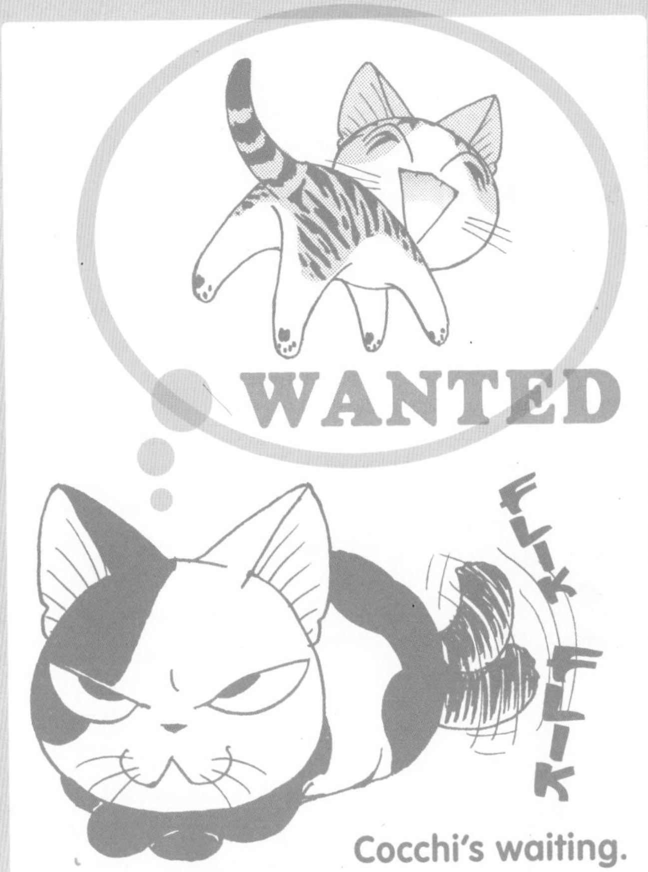
WANTED
FLIK FLIK
Cocchi's waiting.
That Chi...what is she up to?!

Chi's Sweet Home, volume 8

Translation - Ed Chavez
Production - Hiroko Mizuno
Tomoe Tsutsumi

First published in Japan in 2011 by Kodansha, Ltd., Tokyo
Publication for this English edition arranged through Kodansha, Ltd., Tokyo
English language version produced by Vertical, Inc.

Translation provided by Vertical, Inc., 2012
Published by Vertical, Inc., New York

Originally published in Japanese as *Chiizu Suiito Houmu* by Kodansha, Ltd., 2009-2010
Chiizu Suiito Houmu first serialized in *Morning*, Kodansha, Ltd., 2004-

ISBN: 978-1-935654-35-3

Manufactured in China

First Edition

Second Printing

Vertical, Inc.
451 Park Avenue South, 7th Floor
New York, NY 10016
www.vertical-inc.com

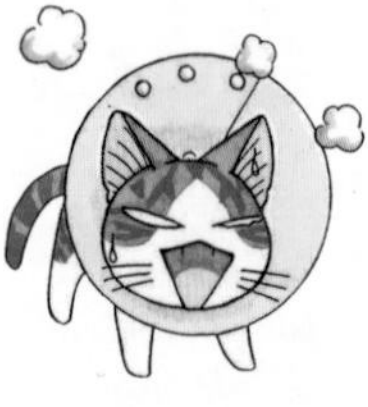

Special thanks to: K. Kitamoto